Also by William Fezler, Ph.D.

Creative Imagery

The Good Girl Syndrome
(with Eleanor S. Field, Ph.D.)

*Breaking Free: 90 Ways
to Leave Your Lover & Survive*

*Hypnosis and Behavior Modification:
Imagery Conditioning*
(with William S. Kroger, M.D.)

William Fezler, Ph.D.

A FIRESIDE BOOK

Published by Simon & Schuster Inc.

New York | London | Toronto | Sydney | Tokyo | Singapore

Imagery for

Healing,

Knowledge,

and Power

Fireside

Simon & Schuster Building
Rockefeller Center
1230 Avenue of the Americas
New York, New York 10020

Designed by Chris Welch
Manufactured in the United States of America

1 3 5 7 9 10 8 6 4 2

Library of Congress Cataloging in Publication Data
Fezler, William.
Imagery for healing, knowledge, and power / William Fezler.
p.   cm.
"A Fireside book."
1. Imagery (Psychology)   2. Self-actualization (Psychology)
3. Imagery (Psychology)—Therapeutic use.   4. Medicine,
Psychosomatic.   I. Title.
BF367.F53   1990
615.8'51—dc20   90-9657
                                                     CIP

ISBN 0-671-69487-1

Acknowledgments

I would like to express my heartfelt thanks to my editor, Barbara Gess, a kindred spirit, who knew what I was trying to say when no one else seemed to understand. Her editorial labors over the manuscript will forever be appreciated. My thanks are due also to my literary agent, Mel Berger, for the energy he gave to this project. To Liza Wright, my publicist, I am grateful for her support.

To William S. Kroger, M.D.

Contents

[On first looking through inverting lenses] . . . the parts of my body were *felt* to lie where they would have appeared had the instrument been removed: they were *seen* to be in another position. But the older tactual localization was still the *real* localization. Soon, however, the limbs began actually to feel in the place where the new visual perception reported them to be. . . . The seen images thus became *real things* just as in normal sight.

—*G. M. Stratton*

Suggestion does not consist in making an individual believe what is not true: suggestion consists in making something come true by making him believe in its possibility.

—*J. A. Hadfield*

If ye have faith as a grain of mustard seed, ye shall say unto this mountain, remove hence to yonder place; and it shall remove; and nothing shall be impossible unto you.

—*Christ*

Our truest life is when we are in dreams awake.

—*Henry David Thoreau*

Introduction

I mages, what you imagine, can heal you, lead you to the higher knowledge that is buried deep within you, and supply you with the power and energy you need to soar to greater levels of experience. It is my hope that you will accomplish all of this by practicing the images in this book.

I will teach you how to use imagery to create profound relaxation, negative hallucinations, and sex energy that will give you healing, higher knowledge, and ever-increasing power. You will learn how to use these phenomena to intensify and expand all the positive aspects of your life while shutting out and eliminating the negative. This will give you an emotional understanding of how much "perceptual" control you have over the positive and negative aspects of your world.

I'll show you how to apply what you are learning to helping yourself with a wide range of problems including: boredom, burnout, irritating distractions, drug abuse, smoking, overweight, alcoholism, depression, phobias, sexual dysfunction, pain, insomnia, anorexia, anxiety attacks, gastrointestinal disorders (such as colitis, ulcers, heartburn, and nausea), skin disorders, asthma, flu, high blood pressure, diabetes, and even lupus, cancer, and AIDS. You'll also learn how you can use imagery to improve your life in many other ways: rejuvenating and bolstering your seeing, hearing, touching, tasting, and smelling; helping your work efficiency, memory, concentration, creativity, confidence, energy, motivation, and athletic prowess; learning to get over a lover, relate to others, and feel loved.

Beyond the healing and improving of practical areas of your life, your range of perception will grow within your sensorium of five primary senses, and "extra" senses will appear as well. New vistas of knowledge will open to you as you embark on a journey into an expanded, extraordinary reality. You will learn to give yourself an intuitive, emotional understanding of the cosmic principles governing the physical universe, the foundation for the manifestation of thought into reality.

I will show you how to generate the power required to propel you into this extraordinary reality of higher knowledge and experience by using imagery to channel the energy of your basic life force. The most readily available, easily accessible form of this force is your sex energy. It is the purest, most basic, vital energy of your life force. You will learn how to create erotic imagery to raise sexual energy that you can then transmute to do healing and self-improvement, or to access higher knowledge. All these things take increased energy. Just as it takes energy to catapult an electron into a new orbital to form a new element, so it takes energy to catapult ordinary consciousness into higher extraordinary awareness. Higher energy yields greater concentration, a higher state of consciousness, and increased power to make a positive change in your life. When you create and channel your sexual energy for the purpose of healing and attaining higher knowledge and experience through raising your consciousness, your result is what I call "spiritual sexuality."

It is not your sense of your sexual energy per se that is most important for your purposes here, but *where it takes you*. The explosion of the psychic orgasm that I'll teach you to create in the pages that follow will transport you into a new place of awareness. This "psychic orgasm" may or may not be accompanied by a physical climax. In any event, you will feel a tremendous amount of energy.

It is the afterglow, the profound relaxation, the altered state that follows your release of energy that is most valuable to you for healing and tapping new sources of higher knowledge and experience. Like the rocket releasing power to transport itself into other dimensions of space, you too will find yourself and your world transformed.

Colors intensify, radiate. You may see creation bathed in a golden light. You can actually feel an etheric, silken texture to the air. Smells and tastes are fresh, pure, clean. The quiet is sublime. There is a dreamlike fairy-tale quality to your world now, as if reality were your own dream, your own creation, just as a dream is. You feel floating, loving, a part of everything, as the creator is an integral part of his dream. It's a world so personal, close, loving, intimate—you feel it is yours alone. Your mind is clear; completely positive, receptive, loving.

It is not the world that has changed, but your perception of it. You are processing it from a higher state of consciousness. Wouldn't you like to perceive like this more often? All the time if possible? Can you imagine being sick or depressed or unhappy in a world experienced like this? It is not possible to raise your consciousness, your level of perception, without healing and feeling better and happier in the process.

Your vehicle to this wonderful state of being is a progressive series of twenty-nine *sensory images*, mental pictures vivid in all five senses, that I have designed to share with you in this book. These images are presented in ascending order of complexity, like piano lessons, each one taking you a step closer to channeling your energy in the production of a stronger mind, body, and spirit. They average a page in length, five minutes on tape if you choose to read them into a recorder for practice rather than recall them from memory. The images have been standardized on several hundred patients in the last nineteen years, and finely honed on the basis of feedback given by psychiatrists, psychologists, and physicians in more than two hundred seminars I have conducted personally.

These twenty-nine images comprise a segment, Images #34–62, of a growing progression of over four hundred images designed for healing and higher knowledge and experience. The beginning of this progression, Images #1–33, is described in my previous book, *Creative Imagery.* I've provided a special image, *Woods Scene,* and exercises related to it in *Imagery for Healing, Knowledge, and Power* that prepare you to start at Image #34 in the progression.

These images are different from those in my earlier book in that they specifically teach you how to create the life force energy and focus it into the achievement of your goals. In addition to this powerful imagery progression, I've devoted an entire chapter to showing how to construct your own images to produce valuable phenomena that can be used for healing and getting what you want in life.

Imagery for Healing, Knowledge and Power is thus a blueprint for physical, emotional, and spiritual growth. It provides a definite method of change—a *progression* of images of ascending complexity—along with many specific images for dealing with particular problems, and strategies for constructing your own images to induce healing and mind-expanding phenomena. The series of images introduced here provides lessons to take you further than you've ever been before, through self-creation of positive feelings, self-healing, and channeling of life force/sexual energy to explore new psychic geography.

As the chapters progress, so will the effects you will be able to derive from them. I hope that the lessons on health will benefit all of you and that the more advanced material will help each of you discover for yourself the knowledge, power, and extraordinary reality that is your heritage. Let's get started creating an infinitely more positive personal reality.

one

Profound Relaxation

The foundation of healing, the attaining of higher knowledge, raising of your energy, and heightening of your positive experience is your achieving a state of profound relaxation. In such a state you are free of disease-breeding stress and negativity and clear to receive the positive influences so conducive to your physical and emotional healing and your spiritual growth.

Because I want this book to be a vehicle to your own positive *experience,* I'm going to start you out right away on the road to creating better feeling states. Your journey begins with learning to create a state of profound relaxation that will pave the way to creating an ever more positive and expanding reality.

Before I tell you all the wonderful things you can do with a self-created state of profound relaxation, I want you to *feel* the state of being I'm talking about. At that point, everything I have to tell you will take on a higher meaning because you will have experienced much of what I'm telling you about. As we progress you will learn to create more new experiences that will give these words even greater meaning because you will have an experiential reference for them. A word is meaningless if you have not had the experience the word denotes. Your experiencing of profound relaxation will thus be your first step toward achieving an emotional, experiential understanding of the principles governing the universe and the perceptual relativity of what we call reality.

Self-Hypnosis

To help you experience this state of profound relaxation I'm going to teach you the technique of self-hypnosis. Hypnosis, by definition, is a state of increased concentration. You achieve it primarily by clearing your mind, so that any positive affirmation you give yourself while you are in this state will not be undermined by a negative, competing thought. The hypnotic state that you will be experiencing is a very positive level of being. It feels wonderful. All cares and fears will fade as your mind clears and a marvelous sense of relaxation overtakes you.

The hypnotic technique that you'll be learning could just as well be called a relaxation procedure. In fact, many times when my patients are afraid to be "hypnotized" I simply say I'm going to relax them, but I use the same method I would if I were calling it hypnosis. I just want to make it clear that the relaxation technique that follows is also the technique for self-hypnosis.

Before I show you how to actually create your own hypnotic state of profound relaxation, I'd like to share with you some of the things I tell all my patients to prepare them for learning to hypnotize themselves. First of all, since hypnosis is a state of increased concentration, you will be more aware, not less aware, in this wonderful state of mind. Even though its name is derived from the Greek *hypnos,* which means "sleep," hypnosis is completely the opposite of sleep. You gain more control, not less, by creating this state. You attain a pinpoint specificity of response and a clarity of thought that you could never achieve in a sleep state.

The increased awareness you gain from creating a hypnotic state manifests itself in a lowering of your positive sensory thresholds. A sensory threshold refers to the level of intensity a stimulus must reach before you can perceive it. A lower threshold means you are more sensitive, a higher threshold means you are less sensitive. In essence, the hypnotic state makes you more sensitive to the beauty of the world. The grass will look greener, the sky bluer. Food will taste better. Flowers will smell sweeter. The touch of your body against the couch will be heightened. Sounds, such as the tape you might make of this procedure to induce this state, will be louder. All in all, the positive aspects of reality will be intensified.

Since one of the objects of practicing self-hypnosis is to attain greater control of your perceptual reality, you will be in control at all times throughout the procedure. There is never a point where you can't open your eyes, get up, and walk out of the room if you desire.

Hypnosis cannot be used to make you do something you don't want to do. You can use it to remove inhibitions and blocks that stand between you and your goals, but not to go against yourself. This state *is* yourself.

You go into the hypnosis on your own and you come out on your own. The hypnotist, or the self-hypnosis technique, only serves as a guide, a source of instruction that you choose to follow for as long as you wish. The worst thing that can happen when you begin mastering self-hypnosis is that nothing will happen. Also, it is always easy to come out of the state. Since maintaining the hypnotic state requires concentration, the state dissipates as soon as your concentration lapses. If you fall asleep while practicing, that is fine. Your hypnotic state will merge into sleep and you will awaken more refreshed than you would from a normal sleep.

You will most likely remember your entire hypnotic session, at least when you first start practicing. In time you may experience hypnotic amnesia, where you forget segments or even all of your session. This is good. Amnesia is a sign of a deep hypnotic state. However, absence of amnesia does not mean you haven't attained a good depth. In other words, you can't have amnesia and not be in a deep state, but you can be in a deep state and not have amnesia.

Traditionally, hypnosis was called "a state that bypasses criticalness." This means that the images and affirmations that you create for yourself while you are in this state go straight to your subconscious mind without your conscious mind there to filter or negate them. For example, if you wish to stop smoking, you can visualize yourself effortlessly resisting a cigarette and tell yourself while you are in a hypnotic state, "I am a nonsmoker," and this image and affirmation or suggestion will be uncritically accepted by your subconscious without your conscious mind there to ruin your good intentions by answering back with a counterproductive message, such as, "What are you talking about? You've never been able to stop smoking. You've already had a whole pack this morning!" If you have the good fortune to be amnesic, to forget that these images and suggestions were given, they are even more powerful. In a state of amnesia your doubting, analytical mind is shut out altogether.

People often ask me whether there's any difference between the hypnosis a clinician or stage hypnotist would do and the hypnosis you create yourself. There isn't. They are all the same. In fact, all hypnosis is self-hypnosis. The therapist, stage hypnotist, or cassette you may have bought in the bookstore all serve simply as your guide or instructor. The state, once you achieve it, is the same—which is not to say, however, that certain ways won't work better to get you there than others.

I think that most people's greatest fear is probably that they won't be able to be hypnotized. Don't worry. You *can* be hypnotized. Forget about the percentages you may have read or heard about that say somewhere around ten percent of all subjects are unhypnotizable. I've found this to be simply untrue. Hypnotizability scales, like IQ, primarily measure your current ability, not potential. Perhaps ten out of one hundred people won't be hypnotized the first time, but that doesn't mean they won't achieve this state the next time they try. In fact, people who have trouble entering a hypnotic state at first often surpass early bloomers later on down the line. In any event, the state is accessible to everyone. It's a level of awareness you *learn* to reach. Some may learn it faster than others, but we'll all get there eventually.

Since hypnosis is a state of heightened awareness and self-control, there's nothing you can't do in this state, and do better than you can do it in your normal state. You can give a speech, pass an exam, even make love. Your performance will be better because you have eliminated competing negativity and noise from your mind. Now let's get started!

Creating a Hypnotic State

I'll be giving you the words for self-hypnosis in their entirety so that you can use this technique to clear your mind and achieve profound relaxation. You can memorize this procedure or you can read it into a cassette recorder and play it back for practice.

If you choose to use a tape, I suggest you alternate your tape sessions with sessions creating the hypnotic state from memory. Tape makes it easier for you to remember the technique, but memory allows you to linger over different segments of the procedure. For example, you may just be beginning to feel a numbness in your legs by recalling what it felt like during times when they were asleep, when the tape goes on and you have to move on with it.

Most importantly, really try to recall the sensations that are being suggested to you in the following technique. Creating a hypnotic state and the marvelous phenomena that will come out of the images that follow is an active process, requiring you to retrieve information from the data stored in your brain. You can use this information to achieve healing, knowledge, and power. You only need to tap it. Here is how.

Technique for Self-Hypnosis

Seat yourself in a comfortable chair with your hands resting in your lap and your feet on the floor, or recline with your hands at your sides. Fix your eyes on a spot on the ceiling above eye level.

Begin counting to yourself slowly from one to ten. Direct your attention to your eyelids and, between numbers, tell yourself repeatedly that your eyelids are getting very, very heavy, and that your eyes are getting very, very tired. Again and again say: "My lids are getting heavier and heavier. I feel my lids getting so heavy, and the heavier they get, the deeper relaxed I will become, and the better able I will be to follow all suggestions I give myself. My lids are getting very heavy. It will feel so good to close my eyes."

By the time you count to two, think of enough suggestions like the ones just mentioned so that you actually feel the heaviness of your eyelids. When you are sure that your lids are indeed heavy, count to three and let your eyes roll up into the back of your head for a few seconds. Then say, "My lids are now locked so tight that I doubt very much that I can open them. My lids shut tighter and tighter, and as my lids lock tight, I begin to feel a nice, calm, soothing, relaxed feeling beginning in my toes, moving into my legs and into my thighs as I keep counting. It's the same feeling that I have in my jaws when my dentist injects novocaine into them; the same feeling that I have when I fall asleep on my arm; the same feeling that

I have when I sit too long in one position; the identical feeling that I would have in my legs if I sat cross-legged on them for very long. A numb, wooden feeling starting in my toes is beginning to move up, up, up from my toes into my legs."

Next, count to four and say, "By the time I have counted to five, my legs from my toes to my thighs will be just as heavy as lead. I can feel my legs relaxing from my toes to my thighs. I can feel them getting heavier and heavier and heavier . . . five. They are so heavy now that I don't think I can move them." Then double back for repetition. "My eyelids are locked tight, so tight that I don't believe I can open them. My legs from my toes to my thighs are completely relaxed." Each time you retrace these suggestions, you stamp in the learned response pattern.

You continue in this way, "By the time I have counted to six and seven, my fingers, hands, and arms will be very, very heavy. I am beginning to feel that same numbness moving up from my fingers to my shoulders. A heavy, detached feeling is moving up from my fingers to my hand, to my wrist, past my elbows, up to my arm, to my shoulder. Both my arms, from my hands to my shoulders, are getting very numb—a heavy woodenlike numbness. When I have counted to seven, my arms will be just as heavy and relaxed as my eyelids, and as numb as my legs are now, as if I had been sleeping on them."

Don't worry if you forget the exact words. The exact words are far less important than the effect that you are trying to achieve: a feeling of numbness all the way from the fingertips to the wrist, to the elbow, to the shoulder, to the neck. In practice, this may be a bit more difficult to accomplish in the first few sessions at home, but the feeling will come faster in subsequent attempts. It is most important that you never become discouraged and that you not tire yourself by spending more than thirty minutes a day in practice.

When you finally reach the point where, by the count of seven, your limbs are sufficiently relaxed, you repeat again all the suggestions you have given yourself going back to your eyelids: "My eyes are locked so tight that I doubt that I can open them. My legs are so heavy that I don't believe I can move *them. My arms are so heavy that I cannot lift them." Then add: "And, by the time I have counted from seven to eight, my trunk will be relaxed."*

Now go back to the lids, legs, and arms. Then say, "By the time I count from eight to nine, my chest will have relaxed, too. With every breath I take, I can just feel myself going deeper and deeper into a relaxed state. My back and abdomen are getting very, very numb. I can feel the muscles in my chest completely relaxed. I can't open my eyes. I can't move my legs. I can't move my arms. I feel my whole body relaxed, thoroughly and deeply. It is so refreshing to remain in this deep, quiet state.

"I will now relax my neck and head, so that, at the count of ten, I will be completely relaxed from my head to my toes. I can feel that with every breath I take I am becoming calmer and more deeply relaxed . . . more and more deeply relaxed . . . into a calm, soothing, refreshing state. Everything is just getting more and more relaxed. I feel as if I am floating away . . . falling deeper and deeper . . . not asleep, but just thoroughly relaxed . . . ten. I am completely relaxed. My eyes and limbs are as heavy as lead. My entire body feels numb, heavy, wooden-like, as I go deeper and deeper.

"I am now going to count to three. At the count of three, I will open my eyes. I will be completely relaxed, totally refreshed . . . one . . . two . . . three."

You have now experienced the state of profound relaxation that will serve as your entree to mastering the sequence of images comprising this book. You will find it helpful to do this exercise for ten minutes three times a day for a week before starting to develop your powers of imagery. Your mind will then be clear and ready to receive the sensory data you will feed it in the process of creating imagery.

People often wonder at this beginning stage whether they have in fact achieved a hypnotic state. I would say first off to not worry about it. Doing the above exercise will inevitably lead in time to the mental state you desire. It's best not to worry yourself looking for signs. However, if you insist on looking for "proof" there are certain reactions typical of the hypnotic state.

The most common initial reaction is one of incredible relaxation. You may not feel strangely different, but you definitely will feel relaxed. The suggestions for numb, woodenlike sensations in your extremities usually take hold quite soon, and you may notice a heaviness in your limbs, difficulty moving them, and a reluctance to get up. Your arms and feet might tingle afterward, as they would if they'd gone to sleep and were now waking up.

As you begin practicing self-hypnosis, your sense of relaxation will increase and you may experience dissociation, the beginning of a change in your sense of your body boundary. Your legs may feel crossed when they aren't or your hands may feel they are at your sides when in fact they're resting on your stomach. As your sense of dissociation increases, your body may feel like its arching or even rising off the couch. In its most extreme form, dissociation makes you feel as if your mind is separated from your body, rising to the ceiling or leaving the room to travel.

The most apparent sign of a hypnotic state that an observer would look for would be a rapid trembling of your eyelids, but you will not be able to feel this or see it since your eyes are closed. An observer would also see a masklike quality to your features, as lines and shadows fade due to the deep relaxation you are able to create. This observer would also note that your breathing becomes deeper, slower, and more regular, though most beginners are also unaware of this.

As you become more proficient with creating self-hypnosis you may wish to abbreviate the technique, till the mere blink of your eyelids triggers the state. You may shorten it to your liking, but personally I prefer to always keep three elements:

1. While looking at a spot, say to yourself, "My lids are getting very, very heavy."
2. Close your eyes when your lids feel heavy and roll your eyeballs back for thirty seconds while saying to yourself,

"My lids are locked so tight I doubt very much that I can open them."

3. Relax your eyeballs and imagine a rhythmic wave of relaxation starting in your toes and washing through your legs, arms, stomach, chest, neck, and head.

The rest of the technique is frosting on the cake, but it is important that the first two suggestions you tell yourself come true in order to convince yourself that your next suggestion, such as, "I eat only foods that are on my diet," will also come true. Affirmation #1 must come true because the physical process of staring at a spot makes your lids tired. Affirmation #2 inevitably manifests because when your eyeballs are rolled back it feels as if you can't open your eyelids.

In addition to eliminating stress and simply making you feel better, the profound relaxation you are able to create through the self-hypnosis technique has many other beneficial applications. We are now going to take a look at what these benefits are.

Profound Relaxation Heals

Many cures and amazing results can be brought on by your use of relaxation alone. Relaxation raises your pain threshold and lowers your pleasure threshold. In other words, relaxation makes you less sensitive to pain and more sensitive to pleasure.

Mandy, a thirty-nine-year-old lab technician, got severe cluster headaches at work whenever she felt the rest of the staff wasn't doing their share of the work. "I'm always willing to take up the slack," she said. "I'm a good worker. If someone else is behind on their job I'll pitch in and help out. I just don't like being taken advantage of. There's a couple of people in the office that will do anything to get out of pulling their share. It really burns me. Especially because I don't think the doctor appreciates how much I really do."

I taught Mandy how to induce the profound relaxation of self-hypnosis on the spot, in the situations where she needed it most. First I asked her to practice the technique for a week, just as I described it to you. I then told her to practice opening her eyes after the eyeball roll and finishing the procedure with her eyes open. I ask you to practice with your eyes closed only because there is less distraction that way. If you want to use hypnotic relaxation in an everyday situation you will probably need to keep your eyes open in order to function. Once Mandy mastered waking hypnosis (eyes open) at home, I asked her to get used to creating this state at work, under normal, calm conditions. Finally I asked her to create this state in situations that normally would make her angry.

"You always have three options whenever something is bothering you," I told her. "Get away from it, change it, or change your reaction to it." Mandy didn't want to quit her job so the first option was out. She did try changing the way the staff shared their work load by requesting they meet regularly to discuss problems, and that helped to a point. What she wasn't able to modify further, Mandy changed her reaction to. She was able to feel relaxation rather than anger at the work situations that were beyond her control to remedy. "No more headaches at work," she finally reported. "Whenever something arises that used to tick me off, I just take a deep breath and go into my relaxation that you taught me how to do."

While Mandy used relaxation to make herself less sensitive to the negative stimuli that were causing her headache pain, Tracy, a thirty-three-year-old ticket agent, used it to make herself more sensitive to the joys of sex. "I never could understand what all the hoopla was about sex," she told me in our first session together. "It sure didn't do anything for me. Wake me when it's over was my attitude. Guys would get so excited and make such a big deal over it. They'd ask if I'd enjoyed it and I'd just go along with them and say it was great. But I don't want to do that anymore. I think I'm shortchanging myself. Not even so much by missing out on sexual pleasure as by not being able to be honest with myself and my partner.

When he asks how I feel I want to be truthful. And I want to be able to say I enjoyed it."

As Tracy began learning to relax herself she found she was becoming more open to all positive sensation. "I enjoy everything more now," she reported, "the sound of rain on the roof, the smell of a flower, the feel of my bath, a good meal, the beauty of a sunset—all the things that I used to love as a child are coming back to me. I realize now that somewhere down the line I must have started shutting off to the world, not just to sex, but to everything."

Tracy's self-induced relaxation made her more sensitive to all positive stimuli and allowed her to open herself to the beauty of the world. This beauty included her experiencing of her sexual feelings. "I guess I was just too uptight to feel anything," she said. "Now it's glorious. I can't believe my energy. The more pleasure I feel, the more energy I have." You will find this is also true for you. As your ability to relax grows and your sensitivity to pleasure increases, your energy level will rise. Pleasure, whether it be sexual or nonsexual, in any or all of your senses, always gives you energy.

Profound Relaxation Increases Knowledge

He who is without concentration is most certainly without knowledge. Relaxation counters negativity and removes the noise of competing thoughts from your mind. It is thus a great boon to increasing your powers of concentration and achieving the knowledge this ability to focus ensures.

Jerry, a nineteen-year-old college sophomore, complained that he wasn't able to concentrate on his coursework. "I'm so scattered," he said. "If I really like the subject I'm okay. But if it's something like government or social science, my mind is all over the place. I think about my girlfriend, my job, what I'm going to do over the weekend. Before I know it, I have no idea what I've been reading. I've just been turning the pages and I have to go back and start all over again."

After creating relaxation three times a day for a week using the self-hypnosis technique that I taught him, Jerry reported, "It's amazing. I feel more focused, more centered. My mind isn't as cluttered. Studying is nowhere near the strain it used to be. It's easier. My mind doesn't *want* to escape the way it used to. Maybe that's a reason my concentration is better. Anyway, I'm sure doing a lot better with the classes that used to bore me."

Sometimes your concentration and study habits may be good when you are learning the material, but your memory fails you when it comes time to retrieve this information. This is often the case when anxiety—such as performance anxiety over a job interview, a new work situation, or an exam—blocks the concentration necessary for accessing the data you need.

Martin, twenty-seven, was a law clerk in a prestigious firm where he hoped to be hired as a lawyer once he passed the California bar exam. The three days of testing that comprise this test are notoriously difficult, and Martin had already failed twice. "It's not that I don't know the material," he explained to me. "I just can't seem to be able to remember it when I take the exam. I get myself all psyched up to come on aggressively like Rambo, but then I choke. Nothing comes to mind. It's awful!"

Martin practiced the hypnotic clearing procedure three times a day for two weeks before he took the bar exam for the third time. This time he passed. "That relaxation was great," he smiled. "I can't believe how much easier it is to think when I'm relaxed instead of all tensed up. It's funny, I always used to believe I wouldn't do well unless I was really revved up, coiled tight like a spring. Now I see that what I mistook for a sense of preparedness was just a lot of nerves. I function much better when I'm relaxed." You too will discover that you learn and retrieve information far more efficiently in a state of profound relaxation.

Profound Relaxation Builds
Power and Performance

It's strange that relaxation, which makes you more sensitive to all things positive and thus raises your energy, is often mistakenly associated with the thought of low energy. Relaxation does *not* mean low energy. Quite the contrary, it spells high energy. A prime example of this is the yogi, who, although he is generating tremendous energy through his intense concentration, is in a state of physical immobility and profound relaxation.

Nothing depletes your power more than negative images and affirmations. Positive thoughts build power. Negative thoughts destroy power. Probably no disorder is more characterized by low energy than depression. You can eliminate depression by learning to create profound relaxation and the heightened positive sensuality and energy that ensues from it. Cole, a thirty-two-year-old criminal attorney, complained of chronic depression that was becoming so incapacitating that his job was in jeopardy. "I feel so down in the morning," he said, "there are times when I can't get out of bed. I just think, 'What's the use? Why get up?' I used to tell myself I'd feel better once I got going and usually that was the case, but lately the depression lasts through the workday. I'm too depressed to fight it anymore and it scares the hell out of me. I see myself alone sleeping in the street somewhere. That's what'll happen if I can't keep going to work."

The first benefit that Cole received from my teaching him to induce deep relaxation was the return of his sex drive. By making him more sensual, the relaxation had also made him more sexual, thus raising his level of sexual energy. "I haven't felt horny in years." He smiled. "It's the first time in a long time I've felt like doing *anything!*" Sex energy is a powerful force and in Cole's case it paved the way to dispelling the low-energy apathy of his depression. In Chapters 6, 9, and 10, you will learn how you too can use your sex energy to banish negativity and effect healing.

Many people, like the law clerk Martin, labor under the misconception that their performance level increases with their anxiety level. They equate tension with being on the alert, ready for anything that comes along. This is an atavistic response related to survival, dating back to the days when our ancestors needed to be continually on guard for predators that could spring upon them at any moment. In today's world this mode of existence is totally maladaptive, and you need to test reality by forcing yourself to work in a relaxed state. Research shows that you'll perform much better when you are relaxed than when you are "geared up" to come on strong. Your performance *increases* with your level of relaxation.

Jackie, a thirty-two-year-old court reporter, said she was depressed because she was lonely and couldn't make a relationship work in her life. "I'm so exhausted when I get home from work," she said, "I can't muster the energy to go out and meet someone. By the time the weekend comes it's all I can do to make it home on Friday, I'm so drained. Then when I do go out on Saturday I'm so desperate knowing I won't have another chance for a week, I stress out and blow the whole thing." As I've treated many court reporters for work-related stress, I know that court reporting is a high pressure job; but I also realized that Jackie's work was taking a higher toll than it should. There was no need for her to feel so down at the end of every workday.

After Jackie learned to create profound relaxation by practicing self-hypnosis at home for a week, I asked her to practice five-minute refresher sessions while she was at work. During her lunch break she would slip off to the restroom and recharge herself with relaxation. "It's marvelous," she reported. "Once I got the knack of creating a positive altered state, I found I could bring it on more and more rapidly. Those mini-sessions in the washroom really got me through the day with energy to spare. What surprised me most was how much my increased relaxation improved my performance. I type much quicker now and that eases the pressure and my fears that I might miss transcribing some of the dialogue going on in the courtroom. I'm able to go out two weeknights a week now and Saturdays are no longer the main event. That's nice. I've finally got plenty of time and energy to meet someone special. All I needed was the energy!"

Your ability to create profound relaxation will not only increase your power and performance at work, it will help you at play as well. Mac, sixty-two, retired early from the air force so that he and his wife Edna, sixty-five, could relax and enjoy life before they got too old to do all the things his rigorous career had kept them from pursuing fully. "I most looked forward to getting out on the golf course every day," he said. "But I just don't have the stamina to go the full eighteen holes. Edna has no problem and she's three years older than I am. I saw several doctors and they say there's nothing wrong with me. I'm in great health. Why am I so pooped out?"

I smiled. "Just because you've retired, that doesn't mean you'll automatically relax," I said. "Tension has become a habit with you. You've become so used to pushing and being wound up these past forty years that it's been imprinted on your brain as a normal mode of reacting. You need to learn to go into a different mode. You need to learn to relax."

As I did with Jackie, I first suggested that Mac practice creating profound relaxation using self-hypnosis for a week, before he incorporated it into recharging periods on the golf course. To begin, I asked him to take a five-minute time-out after every three holes for an abbreviated self-hypnosis session with his eyes closed or open, whichever worked best and he felt most comfortable with. In a month, Mac was able to cut down to one five-minute recharging session after the ninth hole and finish the game easily. To this day he maintains this strategy. "What I really like about this technique," he reported, "is that it not only gave me more get-up-and-go, it improved my golf game. I had a bad habit of being so eager to see how well I was doing I'd look up too soon during my swing and throw the whole shot off. I guess the relaxation improved my concentration to the point I could hold it long enough to complete my swing." You can't concentrate without energy and you can't maintain energy unless you relax. All these forces work together to create an effect greater than the sum of its parts.

The Synergistic Effect of Increased Relaxation, Healing, Knowledge, and Power

The increased energy you will gain from developing your facility to create profound relaxation promotes not only greater powers of concentration and information retrieval, but your attaining greater healing and higher knowledge as well. The way relaxation and energy work together to effect healing can be seen in the mind-body connection. A relaxed, energized mind leads to a healthy body.

Among the first to demonstrate the axiom that energy-depleting negative emotions can cause illness was Hans Selye at the University of Prague in the 1920s. Selye discovered that chronic stress suppressed the immune system, which is responsible for engulfing and destroying cancerous cells or alien microorganisms.

Selye's findings were later confirmed by other researchers, such as Dr. R. W. Bathrop and his associates at the University of South Wales, Australia, who found indications of depressed lymphocyte function, a critical measure of the potency of the body's immune system, in persons who were recently bereaved through death of a spouse. Dr. J. H. Humphrey and his associates at the British Medical Research Council demonstrated that the body's immunity to tuberculosis could be greatly affected by hypnotic suggestion. Dr. George Solomon of California State University discovered that incisions in the hypothalamus, the portion of the brain considered most directly associated with our emotions, resulted in a suppression of the immune system.

Meryl, a twenty-eight-year-old high school teacher, provides an excellent example of how important relaxation can be to maintaining health and combating illness; the relaxation-created energy she was able to produce helped her to heal. "I was always sick with colds and flu until you taught me to relax," she told me. "I think I've been chronically ill since childhood. I continually missed school because of colds and sore throats along with all the other common childhood diseases like mumps, measels, chicken pox, whooping cough. Mother always shrugged it off by saying my resistance was low. I'm sure that was true, but the thing was, nobody in my family ever stopped to ask *why* my resistance to disease was so poor. They just said not to worry, someday I'd grow out of it and become a healthy adult, but I never did. In fact, my frequency of illnesses increased."

I learned that from childhood on, Meryl had always been a worrier. In grade school she worried that the kids were making fun of her and that her teachers didn't like her, even though she had many friends and got excellent grades. In high school she worried that men weren't really attracted to her and that her female classmates thought she was too much of a prude, even though she had several boyfriends and was quite popular. Today she worried that her students were bored by her and that her husband of five years, Jack, would tire of her and become unfaithful, although once again there was no evidence to indicate any real basis for her concerns.

"The first thing I noticed was how much more energy I had," Meryl said after practicing the self-hypnosis technique for a week. "All that worrying was plain wearing me out. I can't believe the amount of pep I got from just learning to relax." Meryl's increased relaxation and energy worked synergistically to reduce her stress and strengthen her immune system. She continued practicing self-hypnosis a minimum of once a day, and her frequency of illnesses decreased to the point where, one year from the start of her practice, she hadn't been sick once in nearly six months—a dramatic reduction from an almost continual state of pathology.

Relaxation and energy also work synergistically in helping you to attain higher knowledge, an emotional understanding of the principles governing the universe. Norman, a forty-five-year-old sales representative, complained that he was tired of doing the same old thing day after day. "Routine is a killer," he said. "Every day it's the same. I get up, put on my socks, make my breakfast, floss my teeth, shower, dress, get money, get keys, race to car, fight traffic, battle the attendant for a space in the lot . . . and so it goes day after day, year after year. It's so boring I can't focus on it. I'm always looking ahead, chafing at the bit to get on to the next part of my schedule."

"You have to take responsibility for your own boredom," I told Norman. "The world hasn't changed. It's as exciting as ever. It's your perception, not the world, that's dragging you down. You have the power to experience things with as much wonder and enthusiasm as you did the first time you experienced them. Reality is a function of your perception. You control whether you will perceive the elements comprising reality as positive or negative."

"I believe it," he answered, "but so what? What can I do about it?" I needed to give Norman an emotional understanding of something he already intellectually knew was true: that his experience of the world, be it good or bad, was within the realm of his perceptual control.

After Norman practiced creating relaxation for a week using the self-hypnosis technique, I asked him to begin incorporating it into his daily routine. "Whenever you find your mind racing ahead, jumping on to all the stuff you need to get through before your day is done, I want you to stop, take a deep breath, and recall the sense of relaxation you were able to create in your practice sessions. A sensation that you have experienced most recently is the easiest to recall and your current practice of creating profound relaxation ensures that this experience is at the forefront of your memory banks. Continue creating relaxation by recalling it until your mind is still. Then focus totally on the task at hand. If you are in the process of tying your shoelace, give your total, undivided attention to that activity. Tying your shoelace is the only thing in the world that matters to you at that point in time."

Relaxation centers you. It puts you in the moment. The moment is pure experience without the negative competition of memory to tell you that you've tied your shoelaces a million times before. Experience is never boring. It takes memory to make you feel something is routine. How else would you know you'd done it before?

It took Norman several months to learn to relax sufficiently to quiet the competing stimuli of memories and focus his attention on reality, the pure sensory experience of what he was doing at the time. But once he was able to accomplish this, his life never seemed routine to him again. "I not only look forward to each new day," he recounted, "my sales have improved tremendously. My mind is focused in the moment and I'm able to sense my customers' needs because I'm paying attention to them. This greater awareness gives me greater knowledge that I can use constructively to satisfy my clients."

You too will discover that profound relaxation puts you in the sensory moment, undistracted by the competing stimuli of noise and negativity. This grounding gives you a heightened knowledge of what is going on around you, an awareness of an expanded, more beautiful reality. As Norman put it, "Everything looked beautiful when I relaxed. The deeper my relaxation became, the more fascinating the world appeared. Things I previously overlooked actually became profound to me. If I took the time and made the effort, just looking at a drop of water forming on the bathroom faucet could become a beautiful, even mystical experience."

The world is a beautiful place if you just allow yourself to process it. Learning to clear your mind through the creation of profound relaxation is a beginning. Charging this clarity of thought with energy and power will take you higher. You will soon see how to use imagery, your imagination, to create this power.

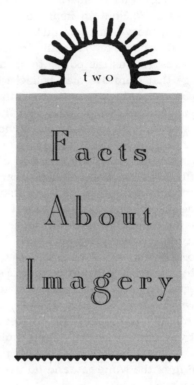

two

Facts About Imagery

Your imagination makes you remarkable. It enables you to transcend the barriers of time and space. This chapter contains answers to some of the most frequently asked questions I receive on *how* to imagine. I'll give you tips and pointers for practicing imagery, things I learned not only through my own experience, but from feedback from hundreds of patients and students whom I've taught to create images vivid enough to make a change in their lives. The remaining chapters will tell you *what* to imagine. But first let's take a closer look at why imagery is becoming such an important tool for positive change in the lives of people today.

The ability to imagine is as old as mind. It is the basis for what we call consciousness. It gives us our concept of past and future. Without an image or recording of past experience—a memory—there would be no past and no future. Time itself is dependent on our ability to imagine.

Images give us the power to span time. Thus it was not strange that primitive man believed that images could give him control of his own destiny and the destiny of others. The famous Lascaux cave paintings portray imagery as a symbol of mastery over the environment. Vivid impressions of leaping bisons were traced upon the cavern walls to give man control over the hunt. Mental impressions of these beasts projected visually from the cavern wall gave early cave dwellers a sense of control over the "real" animals they were imagining.

The power of imagery was used in decorating the tombs of the pharaohs. It provided a homelike atmosphere for dead royalty in the world beyond.

For the first half of the twentieth century, psychology and psychiatry practically ignored man's imagery and fantasy processes. America's emphasis on materialism and technology was reflected in the way it viewed man and his functionings in a rapidly changing world. It seemed that the only thing worthy of study was that which could be *seen,* the overt response. Research focused on the bar press of the pigeon, maze running of the white rat, and lid twitches of the conditioned human eye.

Then, in 1949, a new line of research led to unexpected results that dramatically changed the course of psychology. A physiological psychologist, D. O. Hebb, began to systematize behavior in relation to the neural organization of the brain. To accomplish this he used sensory deprivation.

Subjects' contact with reality—essentially the outside world—was severed by eliminating their senses. Halved Ping-Pong balls were placed over their eyes to remove sight and their ears were plugged to eliminate sound. Bodies were bound and insulated to deaden touch. They were placed in chambers where there was little or no sensory input. Sight, sound, touch, smell, and taste were obliterated.

To the researchers' dismay it was discovered that it was virtually impossible to eliminate a subject's perceptual world. Five to seven hours after sensory deprivation was induced, subjects involved in the study *began to create their own reality*! They hallucinated in all five senses. Their perceptual world was every bit as vivid and "real" as the one they were being experimentally cut off from. In other words, when stimuli from the external environment were reduced, internal activity increased drastically! This pointed the way to a dramatic insight: the mind literally could create its own world. Then it was time to direct attention back to sensory processes in the brain.

Psychologists now realized they had to change the thrust of their research. However, they still faced the problem of measuring the unobservable. After all, calibration is the core of hard science; psychologists wanted to be accepted alongside the respected sciences of physics, biology, and chemistry.

Imagery received another boost in 1953. Researchers in the field of neurophysiology discovered exciting data in relation to the sleep cycle. Human thought during sleep could be followed using elaborate instrumentation, including polygraphs. The dream was no longer something that only its creator could observe. It could now be followed in the scientific laboratory.

The most recent scientific development to bring a convergence of focus on mental imagery is computer technology. Initiated by the brilliant observations of Norbert Wiener, the father of cybernetics, the possibility of simulating human processes via computer prompted psychologists to undertake the systematic study of long-term memories, expectations, and hierarchies of plans.

This refocusing has brought about some amazing changes in the area of psychotherapy. Man's ability to create his own reality has staggering implications for the field of mental health. A wide range of mental and physical problems are now being treated using appropriate imagery.

That positive, appropriate images cure, and negative, inappropriate images destroy is an indisputable fact. Positive images relieve worry, pain, and tension, thus contributing to general well-being. As your anxiety is reduced, you are more resistant to disease and healthier in mind and body. Excessive rumination on negative images, on the other hand, produces disastrous results to the nervous system, resulting in bad digestion, ulcers, and high blood pressure.

Close examination of psychological data and medical research conclusively shows the healing power of imagery. In the late sixties the International Congress of Mental Imagery Techniques was formed to study and develop the use of healing imagery throughout the world. In 1977 the first edition of the *Journal of Mental Imagery* was published to provide a forum for the hundreds of laboratory and clinical studies being conducted on mental imagery.

Imagery is the key to controlling your conscious environment. Let's now take a look at some of the most often asked questions about how you can use imagery to effect positive change.

How Do You Create an Image?

You have images running through your head all the time. Elaborate sequential sets of images are often referred to as daydreams. While you may not indulge in daydreams, you do nonetheless fill your days with plans, expectations, and hopes, all of which are images. At night your imagery takes the form of dreams, although you may not remember all of these fantasies. As Shakespeare said, "We are such stuff as dreams are made of." Consciousness itself is imagery.

The question then is not whether you will create an image, but rather how you will control or determine what imagery is to influence your life. Your ability to concentrate your attention is a determining factor in the creation of your imagery.

The progressive series of images in this book will teach

you to concentrate. It is simply a matter of practice for you
to develop control over what you concentrate on and imagine.
Controlled imagery, like anything else that you learn, is a
gradual process of development. You possess the power of
imagination and you will, with practice, harness that power
to do your bidding.

What Is an Image?

An image is defined as "a mental representation of an actual object." It is thus a mental representation of "reality."
Every sensation you've ever experienced is recorded forever
in your brain. You have the ability to relive any of those sensations as vividly as the first time they entered your consciousness. We know this from research involving the
stimulation of the brain through electrodes. Penfield, a great
neurosurgeon, showed that electrically stimulating a certain
area of the cortex will produce a taste, smell, sound, vision,
or tactile sensation so real it cannot be discriminated from
reality. There is a story in the science-fiction literature of a
man whose brain was removed and stored in a vial where it
was appropriately stimulated to make the man believe he still
had a body. While this story sounds fantastic, it *is* possible.
Many philosophers claim that all material things are illusion,
that there is *only* mind. The philosophy that states there is
no world independent of your perceiving it is called solipsism
and is opposed by materialism, the doctrine that physical matter is the only reality and can exist independently of consciousness. If solipsism is the truth, "reality" and the image
are one.

While it is debatable whether the image and reality are one,
no one would dispute the assertion that they influence each
other enormously. What you experience in the world outside
influences your internal reality and what is going on in your
head affects the way you relate to that which is outside. A
more positive internal environment will lead to a more positive
external one. When you *feel* good the world looks beautiful
and when you *feel* bad the earth is ugly.

How Do I Make an Image Real?

For an image to seem real, you need to experience it in all five senses. Reality comes to you through five senses. The only difference between an image and reality is the *source* of the stimulation or data. Reality comes from outside your head. Images come from inside. You can perceive both with equal vividness.

When you create an image you draw on past sensory data that has been recorded in your cortex. You can retrieve data from this sensory memory bank and play it back in a staggering array of new combinations and permutations. You do not have to project it back into consciousness in the same sequence or combinations in which it entered. For example, you could play back the reality of a white bird sitting on a blue table as a row of twenty winged white tables with no bird present. Fantastic as this image may seem to you, it does have a basis in reality.

As your range of experience increases, so does the amount of information at your disposal for creating new images. Your retrieving a bit of sensory data to make an image feels no different to you than your *trying* to remember a fact or a figure. If the image you desire to create calls for you to be walking along the beach, work at recalling what it felt like for you to walk on a beach. If you've never been on a beach, recall hot sun, wet water, white sand, and the taste and smell of salt from other separate experiences, put them together, and *create* a memory of your walking on the beach. It's that simple! You can reorganize bits from your past in any way you wish.

To make your image real, therefore, you focus on the sensations called for in its production and *remember* times when you actually had these sensations. The process of remembering will trigger the recording. Sometimes this takes a lot of energy. Remember the time you struggled to recall a certain date? At first it was buried somewhere, but with determined effort you were able to get the material to surface. Your retrieving a certain smell or sound is the same process.

If you're having difficulty trying to create a sensation in an image and it's available to you in reality, go find the real thing. Then try to remember it. For example, if you're trying to stop eating chocolate cake by imagining yourself able to resist it, and you cannot remember what chocolate smells like, go sniff the real thing and immediately attempt to recall the smell for your image. A recent memory is always easier to bring back.

How Do I Strengthen an Image?

Your images become more vivid with practice. However, a technique you can use to speed up the process is to practice concentrating on one of your senses to the exclusion of the others. A blind man has supernormal hearing because he has given this sense more attention. A sculptor focuses on touch, a gourmet on taste, a perfumer on smell, a musician on sound, a painter on sight. They *develop* these senses by paying more attention to them.

You can develop a sense in an image by concentrating on it. If for example you are able to create the image of a beach in vivid detail except for the smell of salt air, imagine *only* the salt air. Create a beach image where the waves are silent, the night black, and the water out of touch. Your only clue to being on a beach is the smell of salt air.

You can heighten the reality of an entire image by imagining it in only one sense at a time and then putting all the senses back together for the final revitalized result. You will see that this technique is especially useful for increasing your powers of sexual imagery.

Is the Average Person Good at Imagery?

Yes. Images run through your mind all the time. Imagery therapy consists of your simply learning to control *what* particular images you wish to play. This requires your concentration. If concentration is psychotically impaired, as it is in schizophrenia, it will be more difficult to focus on the imagery. But even schizophrenics are able to benefit from specially tailored images which more closely approximate their "bizarre" thought patterns.

What Makes One a Good Subject for Imagery Techniques?

Intelligence, the power to concentrate, and the ability to relax make you a good subject. The self-hypnosis technique that I gave you in Chapter 1 will enable you to relax. Your practice and repetition of the images will improve your concentration. As for intelligence, your IQ would have to be extraordinarily low for you not to be able to create *any* images. Researchers now believe that even white rats have some form of images running through their tiny brains.

How Should I Give Myself an Image?

You can tape-record the images in this book exactly as I wrote them and simply follow their directions on playback. However, if you choose to rehearse your image from memory it's important for you not to verbalize it. For example, if you have an image of yourself walking along the beach, don't say to yourself, "I am walking along the beach." *Just be there.* Feel yourself there. There's no need for you to say, "I am there." When you remember a past good time at a party the memory doesn't speak to you, saying, "I am once again at that party." You simply remember it. However, when you work with the self-hypnosis technique, it is all right to say to yourself, "I am now feeling a sense of relaxation moving up from my toes," etc.

Many people report that the first few times they practice imagery it is as though they are seeing themselves in the image on a movie screen. They ask, "Should I see myself or actually be there?" *Be there!* But don't be alarmed if at first it's like watching yourself in a movie. With practice your sense of detachment will subside.

Should I Use a Tape or Rely on My Own Memory?

If you tape either the self-hypnosis technique or the images, only use the tape every other time you practice. Tape and memory have their own individual advantages. A tape allows you to relax and let go without worrying whether you will remember all the salient details. Your creating an image from memory gives you a greater sense of independence and self-control. It also lets you go at your own rate. Certain senses in an image take time to conjure up. You may just be beginning to get the smell of a salt-air breeze when your tape goes on to the vision of a sunset. If you had had a little more time to linger, your image would have been more vivid.

If you do well practicing from memory alone, that is great! If the images you are working on appear difficult and nothing seems to be coming, try taping them. I seldom suggest that a client tape the images on his first visits. It's only if he reports that he doesn't think he's getting anywhere that I will suggest a tape. You may find that if you have trouble practicing from memory alone, a tape can work miracles. But remember, if you rehearse only from memory, that is excellent. If you use a tape, alternate it with memory.

What If I Don't Get It?

Relax. You will. In time. Your images always become more real with practice. Tell yourself that it's not important to get it, that it's okay to fail. Even if mastering a particular image to eliminate a certain problem is terribly important to you, *tell yourself* that you do not care whether the image seems real or not. This is a hard lesson for many people to learn, but it's at the point where you let go, where you do not force it, that it will all come together. Be patient. Do not allow yourself to make it too important. That is part of your exercise.

Clara, a forty-two-year-old housewife suffering from constant and excruciating back pain, illustrates how you can use the technique of "paradoxical intention" to remain patient.

Clara had been on medication for many years and said she "couldn't live without it." Her internist, fearing she was becoming addicted, was gradually cutting her dosage and she was certain she couldn't go on. She'd said on her first visit that imagery was her last hope. If it didn't work she was going to kill herself.

For several months Clara and I worked at getting her to imagine that her back was immersed in ice, totally numb. Occasionally she would experience a tingling, the beginning of anesthesia, but then she would lose it. Finally she said she was giving up. There was one more image I wanted to try on her, but she refused, saying she'd only come to tell me she was quitting. Treatment was hopeless. "Great," I said, "it isn't going to work. Who cares? Let's try it one more time just for the heck of it. This is your last visit, so what difference does it make?" In less than five minutes, Clara's back went stone numb. It went numb because she could let go and allow the image to take over.

Whenever you find yourself becoming too impatient for positive results you may find, like Clara, that giving yourself affirmations such as, "I don't care if I get it. It doesn't matter. I don't care," will help you to reduce the anxiety you are creating by your impatience to succeed and allow you to achieve success after all. Telling yourself that you don't want the very thing you do want, in order to reduce the stress of pushing too hard, is called "paradoxical intention." You may find it a useful tool whenever you become too eager for mastery.

There's a fine line between trying and pushing. Imagery *does* take energy, it does take work. You can't just lie there with the tape going and doze off, as some of my clients have been prone to do. But you also cannot force the issue and will the image to become real. Active recall, not brute force, will make an image materialize. Don't grit your teeth and flex your muscles to get an image going. Direct your total attention to the immediate sensations called for in the image, not to the goal you wish the image to achieve. Don't anticipate. Without anticipation there could be no worry. Without worry it will all happen.

How "Real" Must My Image Be to Get Results?

Not very. I am continually amazed at the great results obtained by people who claim they "can't see a thing" when practicing their images. Obviously something is being shaken up in their heads when they do these imagery exercises, even though it may not *seem* like it to them at the time. Though they report that their imagery is weak, they are nonetheless no longer smoking, drinking, overeating, ejaculating too soon, or doing whatever it is that they were imagining overcoming.

Will I Be Aware of What Is Going on Around Me During an Image?

Usually yes. As your concentration on the image increases you will begin to shut out extraneous competing stimuli and you will not attend to environmental distractions. However, for the most part, two realities will coexist. You will still retain a vague knowledge that you are "really" lying on a couch in your bedroom, or wherever you happen to be during your practice session. As you become more proficient, you may have flashes, moments when your image takes complete hold, when for a brief, shining moment your old reality is totally out of consciousness.

Will I Always Remember What Happened During an Image?

In lighter stages of imagery two realities coexist and you remember everything that occurred in the image. As your imagery becomes more vivid and your concentration intensifies, bits and pieces may not be remembered, and in some cases you may be "blank" for your entire image. Often it returns to you later.

This amnesia is spontaneous and occurs whether you desire or suggest it or not. It is a remarkable feat to spend five minutes listening to an image and, immediately upon coming out of it, not remember it at all. It is even more remarkable to give yourself an image from memory and then not remember whether you gave it to yourself! This does happen, however, and it should be a cause for celebration. It's a sign that your image was very real. Your present reality and the reality of your image are so clearly defined at this stage that the two are mutually exclusive. You can no longer process them simultaneously.

Often when you return to your "imagery reality" you will remember things from other images that you were unable to recall in your "normal reality." While amnesia is proof positive of strong imagery, in over half of the cases it does not occur, and you shouldn't take its absence as an indicator that your concentration is weak. As with self-hypnosis, the presence of amnesia indicates strong concentration, but its absence indicates nothing.

What If There's Something in the Image I Don't Like?

As you will see, some of the images are designed expressly so that you won't like them. They ask you to experience unpleasant sensations that you can pair with things you like too much. This procedure is called "sensitization." You imagine something you hate, such as the smell of vomit, in conjunction with something you crave, such as cigarettes, so that you will come to hate cigarettes as much as the vomit.

On the other hand, if the image is intended to be pleasant and to relax you, but you find some of it aversive, you can change it. For example, even though most people enjoy walking along the beach, you might not. Perhaps you burn easily and the thought of a blazing, yellow sun is not attractive to you. *However*, rather than removing the unpleasant elements from this type of image, it is better that you *make them positive*. You have the power to make anything pleasurable. It's *your* image. You created it. *In this image* you *love* a blazing, yellow sun. That's the exercise!

Once you are able to make disliked objects in an image

more attractive, you will be able to change their valence in reality also. This is an invaluable lesson. The negativity of an experience is a function of your perception. You *make* it what it is. You have the power to imagine being sawed in half by a chain saw and enjoy it. You also have the power to be actually sawed in half and enjoy it, but there's usually no point. I say "usually," because there are times when the power to turn pain to pleasure has great payoffs. The early Christian martyrs signaled to their friends that they were feeling no pain when they were burned at the stake. Some of them in fact laughed in ecstasy. They weren't suffering the pain of corporeal destruction, they were reveling in the sublime joy of spiritual transcendence.

If you *choose* to hate beaches, or tapioca pudding, or people with red hair, or flying in airplanes, fine! That's your choice. But you should also have the power not to hate, not to fear, any object you select. It seems only logical that the fewer things in your present reality that you hate or that make you uncomfortable, the better you will feel. Why nurse a hangup? Anything that makes you feel unpleasant is a hangup. Rather than refusing to imagine an image with oranges because you do not like oranges, why not imagine an image *in which you like oranges?* Oranges will then be one less thing in this world that makes you uncomfortable.

You hate things because you *think* you hate things. Imagine you like them, and you will. It's your choice. Make a list of all the things you don't like. Then create an image for practice in which you see yourself really enjoying them. It'll change your reality. First the thought, then the deed. Change your imagery and a change in reality will inevitably follow.

What If I Think Other Thoughts During My Image?

Don't worry about it. That's par for the course. When you relax your mind and allow images to surface, much irrelevant data is bound to surface with them, especially at first. Analysts have used relaxation and imagery for years in the technique known as "free association" to produce a wealth of thoughts streaming through consciousness. All learning is by association. One thought triggers another, one image triggers another. You will find that as you practice imagery you will have memories of events that you haven't thought of in years. Some may go all the way back to early childhood. Many of these old images can be therapeutic and give you new insights as to why you are behaving the way you do today. Older imagogic data may be playing at a subconscious level and influencing your present life in ways you didn't realize. Once these old images surface, you can deal with them. Reprogramming consists of your reorganizing this old material. Keep the good on tap and stop playing the negative.

So you see that "extraneous" thoughts can be a very beneficial by-product of your imagery practice. In time you will be proficient enough at imagery control to shut old images out completely, if you choose. In the meantime, use them to understand why you are what you are today.

How Long Should I Stay in an Image?

The images in this book usually last between five and ten minutes, but you can stay in an image as long as you like. Longer imagery sessions naturally require greater concentration and are more difficult to maintain. It is not inconceivable to prolong an image over several hours, at which time your diminished concentration or falling asleep would bring you out of it.

Is It Ever Difficult to Come Out of an Image?

No. You won't experience any difficulty in shifting from an image to "reality." You can end an image simply by opening your eyes. You can use any cue you choose as a signal that the image is to end. Common techniques include counting to three, snapping your fingers, or sitting up. If you fall asleep during an image you will awaken later much refreshed. An image requires your conscious, directed attention, and you will not be able to maintain it in a sleep state. An image may be so pleasant that you feel reluctant to leave it—just as you leave any good time with reluctance—but once your decision is made, you will come back to this reality. Your chief concern is getting into the image. Coming out is easy.

How Do I Keep My Image Fresh?

Repetition is the key to learning, and you may have to rehearse images several times before they take effect. There is no set number of times you need to go over a given image. Practice until you get results, if it takes one or a hundred times. While you may continually modify your images in order to keep them fresh, it is also possible to maintain freshness by altering your perception rather than the image. You have the power to maintain the "illusion of the first time." The key to this is, *don't anticipate.* Stay in the now. Concentrate only on the senses involved in the image at the time. Just as a good actor doesn't contemplate his next lines while delivering his present ones, a good imagery subject doesn't flash on the future while conjuring the present. Rehearse an image as if it's the first time you've ever done it. You have no idea what's coming next. That is the exercise!

Can I Make My Own Images?

Definitely! Specific images are delineated for you in this book to serve as models for building your own. They have been found to be particularly effective for the treatment of certain problems by a trial-and-error procedure used on a large patient population. They are images that work best *on the average.* After practicing with the standard images you may modify them to meet your individual needs as well as construct completely new images of your own.

Why Is an Image So Powerful?

Because that's all there is. Consciousness is an image.

Can I Use Images the Rest of My Life, After I Solve a Particular Problem?

Absolutely! Your training in imagery control begins by using specifically constructed images for specific problems, but once you get the hang of it you can branch out to other areas of your life and modify your way of dealing with things in general. In all cases you can use imagery to maximize what you get out of reality.

You can use images to change your entire perceptual gestalt. How you view the world today is a function of all the ways you've viewed it before. When an infant sees fire for the first time, his only impression is redness. He gets closer and a new impression is added: warmth. From this point on, whenever he "sees" fire his visual perception is altered by his "knowledge" that the fire feels warm. His memory or image of the fire's tactile impression influences his visual perception indefinitely. Your previous images or memories in all five senses influence every sensory impression in every sense modality that you have thereafter.

As years pass and you store millions upon millions of bits of sensory images, they come to exert an enormous influence on the way you perceive reality, on the way your cortex "interprets" sensory stimuli. Your present sensation is distorted by this huge block of sensory data. If you keep adding negative impressions to this block, your reality will be distorted on the negative side. If you *choose* your programming, allow only positive data access, or at the very least *increase* the amount of positive data you process, you will shift this library of data to the plus side—and along with it, your perception of reality.

Contrary to popular opinion, a negative experience is *never* good. Even if you do "learn" from it, whatever that means. The only thing ever learned from a bad experience is that you should not have had it in the first place. Suffering does not build a healthy character. It only makes your perceptual gestalt more negative and blackens your reality. I'm going to show you how to use imagery to fill your consciousness with positive, motivating, energizing thoughts. They will produce a bountiful harvest in reality.

How to Create Your Own Imagery

Before I give you the images that I've found to be so effective in evoking healing, higher knowledge, and power, I want to tell you how to create your own imagery. The foundation for all imagery techniques is to imagine whatever it is you want to have happen. If you wish to be healthy, mentally picture yourself, using all five senses, as vigorous and robust. If a particular career is your goal, envision yourself already in that career. If wealth is your desire, visualize yourself rich, secure, and happy. You create a desired effect in reality by first manifesting it in mind.

To help you attain the effects you desire I'll instruct you in three kinds of imagery:

1. Imagery to eliminate a specific problem or achieve a final goal
2. Imagery to produce a phenomenon that can serve as a means to your final goal
3. Imagery to strengthen your powers of imagery so that you can perform the first two types of imagery more effectively

Let's begin by looking at the first kind of imagery so that you can learn how to create an image to cure a definite problem or attain an ultimate goal.

Imagery to Achieve Ultimate Goals

When you create an image to achieve an ultimate goal you imagine that you have already attained your goal. While the basic principle sounds simple there are many ways of going about it. In the following pages I've presented some common goals you might have for physical and emotional healing. Use the self-hypnosis technique to clear your mind before practicing any of the imagery exercises.

Alcoholism, Drug Abuse, Smoking, and Weight Control

If your goal is to get off a harmful substance such as alcohol, drugs, cigarettes, or food that is unhealthy and/or making you gain weight, there are two types of imagery you can use to eliminate your problem, positive or aversive. In both cases you visualize the final goal, yourself as a person who no longer desires the substance you want to eliminate from your life.

Personally, I prefer the positive approach to the aversive

one, and I start my patients out with positive imagery and advise that you do the same. You can begin your positive approach by imagining that you are in the place where you are most likely to engage in the behavior you wish to eliminate. An alcoholic might imagine a bar, a cocaine addict a party situation, a smoker his desk at work, an overweight person the kitchen. Really put yourself there vividly in all five senses. Ask yourself, "What do I see? What do I hear? What do I feel? What do I smell? What do I taste?" You might even ask yourself what you just finished doing—such as getting home from work, shopping, or talking to a friend or relative—as these activities contribute to your present state of mind and set the scene as much as the physical environment. Fill in your psychological environment as well, the thoughts streaming through consciousness, your present mood and feelings.

Next see the substance you want to turn off to on a bar, table, or floor directly in front of you. Take your time recalling what it really looks like and be specific. If it's alcohol, what kind of alcohol? What are you most likely to drink? Scotch, vodka, whiskey, gin? Is the bottle there? What brand are you drinking or smoking? What bad food are you eating? Be specific. Is it chocolate? Chocolate what? Cookies, cake, candy? You can get by with giving yourself a general affirmation such as, "I avoid all foods with cane sugar," but there is no such thing as a general image. There is no way that you can imagine all things with cane sugar on the table before you. In order to effectively create an image you have to know *exactly* what is in it.

Now imagine yourself picking up the substance you wish to eliminate from your life. Really *feel* it in your hand; the wet, cold surface of the martini glass, the soft, powdery cocaine, the dry texture of the cigarette wrapper, the gooey mass of the chocolate bar.

Sniff the substance. Really smell the brandy, hashish, tobacco, or cream cheese that you will be turning yourself off to. Take your time. Think. Remember. Handle the substance and listen to the sound it makes: a tinkling liquor glass, rustling of marijuana leaves between your fingers, crinkling of a cigarette wrapper, breaking of a chocolate bar.

Now imagine that you effortlessly set the substance down and leave the room. The moment you are out of sight, sound, touch, and smell of the substance, imagine feeling fantastic. Place yourself in the most wonderful spot you've ever been or the place you've always wanted to go. You might visualize the beaches of Tahiti, a tropical lagoon, a long-remembered night with friends around a campfire or in a forest. Again, make this place real in all five senses.

You may not realize it, but what you've just done is imagine yourself as the person you want to be, a person who effortlessly resists an unwanted substance and feels absolutely marvelous for doing so. In the positive approach you experience the substance in all senses except taste since you imagine having no desire to ingest it. Then you effortlessly put it down and walk away from it. You reward your act of effortless resistance by imagining yourself in literally the nicest place imaginable.

Although our primary concern throughout this book is imagery, I will on occasion suggest affirmations you might like to try in conjunction with your imagery if they are particularly appropriate. In this case, when you imagine setting the substance down you might also tell yourself, "I resist rum [heroin, cigarettes, pasta, or whatever] effortlessly." With alcohol, drugs, and cigarettes you might also respectively add, "I am a nondrinker [non-user or nonsmoker]." I wouldn't suggest calling yourself a non-eater, no matter how much you wish to lose weight. However, you can tailor a similar affirmation for weight control if you make it more specific, such as, "I am a non-eater of chocolates."

I'd suggest using an aversive imagery approach to substance abuse, including smoking and weight control, only if the positive method fails you, and only if you don't find such a technique objectionable. Please don't force yourself to do something you don't want to do. There are many imagery options available to you. Although aversive imagery may give you faster and more dramatic results, its effects often don't last as long as the ones attained using the positive imagery approach that I just outlined.

The aversive imagery approach, or "covert sensitization," as it is often called, begins the same way as the positive imagery approach. Imagine yourself vividly in all five senses in the location where you are most likely to partake of the substance that you wish to eliminate from your life. Imagine experiencing the substance through your senses of sight, hearing, touch, taste, and smell. At this point the procedure changes. Instead of effortlessly resisting the substance, you begin consuming it. Really imagine its taste—the sharp bite of tequila, the metallic taste of crystal, the bitter flavor of tobacco, the sweetness of a jelly doughnut. Imagine that you keep ingesting the substance and that with every sip, snort, smoke, or bite, you have a growing sense of nausea. Continue recalling the sight, sound, touch, taste, and smell of the substance and pairing it with the nausea.

Now imagine that you throw up. Visualize it graphically in every detail. Hear the vomit pour from your mouth as from a faucet and splat upon the unused portion of the substance that you are abusing. See yellow and green gobs of puke and slime floating in your drink, soaking into your cocaine, absorbing through your cigarette paper, mixing with your non-dietetic foods. Feel the slime running down your face and hands. Taste and smell the rancid, sour puke mixed with the taste and smell of the alcohol, drugs, cigarettes, or unhealthy food.

You may end your image here, but I suggest you stop on a more positive note in what is called an "escape relief" paradigm. At this point you imagine getting up, leaving the room, and immediately being transported to the most wonderful place you can imagine, just as you did to end the positive imagery approach. You are thus rewarding yourself for removing yourself from the presence of the unwanted substance, as well as punishing yourself for consuming it.

Although aversive imagery, like positive imagery, entails

your imagining yourself as someone who no longer desires the substance, you can see that the means of doing this are quite different. Here you are punished before you turn off. Before, you are already turned off when the image starts.

The key to effectively using an aversive imagery approach is to imagine pairing something unpleasant with whatever it is you wish no longer to like. I used vomit to illustrate the method because it is the aversive stimulus I use most often. You can pair anything you dislike with something you like too much in order to turn yourself off to it. I recall a woman in her forties who imagined wrapping brownies in her husband's old smelly socks to turn herself off to chocolate. A nineteen-year-old cocaine addict imagined snorting coke in the presence of the rotting corpse of a friend who had been found thawing in the spring after he was shot in a fall hunting accident. Be creative. As noted above, I personally prefer the positive approach, but I've seen many cases of dramatic results achieved through the aversive technique when all else failed.

Drug Abuse

There is one imagery technique especially suited for the treatment of drug abuse that I'm not including with alcoholism, smoking, and weight control. Instead of creating an image to change your self-perception to that of a person who no longer craves the drug, you create an image that gives you the same effects as the drug, to be used as a substitute for the drug.

To begin, make a list of all the feelings the drug produces in you. Cocaine, for example, may give you a racing sense of high energy. You may feel wonderfully optimistic, believe you can do anything. Marijuana may give a sense of mellowness. Perceptual alterations in form and color might be your experience with LSD. With heroin, the world may become dreamy, as you slip into a euphoric relaxation.

Really give this list your full concentration, pinpointing

the drug state in vivid detail. Ask yourself, "What do I feel like on this drug? What do I like about it? How is it different from my normal reality?"

Once you've listed the specific effects that the drug has on you, think of what kind of image you could create to produce the same or similar effect. If high energy is an effect you want to induce with your image, consider what would make your adrenaline flow: vigorous activity like running, jumping, wrestling; exciting, dangerous situations such as body surfing, mountain climbing, white-water rafting; wild sexual encounters.

If mellowness is the effect you wish to feel, think of what, other than the drug, has given you this feeling: the relaxing calm after a strenuous physical workout; the sweet sense of peace right before you drift into slumber after a good but tiring day; that wonderful feeling that steals over you when a hush falls and you have a quiet time.

If you enjoy the hallucinogenic effects of LSD, create an image with psychedelic colors and melting, altering forms. If it's a dreamy, relaxed state you're after, you might create an image of floating in a mist or on a cloud, or of shrinking down to nothing, free of your body, to achieve the phenomenon of dissociation, which I'll soon describe in detail. Once you've created an image that produces the effects on your list, go into this image whenever you crave the effects of the drug that you have been abusing.

Marla, a twenty-eight-year-old heroin addict, had a $150-a-day habit. She used four times a day, and was so sick every night she couldn't sleep. "The first time I did heroin it was so dreamy and relaxing. I kept using it once in a while for five or six years, no problem. Then I just stepped it up to every day. It took me a month to get sick. Two years ago I would have said there was no way in hell I'd be strung out. It won't happen to me. But it's hard when it's right there.

"Methadone didn't work. I just got addicted to that. If I could just sleep. As soon as I start to relax, the program kicks in: 'You'll be mine till death do us part,' it says. It's like a marriage vow. I get high alone now. I want it all. I don't want to share. I'm not like that. I'm a sharing, giving person. I can't have a supply in the house cause I'd do it all. So I have to get it every day. I can't save it. I don't know why. You can only get so high. I can never get enough. I could have a whole drawer full and still be looking on the floor for more."

Marla had described her initial high as "dreamy and relaxing." I asked her if there was any other experience that she could conceive of as being like this. "Becoming air," she said. "Evaporating." She set the scene of her image by a pond in a redwood forest. Then she imagined that a band of elves wrapped her tightly in a gossamer twine, binding her tighter and tighter. Suddenly a glorious turquoise butterfly appeared. He took the end of the twine and flew high into the sky, spinning her like a top, releasing the pressure with such a force that she exploded, diffusing over the wooded pond, becoming one with the summer breeze. Marla was able to re-create a sense of evaporation akin to her sensation of heroin use by practicing this image. It took over a year, but in time her imagery-induced effects became a viable substitute for the drug, and she no longer uses heroin.

Anorexia

Just as you can use imagery in conjunction with your diet to turn yourself off to food, you can use it to become more attracted to eating as well. This is something you may want to do if you have trouble gaining weight or are anorexic.

There is one imagery technique that I find particularly effective for increasing the desirability of food. Pick a particular food that you want to eat more of or put back into your meals. If you've been anorexic long, you'll most likely choose a food that is both nutritious and high in calories as you'll want to start gaining weight soon. I often suggest to my anorexic patients that they begin with a high-calorie fruit such as bananas, which are easy to digest and are not as repugnant to them as more greasy or fatty foods may be.

Next, think of a wonderful place you've been, or where

you've always wanted to go, as you did in the last section to reward yourself for resisting undesirable substances. When you've created this scene, vivid in all five senses, incorporate your eating of the specific food you selected into your image. For example, if you're concentrating on eating more bananas and the place you've always wanted to go is Tahiti, imagine a banana tree midway through your image along with your picking and eating bananas from this tree and loving every mouthful. It's important that you really envision enjoying the experience of eating the banana, because that is your goal, to *like* eating bananas.

After you've practiced this image for a week, it's time for you to actually eat while you are in the image. Take a real banana and place it by your side, within your reach, while you induce self-hypnosis and begin creating your image. When you come to the point in your image where you pick the banana, reach for the real banana by your side. Then, when you imagine eating a delicious banana in Tahiti, eat the real banana. Directly use your imagery to enhance reality. When you're done eating the banana, finish your image and bring yourself out just as you would bring yourself out of any hypnotic or altered state, by saying to yourself, "I am now going to count to three. At the count of three, I will open my eyes. I will be completely relaxed, totally refreshed. One ... two ... three."

If you select a food that needs cutting or other preparation, I suggest you do this ahead of time so you only need to concern yourself with eating the pieces during your image. If the food is normally eaten with a fork or spoon you might find it easier to use your fingers for this exercise; however, with a little practice you'll soon become adept at using a utensil with your eyes closed. Another option is to slowly open your eyes during the eating portion of the image, all the time continuing to focus your attention on the sensations comprising Tahiti. Just as waking hypnosis—hypnosis with your eyes open—is possible, so is waking imagery. You definitely have the power to use imagery to override reality, even with your eyes open, as we'll examine in depth later in our exploration of positive and negative hallucinations.

Athletics

Imagery is now being used to train Olympic contenders throughout the world. The key, again, is to imagine what you want to have happen. Envision, in all five senses, the athletic form you wish to demonstrate. Then match it in reality. If you are going to use imagery to help you excel in sports, it is especially important that your image be specific. You must know the correct form before you can visualize it. You know what the experience of resisting a cigarette is, but you may not be knowledgeable of the mechanics of a good golf swing. That is why I recommend you seek expert coaching in conjunction with your use of imagery to improve your athletic prowess. The athletic form you imagine must be correct.

It seems that every sport has its classic areas of error. When serving in tennis, players often reach for the ball rather than waiting for the ball to come to the racket. Golfers bend their arm during their drive. Basketball throwers don't follow through with their aim. Baseball hitters step into the ball. Once you find your area of error, imagery can be invaluable to you in correcting it.

The concept of combining mind and body to achieve a super athlete has gained great popularity in America in the last ten years, although it is certainly not a new concept. The ancient Greeks were masters in achieving a spartan discipline to merge mind and body into a single, powerful athletic machine. Nowhere has the relationship of mental concentration to physical performance been more highly developed than in the oriental disciplines of karate and jujitsu. But in America the idea of "Zen sports" is relatively new. We are only beginning to put our minds into our athletics.

The method of mentally mastering your body to achieve athletic excellence is really quite simple. Once you know the athletic form you truly want to manifest, imagine yourself successfully performing in that form. Research has shown that you can make more baskets simply by mentally rehearsing successful free throws ahead of time.

Most often the accurate mental rehearsal will lead to its manifestation without your having to use imagery *during* the sport itself. However, just as you can eat in an image to eliminate anorexia, you can also perform in an image to excel at a sport. In my college years I was a lifeguard and swimming instructor. A classic error that many of my students made in learning the breaststroke was that they pulled with their arms and kicked their legs at the same time. The correct form is: pull, kick, glide. Pull your arms. *Then* do your frog kick. Then glide.

Mental rehearsal was not always enough to manifest the correct form. When it was insufficient, I asked my students to hold the right image during their actual swimming, to literally merge realities, bringing their reality up to match their image. They were to imagine themselves lying prone, facedown in the water, while they were actually doing this. Then they were to imagine pulling their arms down through the water to propel themselves and lifting their heads to breathe. When the arm stroke was finished they executed a frog kick while resting their faces back in the water and gliding. The object, once more, was to produce an image so vivid it overrode reality. In this case the image became reality. A perfect breaststroke became their only option. It was the only pattern in consciousness to follow.

I want to issue you a word of caution about using imagery during an actual athletic performance. While there is little danger other than maybe a mouthful of water in using imagery while you swim, the results of making an error can be greater with other sports, such as skiing. Merging imagery and reality on a ski slope can lead to a broken leg if you don't quite have the hang of it and your concentration lapses. It takes your undivided attention to create and hold the correct image you wish to manifest. This image is much easier to hold in a mental rehearsal where you are lying down undistracted, with your eyes closed, rather than speeding down a ski slope wide-eyed.

If your concentration lapses, and your image is distorted, that distorted image may be what you match in reality. Be very sure of your clarity of thought before using it while performing sports like skydiving or jumping hurdles. Stick to pure mental rehearsal in these cases for a long time before venturing forth into the use of imagery during actual performance. And then use it at first only on the beginner's slopes and low hurdles. Give yourself time, go at a comfortable pace, and you'll be amazed at what a good athlete you can become using the appropriate imagery.

Cancer and Disease

The use of imagery in the treatment of cancer patients came to the forefront in the work of Carl and Stephanie Simonton at the Cancer Counseling and Research Center in Fort Worth, Texas. In their book with James Creighton, *Getting Well Again,* they describe how a person's reaction to stress and other emotional factors may have contributed to the onset and progress or recurrence of their disease. They explain how their program, which includes relaxation, techniques for learning a positive attitude, and visualization, enhances patients' chances for recovery and substantially improves their quality of life.

The Simontons stress that most people who are exposed to known cancer-producing substances still remain healthy. What we need to look at, therefore, is not only what causes the disease, but what maintains health. Mere exposure to a disease does not mean we become ill. The Simontons state, "The body does battle with cancerous cells on a routine basis, and routinely the cancerous cells are contained or destroyed so that they can do no harm." A significant body of research demonstrates that the development of a cancer does not require just the presence of abnormal cells, it also requires a suppressing of the body's normal defenses.

We've already seen, in the pioneering work of Hans Selye, that there is a strong link between stress and illness. Research also shows that the incidence of cancer in laboratory animals is greatly increased when they are put under stress. Finally, more and more findings, including those of the Simontons, show a substantially different incidence rate for cancer among patients with different kinds of mental and emotional problems. Louise Hay in her excellent book on self-healing, *You Can Heal Your Life,* says that she has observed that cancer occurs in people who hold a deep resentment for a long period of time. She states, "To me, learning to love and accept the self is the key to healing cancers."

Self-hypnosis to create profound relaxation in order to remove stress and negative emotions such as resentment, guilt, and self-criticism, is therefore one of my first recommendations in the treatment of cancer. Positive imagery of any kind will reduce your level of stress, thus fortifying your immune system. The images described in the following chapters are all designed to make you more sensitive to the positive and less sensitive to the negative aspects of reality. I therefore recommend practicing the entire series as a means of strengthening your body's defenses and combating cancer.

There are also more specific images you may want to employ in your war against disease, including cancer. This brings us to a current hotbed of medical debate. There are three schools of thought concerning the efficacy of using imagery to treat cancer. The first school believes that it doesn't work, that there is no relation between what you think and the diseases you get, including cancer. The second school of thought recognizes the importance of relaxation and positive thinking for reducing stress and bolstering the immune system. Its adherents believe that positive imagery can help treat disease, because it strengthens the immune response. However, they also believe that it doesn't matter what you imagine as long as it is positive and reduces your stress: imagining yourself relaxing by a brook would be just as effective in the war on cancer as imagining that your cancer cells are being destroyed. They say this latter type of image is also stress-reducing because, if you believe it will work, it reduces your anxiety. Relaxation is the bottom line in the second school of thought.

The third school of thought is in accord with the second on the point that relaxation strengthens the immune system, but its supporters also feel that the content of the image, beyond the fact that it is relaxing, is important. They believe that the mind-body connection is even more specific, that what you see is what you get. In their defense I have to say that if you imagine holding your right hand over a fire, the result is sweating—and, in more dramatic cases, a fever blister on your right hand. Relaxation aids the concentration necessary to achieve the effect, but it does not directly produce the effect. The image of fire produces the blister. The image produces the exact effect imagined.

The third school of thought would therefore support the belief that a specific image of cancer cure will produce that specific result. Again, the method for creating such an image is simple. Decide what form you want the cancer cells to take. You might want to imagine them as monsters in black capes, rotting meat, or even as cells under a microscope. Then decide how you want to picture the agents that will destroy them, namely the T killer lymphocytes, macrophages, or white cells. A powerful guy like robocop, a universal healing white light, an army of voracious, gobbling blue dots that eat everything in sight; you can envision anything you want to destroy the disease.

Now that the characters are set, put the image into action by imagining the good guys (your metaphor for your immune system) totally wiping out the bad guys (the cancer metaphor). Practice this image as often as you find comfortable, but generally no more than three times a day, five minutes each time. If one or both of your metaphors don't seem believable to you, don't pack the necessary punch, or lose their impact, change the image. If your image isn't as vivid as you'd like, you'll find that you can strengthen your powers of imagery by practicing the imagery sequence that begins in the next chapter.

Depression

It's been my observation that one of the primary causes of depression is projecting a negative outcome. Depressed people imagine their future as black. They see themselves never being happy, never getting the things they want and need. If they do conceive of achieving any of their goals, they visualize themselves unhappy in their realization. Money won't buy happiness. Friends won't buy happiness. Fame won't buy happiness. What will? Love? No, love is not enough to make the depressed person happy either. Only one thing can make you happy if you're truly depressed, and that is a change in your state of mind. You need to imagine yourself happy, conceive of your future as bright.

It doesn't really matter much what your images to end depression consist of, as long as you see yourself truly happy in them. Logic would dictate that you rehearse pleasant scenes such as boating, picnicking, or talking with friends, but even if you visualize yourself doing laundry or grocery shopping, the result will be positive if you imagine yourself as happy in these situations. Depressed people can envision themselves surrounded by loved ones at a wonderful party and still be miserable because they take the attitude, "Look, that only proves I'll always be depressed. I've got everything and still I'm unhappy. What a waste." In Chapters 6 and 9 you'll learn how to lift depression by creating sex energy, a force incompatible with the low-energy state of depression, but the best specific image you can create for ending depression is one in which you imagine yourself as happy, no matter what the circumstances.

Phobias

If you wish to create specific images to rid yourself of a phobia, you'll find it effective to construct a hierarchy first.

Divide your phobia into seven steps of increasing difficulty, Step 1 being an activity related to your phobia that is easy for you to do and Step 7 being the one you have the most difficulty with or can't do.

For example, if you have a social phobia that makes it uncomfortable for you to be with people, you might construct a hierarchy similar to this:

1. I'm talking on the phone to my mother.
2. My mother is serving me a meal.
3. I'm talking on the phone to my best friend whom I've known all my life.
4. I'm having lunch with my best friend.
5. I'm at a big party with over a hundred people and nobody knows me.
6. I'm circulating at a large party where only a few people know me.
7. I'm seated at a table for eight where everyone knows who I am, but I only know the host well.

This hierarchy could of course have many variations, but it is one I commonly make for social phobics. Then elaborate each step into an image detailed in all five senses. Practice each image in order, until it no longer makes you uncomfortable to think of it. See yourself relaxed in each step.

Two other common forms of hierarchies are called "temporal" and "distal." In a temporal hierarchy you divide your phobia into units of time. For example, if you are afraid of flying, Step 1 might be to imagine yourself a month from your departure, the time you first notice a twinge of anxiety. Each step takes you closer in time to your takeoff, till you reach Step 7, which could be your boarding the plane or the actual flight. In a distal hierarchy each step takes you closer in space to the feared object or event. If you're afraid of snakes, in Step 1 you might see yourself totally relaxed, standing outside a shop window peering at a snake in a glass cage several yards away. Each step takes you closer to the snake until in Step 7 you may imagine yourself picking it up, still in the same relaxed state that you imagined yourself in for Step 1.

The key to ending your phobia is to imagine yourself re-laxed every step of the way. Continue to practice Step 1 as an image until you are able to do it successfully, without expe-riencing any fear or anxiety. Then practice imagining Step 2 till you get similar results, and so on till you can visualize yourself relaxed in the final step. It's important when you practice this covert desensitization procedure to keep your images or steps separate. Don't look ahead, or you lose the value of the hierarchy. Don't think for a second of touching the snake when all your image calls for is for you to be looking at it through the window. Stay in the now. Imagine yourself relaxed each step of the way, and you will become what you envision in Step 7, a person who is relaxed and no longer afraid in a past phobic situation.

Pain

True to the imagery formula of imagining yourself the way you want to be, a specific image that you would create for pain control would consist of your imagining yourself without pain. There are of course an infinite number of variations on the form this image could take.

You might imagine a specific element taking your pain away. An excellent scene that I often use with patients is to envision oneself in a dazzling, healing white light that absorbs all discomfort. You also might visualize yourself in a vat of magic, soothing liquid that draws out all negativity from your body. A variation on this theme is to imagine the part of your body that is in pain separating, detaching from your body. You can intensify the effect by then imagining the detached section exploding or dissolving into thin air.

Another option is to envision your pain in a metaphor like those described in the section on imagery for cancer. You could, for example, imagine the pain as a murky green light that was completely erased by a soothing blue light.

You might prefer an image where your pain is already

gone. In this case you would imagine yourself moving freely and effortlessly through the routine of your normal day, feeling great. You may also choose to use imagery to produce anesthesia in the afflicted area, a technique I'll describe in the next section on phenomena you can produce with imagery.

Imagery to Produce Phenomena

Now that we've looked at how you can create your own images to achieve a final goal, let's take a look at a second kind of imagery: imagery to produce phenomena that can serve as a *means* to your final goal. Instead of visualizing the end product you desire, you use imagery to create a tool that you can then use to get what you want.

I'm going to teach you to use imagery to create eight such tools or phenomena. They are:

1. Relaxation
2. Anesthesia
3. Time Distortion
4. Dissociation
5. Heat Transfers
6. Sex Energy
7. Age Regression
8. Negative Hallucinations

My first book, *Hypnosis and Behavior Modification: Imagery Conditioning*, co-authored with William S. Kroger, M.D. (published by Lippincott in 1976), gives over ninety pages of bibliography covering the research on these phenomena.

Relaxation

You can use imagery to further deepen the profound relaxation you learned to create in Chapter 1 using the hypnotic clearing procedure. Use the same principles you did to create a positive image to reward yourself for resisting a substance. Using all five senses, recall a wonderful, positive time. It may have been a trip to the mountains, a night on the beach, a high school prom. Re-create it in every detail so that it takes you about five minutes to conjure. Preface it with self-hypnosis so that you are already in a relaxed state, which you can deepen with relaxing imagery.

Or create a completely new image using something that never happened to you, but that you would like to happen. Be as fanciful as you like. You might imagine yourself drifting on a cloud, floating in a sunset, swimming in a tropical lagoon. Again, make it real in all your senses. You'll be pleased to discover that this kind of positive image will serve to deepen the relaxation you've learned to create with self-hypnosis. Even though your ultimate goal may not be deeper relaxation, you will be able to use the phenomenon of imagery-induced relaxation as a tool to help you reach your ultimate goal.

Marshal, a twenty-eight-year-old carpenter, wanted to improve his work efficiency at building construction. "I keep getting laid off," he complained. "My foremen say I'm too slow. I'm conscientious and a good worker, but I can't keep up with the rest of the guys." After some probing I learned that Marshal's chief problem lay with pounding nails. His concentration would lapse and the nails would go in crooked and have to be pulled out. This cost a precious loss of time. "I think I'm just too uptight in the job," he said. "I'm so worried I can't pound a nail straight I choke up and forget what I'm doing. Then I blow it."

"What was the best time you ever had in your life?" I asked Marshal. After a few inquiries as to what I was after, and considerable thought, he answered, "About eight years ago, after an all-night party, I remember leaving the place alone about six in the morning. It was a big house way up in the hills where I'd never been before. When I walked outside it was like another world, all green with canyons and lots of mist. And it was so quiet, not a sound. I remember walking down the road to my car and the mist just swirled in. I couldn't see the house behind me or the road in front of me. It was like I'd died and gone to heaven."

I helped Marshal embellish this scene by filling in the sensory detail. He'd said what his experience looked and sounded like, but I wanted to know more about the touch, taste, and smell of it. I learned that he remembered a wet, warm softness to the mist, a smell of greasewood from the native shrubs growing along the canyon banks, and a faint taste of beer from the night before, a taste he found most pleasant in the context of his experience.

I asked Marshal to practice recalling this scene three times a day for a week. Then I suggested he spend five minutes in his car once he arrived at work to induce self-hypnosis and recall this scene so that he would come on the job relaxed. If he could take five minutes during lunch or coffee breaks to create more relaxation, so much the better. In two weeks Marshal reported, "I was a little nervous at first that someone would see me sitting in my car with my eyes closed, but nobody paid any attention to me. That image really did relax me. I found myself automatically thinking about it, you know, just for a flash, when I started getting uptight. Then I'd relax. It was great. Now that I can keep my mind on my job, I pound straight and stay in pace with the others." Marshal had learned to effectively use imagery-induced relaxation to improve his job performance. If you have trouble keeping your attention on your work you also might find that taking timeouts for imagery-induced relaxation will help you to focus better.

Anesthesia

You have the power to create the phenomenon of anesthesia if you use the appropriate imagery. This phenomenon can be used for many things, including eliminating pain or freezing hunger pangs. When you imagine cold in a particular area of your body, blood actually leaves that area and numbness ensues. You thus can control your blood flow and vasoconstriction by creating images involving cold.

The imagery technique that I use most often in this regard is called "glove anesthesia," a term that refers to your anesthetizing your hand so that you may then transfer that anesthesia to any part of your body where you are experiencing discomfort. To help you make up your own image for creating glove anesthesia, here are some guidelines: Place yourself in any situation where you will logically be able to introduce ice or snow. It could be a house in the winter, a ski lodge in the mountains, or even a kitchen or restaurant where you are about to be served a drink with ice in it. Really envision yourself there, working to make it real in every sense.

Now imagine ice or snow coming into your image. If, for example, you've pictured yourself in a house or ski lodge in winter, visualize going outside into the snow. If you're imagining yourself in a kitchen or restaurant, envision taking out an ice-cube tray or being served a drink with ice in it.

Next, imagine that with your right hand you pick up a fistful of snow or an ice cube. Squeeze it tightly, concentrating on the numb, wooden sensation that is beginning in the palm of your right hand; first the size of a pinpoint, then of a dime, then of a half-dollar, spreading like ripples on a pond. When you actually feel the numbness in your right hand, place your right hand on your right cheek. Let the numbness in your hand drain into your cheek.

Say to yourself, "My cheek is becoming numb, just as if novocaine had been injected into it." When all the numbness has drained from your hand to your cheek, place your hand once again at your side. Then place your hand again upon your cheek and let the numbness drain from your cheek back into your hand. Give yourself the affirmation, "My hand feels numb, like a log with nails in it." When all the numbness has drained from your cheek back into your hand, place your hand again at your side. You can then finish your image by going back inside or drinking your drink or completing whatever other business you may have started.

Practice the anesthesia-producing imagery until you really begin to feel the numbness in your hand and cheek. Then modify the procedure and transfer the numbness from your hand to any area where you may be feeling discomfort. You learn the procedure by transferring numbness from your hand to your cheek because it is easier to create anesthesia in an area that is pain-free and the cheek is a good place to start because it is a part of your body where you would likely have experienced numbness before because of novocaine.

Mike, nine, suffered a broken collarbone when he was hit by a car as he raced to school his first day of fourth grade. He had terrible nightmares for several weeks after the accident. The dreams would cause him to bolt upright in terror and then he'd have difficulty resuming a sleep position due to the pain of his mending collarbone.

I asked Mike to think of the coldest image he could, telling him we really wanted to freeze his pain. "I think that would be the time we skated across the lake," he said. "I'd never skated anywhere but a rink before and I overestimated my endurance. By the time we got across the ice my hands and feet were frozen numb. Then we had to skate back. I'd swear my feet were frozen solid. I couldn't even move my fingers when I got inside."

I told Mike to practice re-creating this image of his skating incident. When he really felt like his hands were ice-cold he was to transfer the cold to his right cheek and then back to his hand again as I have already described. Mike mastered the cold transfer in four days, whereupon I suggested he use this image to create cold in his right hand and transfer it to his collarbone whenever it was causing him discomfort. The technique proved especially effective when he found himself sitting up in bed in the middle of the night after a nightmare. It not only soothed his pain, it calmed his mind as well and enabled him to sleep calmly the rest of the night.

Time Distortion

Time distortion is another phenomenon you can create with imagery to make your life better. Time doesn't really exist. You get your concept of time from the number of events that transpire between one event and another. So, if I froze you solid for a hundred years and then asked you, "How long does it seem since I last spoke?" you'd say, "A second," because nothing had gone on in your head that past century. Because time is a psychological construct, you have the power to manipulate it psychologically. Normally, in your everyday life, you experience time expansion (time seems to be going very slowly) when you are having a terrible time, such as when it's raining, you're late, and your taxi isn't showing up. On the other hand, you experience time concentration (time seems to be passing quickly) when you're having a wonderful time, such as when you're at a party with great friends really enjoying yourself. What you want to be able to do is reverse that natural process. You want the bad times to go quickly and the good times to last forever.

The key to creating your own imagery for expanding time is to imagine that more time has passed in your image than it took for you to practice it. If the image seems real to you, it will feel as if more time has passed than actually has.

You may want to imagine that a lot more time is passing than the average five minutes it takes you to do an image: weeks, years, eons even. Or you may prefer to make it only a few minutes or hours more than the "real" five minutes. Imagining a lot of time is more dramatic and may hold your attention more; however, it may be easier for you to imagine only a few extra minutes or hours elapsing. Experiment. You may find special advantages in each case and use them both.

It's also beneficial to preface your time-expansion image with an appropriate affirmation, such as, "One minute of actual time will seem like ten minutes to me. Time will go by very, very slowly. It will seem like an eternity."

Garth, a thirty-two-year-old fireman, had used marijuana every day for the past five years. "It's starting to impair my judgment," he said. "I started using grass to relax me and keep from getting bored. Sitting around all day waiting for a fire can make you stir-crazy after a while. I thought I had a handle on it, but lately my timing seems to be off. My reflexes are bad. That can be fatal in an emergency where you're trying to save someone from a burning building."

A relaxing expanded sense of time is a common component in the experience of marijuana use. I wanted to show Garth how he could create his own sense of relaxing time expansion without relying on marijuana. I asked him to come up with an image in which a lot of time was passing. "The creation of the Grand Canyon," he laughed, "that took thousands of years." Garth didn't realize it then, but his was an excellent idea. I helped him construct an image where he envisioned centuries of erosion gradually shaping the terrain into one of the natural wonders of the world, accompanied by the sounds, tastes, smells, and feelings that went with it.

If this image seemed totally real to Garth when he practiced, it would seem to him like centuries, rather than five minutes, had passed during his practice session. Naturally the image did not seem that real, but it did afford him at least a twofold expansion of time; the image always seemed to last at least ten minutes. I advised Garth to use his image to create time expansion whenever he felt a craving for marijuana, as a substitute for the effects he normally got from the drug. It worked. In two months Garth was clean.

Britt, fifty-four, a family counselor, mother of two grown sons, married to Irv, fifty-six, a tax lawyer, had a recurring rash that drove her wild with itching. The rash was especially irritated by heat and tight clothing, and Britt found she was increasingly restricting her activities. "I stopped exercising," she said, "because it makes me too hot and I break out. I can't even dance with my husband anymore. In fact it's to the point where I'm afraid to go anywhere nice because it means dressing up and I'm only comfortable in something really loose that looks like hell and I wouldn't be caught dead in."

I taught Britt how to use imagery to create time expansion so that she could prolong the good periods when she wasn't itching. First I asked her to come up with an image where more than five minutes went by. "How about our summer vacation picnics?" she ventured. "We have a beautiful cottage on a lake in Northern California where we vacation in July. Usually we get up early, around six o'clock. We eat breakfast and are out by seven. I help Irv load the boat with cushions, oars, anchor, motor—all that stuff, and off we go. By eight we're at the head of the lake. There's a wonderful beach there that only he and I seem to have discovered. We park the boat on shore and hike through the woods till noon. By then we're starving. We spread out the blanket and have a marvelous picnic! Coleslaw, potato salad, hot dogs, the whole shooting match!" I couldn't have come up with a more tasty image if I'd tried.

You'll note that six hours go by in Britt's image, much less time than it took Garth to create the Grand Canyon, but still far more time than the five minutes it would take Britt to rehearse her image. If you choose to create an image where less than a day passes it can be helpful to periodically notice the time of day as Britt did: up at six, breakfast finished by seven, at the head of the lake by eight, picnic at noon. Other indications of time passing, such as the sun rising and setting, scheduled meals, and activities that take a given amount of time, are also good devices to incorporate into your time-expansion imagery. Britt practiced her image whenever she was free of itching and was able to expand this good time, leaving less and less time for the rash to occur. It was three months since her last flare-up when she successfully terminated therapy.

You may have already guessed that if the key to expanding time is to imagine more time passing, then the key to concentrating time is to imagine less time passing than the five minutes it takes you to do the image. If the image is real to you, the less time that passes in your image, the less time it will seem has actually passed. The possible ranges of time elapsed may, however, seem more limited than what is available to you for time expansion. Possible scenarios lasting more than five minutes may be easier to come up with than those lasting less; I'm sure, however, that the possibilities are infinite in either case.

I suggest prefacing your image with a suggestion for time concentration, such as, "Ten minutes of actual time will seem like one minute to me. Time will go by very, very rapidly. It will seem like an instant. In less than an hour I can accomplish an entire day's work and accomplish it more effectively than I would ordinarily."

Cynthia, sixty-three, a corporate accountant, had chronic spells of depression which were always worse in the morning. She learned to create an image for time concentration that would enable her to shorten these morning cycles. When I asked her to think of an image where the time elapsed was less than five minutes, she said, "What about a detailed story of a feather falling from a bird high in the sky?" I agreed that I liked the premise, and this is what we came up with: "You are lying on your back in sweet, green grass looking up at a clear, blue sky. A robin flies high overhead. See a red feather drop from his breast, glinting in the sun, falling toward you. Feel the warm rays of the sun against your skin. The feather is caught by an undercurrent, zigzagging downward. The heavy scent of sweet peas blows on the wind from a garden nearby. The feather comes closer. Notice the taste of strawberry jam from jam and muffins you had earlier that morning. See the wind ruffle the robin feather as it comes nearer. Roll over on your stomach and keep looking at the feather. Feel the bumpy earth in the grass beneath your stomach. Feel a tickle on your nose as the feather grazes it. The feather lands in the grass."

It would only take about ten seconds for a robin feather to fall from the sky, but it took Cynthia five minutes to imagine it. Much less time passes in the image than passes in reality.

Therefore, since the imaginal time is less than the actual time, the more real the image seems to Cynthia, the less time she will feel has passed. She used this image, prefaced by an affirmation for time concentration, whenever she felt depressed in the morning. The image plus affirmation produced a sense that time was passing rapidly and her depressive cycle was felt to pass more quickly. Again, use time expansion to prolong any positive periods of your life and time concentration to shorten any negative.

Dissociation

Dissociation is a state of euphoric relaxation. In its milder forms you may lose track of your body parts. Your hands may feel at your sides when in reality they are resting in your lap. Or your legs may feel crossed when they're not. In its more pronounced form, dissociation makes you feel as if you are rising off the couch or even separated from your body. Such cases of extreme dissociation have been termed traveling, clairvoyance, astral projection, or, a more scientific term, out-of-the-body experiences (OOBE's).

Robert Monroe, in his classic book *Journeys Out of the Body,* defines an OOBE as, "an event in which the experiencer (1) seems to perceive some portion of some environment which could not possibly be perceived from where his physical body is known to be at the time; and (2) knows *at the time* that he is not dreaming or fantasizing." In all its forms, dissociation produces a powerfully positive feeling and you can use it to your advantage.

There are several ways that you can create images to produce dissociation. One is to imagine that you are standing in the room where you are actually practicing your image. Imagine looking straight ahead and taking in the room in great detail; color of the walls, pictures hanging, pattern of the ceiling. Then turn around and carefully observe the rest of the room in all five senses. Now imagine turning back around and looking down to see a person lying on the surface where you are practicing. This person is lying perfectly still, the absolute picture of calm and repose. This person looks exactly like yourself. Next you turn back around and leave the room. Walk out of the building and into another building. Enter a room that's all white: white walls, floor, and ceiling. Go to the window and look out into the window of the room you just left. See that same person lying there in a state of total relaxation.

A second form of image you can create to produce dissociation is one where you imagine yourself floating up and out of your body. Begin your image by visualizing yourself in an absolutely beautiful place such as a serene garden or by an idyllic brook, wherever you would most like to be. See yourself completely calm, totally tranquil. Then imagine drifting up into the air, leaving the shell of your body still resting in its state of relaxation. Feel the sense of expansion and liberation that comes from no longer having carnal restrictions.

A third form of image, my favorite, involves your imagining your body shrinking till finally there is nothing left at all, nothing but consciousness, that is. This is an excellent way for you to acquire an emotional understanding of the knowledge that consciousness never dies. Matter transforms, but consciousness is constant. I think you'll find this type of image works best if you first place yourself in a beautiful setting before you begin to imagine your body shrinking. Make a little story out of it if you like.

Rob, a fifty-one-year-old investment banker, successfully used the detached, euphoric relaxation of dissociation to counter his fear of flying. He created a beautiful garden that consisted of every plant in the world, very much like the Garden of Eden. Then he imagined eating magic blueberries that caused him to shrink till finally there was nothing left but awareness. There was certainly no need now to fear flying. Imagining himself unrestricted by his body gave Rob a wondrous sense of freedom and euphoria. He successfully used this image on an airplane to counteract his anxiety whenever he found himself starting to worry about the flight.

Heat Transfers

Just as you can use imagery of cold to direct your blood out of a given area of your body to produce anesthesia, you can use your recall of heat to divert your blood into a specific bodily area. Cutting blood off to an area of your body causes it to become numb, as when your arms or legs "go to sleep" from lack of circulation because you've been putting too much weight on them too long. Conversely, directing blood into a specific region of your body wakes it up even more, providing nourishment to the cells and sexual arousal if the body area focused upon is the genitals.

The imagery procedure for a heat transfer is the same as the one you learned for transferring anesthesia, only instead of imagining something cold in your right hand, you imagine something hot, such as holding your hand over a fire or a steaming kettle. You may also simultaneously give yourself an affirmation, such as "My hand is getting hotter and hotter. The blood is rushing to the surface of the skin on my hand." When you feel the heat in your right hand, place your right hand upon your right cheek and let the heat drain from your hand into your cheek.

During this transfer, affirm, "My cheek is becoming flushed. The blood is rushing to the surface of my skin in my cheek." When all the heat has drained from your hand into your cheek, place your hand again at your side. Then put your hand once more on your cheek and let the heat in your cheek drain back into your hand, affirming, "My hand is becoming hot, flushed. The blood is pulsating through my right hand." You may end your image with your hand still warm or you may imagine it cooling off. I prefer that my patients end with their hands still warm, as these are effects you will need to learn to maintain in order to derive maximum benefit from them.

After you've practiced your heat-transferring image for a week, you are ready to transfer the heat from your hand to the area where it is needed, rather than to your cheek. Where you transfer the heat depends upon what problem you are working on. Heat recall is very effective in treating dermatological problems such as acne and psoriasis. In this case you transfer the imagery-induced heat from your right hand to the area of your body containing the skin eruptions. The heat dries the lesions and the increased blood supply nourishes the damaged skin.

Sandy, an eighteen-year-old high school senior, used imagery involving his recall of heat to direct blood to the surface of his face and clear up a bad case of acne. I began by asking Sandy what he wanted to use in his image to make his hand hot. He said that the last time he'd had a hot hand was when he'd taken off the radiator cap of his T-Bird. First we set the scene, as you should do when creating your own images. Establish a positive five-sense setting before introducing the situation that will produce the effect you are after. Sandy started his image by visualizing himself having a great time driving his car on the open road. Then he stopped the car and started to look at the radiator, putting his right hand on the cap. It didn't burn, but it felt very hot. He held this part of the scene until he actually felt heat in his right hand, and then did his transfers. Finally, he jumped back into the T-Bird and sped off, his hand still feeling warm. After practicing this for a week, he was able to transfer heat from his hand directly to his face and dry up his lesions.

In addition to clearing up dermatological disorders, you can use a heat transfer to cure migraine headaches. Headaches are often caused by a congestion of blood in your head and neck area, thus producing the throbbing, pounding pain associated with a migraine. You can get blood to leave the area of your headache by diverting it to your hands.

Edna, a seventy-one-year-old retired telephone operator, learned to direct blood to her hands, thus relieving the blood pressure in her neck and head area to cure her migraine headaches. She created an image in which she recalled a recent trip to Yellowstone Park. Once the scene was established, she envisioned herself holding her right hand over a pool of boiling mineral water she'd seen at Old Faithful geyser. She transferred the heat from her hand to her cheek and then back again, holding the heat in her hand as long as she could to keep the blood from her head area. In two weeks of practice, she achieved control over her headaches.

By transferring heat from your hand to your genital area, you can produce sexual arousal. Arousal in both men and women is correlated with a congestion of blood in the genital region. Susie, thirty-two, managed to become orgastic for the first time with Sean, her husband of five years, by using imagery of heat to divert blood to her genital area and produce sexual arousal. She imagined putting her hand on the hot, wet cement by her swimming pool, once she had a good image going of the pool and its surroundings. When she had mastered the hand-to-cheek transfer, she practiced transferring heat to her genitals, which created a good level of arousal for her. Finally, she was able to do a heat transfer during intercourse by recalling heat in her hand and then placing it on or near her genital area during lovemaking. The added arousal afforded by the heat transfer eventuated in her reaching her first climax with Sean.

Sex Energy

While you can create sexual arousal and sex energy by using imagery that focuses your recall of heat on your genital area and thus diverts blood there, you can also raise sexual energy by creating an image that is inherently sexually arousing. You can base this erotic image on an exceptional past sexual experience or you can make one up, producing the most arousing scene imaginable.

Jake, a forty-eight-year-old orthopedic surgeon, cured himself of impotence with his wife Dora, forty-seven, by learning to create vividly arousing sexual imagery. Jake created an image that was a combination of his best past sexual episodes with Dora. One particularly memorable time, they'd made love in the woods. Another time, they'd used several positions. Another, he'd been away and hadn't had sex in two weeks. Another, she was especially amorous.

Jake's resulting image brought him and Dora together in the woods on a beautiful summer day. He'd been celibate for two weeks and his sex drive was high. She was very eager to see him, and literally attacked. Their energy remained high and they went through a flurry of sexual positions, the mutual attraction and arousal growing all the way, till each was totally satisfied. As Jake continued practicing this image to feed his mind with the arousing thoughts he'd once had about Dora, his sexual interest in her revived and his potency returned.

Age Regression

You can also use imagery to produce the phenomenon called "age regression," to take you back to a past level of better functioning, a time when you were problem-free. To create an image for age regression, recall a specific positive time in your life when you didn't have the problem you are trying to eliminate. Turn that memory into a five-sense image and practice it three times a day to restore the mode of thinking you had before developing the problem.

Marge, a thirty-six-year-old dental technician who had smoked two packs of cigarettes a day for the past twenty years, used imagery-created age regression to take herself back to the state of mind she had enjoyed before she became a smoker. Since Marge started smoking when she was sixteen, I asked her what one of her fondest recollections was from when she was fifteen, the period before she became a smoker. "Playing tag on the lawn with my brothers," she said. "I loved that!" Marge and I created an image of her old home, her brothers, and the joy they experienced playing together.

After Marge practiced this image a week, she said, "I had a different state of mind then. I would never have considered smoking then. Practicing is helping me get that mind-set back. When I have it, I don't even think of smoking." In the mode of thinking that her age-regression image helped her to achieve, Marge no longer craved cigarettes.

Negative Hallucinations

The last imagery-created healing phenomenon that I'll discuss in this chapter is the "negative hallucination." If you experience something in any of your five senses that is *not* there, the phenomenon is termed a "positive hallucination." Conversely, if you do not sense something that *is* there, it is termed a "negative hallucination." You have the power to positively and negatively hallucinate in any or all of your five senses, and both forms of hallucinations occur in your normal, waking life.

Positive hallucinations are most common when you are expecting something. For example, if you are waiting impatiently for someone who is late, you may swear you hear him pull up in the drive or knock on the door (positive audio hallucinations), only to discover there is no one there. You may even think you see a shadow pass by the curtains (positive visual hallucination).

On the other hand, you may be so engrossed in something that you don't feel a tap on your shoulder (negative tactile hallucination) or smell the dinner burning (negative olfactory hallucination). The negative hallucination can be of great value to you in helping you to shut out any unwanted stimuli, such as pain, urges for food, cigarettes, drugs, or alcohol, or phobic situations.

Since the key is always to imagine the world as you want it to be, then in order to negatively hallucinate or shut out any unwanted element from reality, you begin by shutting it out in your image. Imagine the situation you want to change *minus* the undesired element.

If the sound of your neighbor's dog is driving you to distraction, create an image of yourself happy and calm, not hearing any disturbing noises. If a bad case of hives is keeping you from sleeping nights, create an image of yourself restfully sleeping minus the feeling of itching. If the smell of a substance at work, such as printer's ink, gasoline, or ammonia, is making you ill, visualize yourself happy at work, not smelling these odors. If your diet calls for you to eat cottage cheese and you hate it, imagine eating the cheese *minus* the taste. If someone's presence always distracts you at work when you give a group presentation, create and practice an image where you give a great, relaxed speech and don't see your detractor—where he is visually negatively hallucinated.

Ted, a twenty-three-year-old tennis player, learned to tactilely and negatively hallucinate the pain of a healing knee injury. He'd been advised by his doctors to do some light exercise to get the knee back in shape, but said that any movement at all hurt too much, and he'd become a couch potato. I asked him to create an image of what he wanted to have happen. He envisioned himself pleasantly moving around the house, bouncing from sofa to chair, puttering around the garage, watering the lawn, *minus* the pain of his knee injury. In a few weeks, what Ted could eliminate in imagery, he could shut out in reality as well. The knee mended in fine shape. You will learn more of the value of the negative hallucination for healing and spiritual growth in the next chapter.

You are about to begin experiencing a progressive series of images that will vastly strengthen your powers of imagery. This is the third kind of imagery I mentioned. Among the many benefits you will derive from this series is a greatly enhanced ability to perform the first two types of imagery discussed in this chapter: images to achieve final goals and images to produce phenomena.

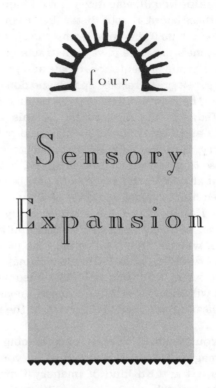

four

Sensory Expansion

Would you like to be more sensitive to all the positive things in life? Gaze with the awe of a child when contemplating a sunset; be ever aware of the soft caress of a breeze against your flesh; discriminate each instrument in a musical piece; savor your food with relish; be moved to passion by the sweet scent of leaves in a forest after a summer rain? Would you like to experience these wonderful things that comprise your sensory reality with an intensity and vigor that eclipses everything else? Wouldn't it be marvelous if positive sensations were all that existed in your life? Wouldn't it be even more marvelous if you could heighten the things that you already enjoy, expand their beauty and joy to a new level of awe and wonder?

On the other hand, wouldn't it be great if you could shut out all that is unpleasant in your reality? Not feel the pain of a tension headache; be impervious to the sound of your neighbor's radio; not attend to the flaws or imperfections you presently see in your home, friends, or lover; refuse to perceive an odor that is foul or offensive; not pick up on flavors that are disagreeable? How terrific it would be to expand upon all that is positive and eliminate all that is negative.

Sensory Thresholds: Controlling Your Senses

The first question you need to answer in order to achieve this desired state is, "How do I focus upon and expand all the positive things that comprise my reality?" The answer to this question will give you a solid foundation for self-healing and personal growth.

You already learned in Chapter 1 that one way you can become more sensitive to the positive and less sensitive to the negative is to deepen your level of relaxation. Relaxation lowers your sensory threshold to the good and raises it to the bad. Let me now elaborate on exactly what a sensory threshold is, so that you can appreciate how scientifically documented the principles I'm discussing with you are.

Every sense you have is "locked in" to a given range of stimuli. You can "see" light only within a very minute range. Infrared at one end of the spectrum and ultraviolet at the other end constitute your visual boundaries. If you were more sensitive, you could "see" an infinite number of other realities in proportion to the complexity of your receptors.

You "hear" only within a minuscule range of sound waves. You cannot, for example, hear radio waves. If you could, you wouldn't need a radio. The same limitations hold for your senses of touch, taste, and smell. Hot past a certain point simply burns. You're not able to say, "That burner feels six hundred degrees while the other one feels eight hundred." In the other thermal direction, cold past a certain point simply produces numbness. You can't discriminate one hundred degrees below zero from two hundred degrees below zero.

Sweet tastes and smells are sweet only beyond a given concentration, and the same holds true for salty, sour, and bitter tastes. Their strength or concentration can vary far beyond your capacity to detect the difference. There are, however, instruments that detect much more than your present sensory powers, so we do in fact know that these differences exist.

A threshold is defined as: "The point at which a physiological or psychological effect begins to be produced (of consciousness)" [*Webster's Dictionary*]. A sensory threshold, therefore, is the point at which a physical effect (light, heat, sound waves, etc.) produces a physiological or psychological effect (sight, touch, sound). The point in the continuum of light waves where you begin to see, or the point in the continuum of sound waves where you begin to hear, is your sensory threshold.

Sensory thresholds vary from person to person. Some people can pick up on light waves or sound waves in a range that others can't detect. The science that studies these effects of physical processes upon your mental processes, psychophysics, is very interested in these individual differences.

A common psychophysical test that you may have had is the one to test your hearing. Tones of various volumes and pitches are sounded into your headphones and you are asked if you can hear them. This is a test of your auditory sensory threshold. It reveals two things. First, how well you hear. Namely, the points in the range of sound waves where your hearing begins and ends. And second, how fine a discrimination you can make within that range. Two sounds are varied until you cannot tell the difference between them in either volume or pitch, although the instrument may show an enormous difference, depending upon how sensitive the instrument is. The smallest interval between two tones that sound different to you is called a JND (just noticeable difference).

JNDs also vary among people. Two tones that sound the
same to one person may be obviously different to another. The
second person is more "sensitive" to sound in this range. JNDs
vary in every sense modality for every human being. Artists
may be more sensitive to colors, sculptors to touch, musicians
to sound, gourmets to taste and smell. So you can see that not
only does your range of perception for each sense vary, so
does your ability to discriminate within it. As a function of
our varying sensitivities, the world may appear quite different
to each of us.

These individual differences should alert you to one very
important fact. *You are capable of perceiving far more than
you presently perceive.*

An Extraordinary Reality

Your areas of possible sensation are infinite. Your limitations and inhibitions are *learned*. You must therefore unlearn
them if you are to grow as a sensual being.

I'm going to show you how to lower your sensory thresholds and become more sensitive in all five of your sense modalities. You will expand your senses and increase your range
of sensory awareness. There are infinite levels of reality waiting to be experienced. Waiting for you to reach out and embrace them.

Imagine if you will that you have only one sense, taste.
What would a world be like where taste was your only sensation? Really try to imagine. The limitations to your knowledge of "reality" would be staggering.

Your only "reality" would come to you from that with
which you had direct physical contact. In order for you to
taste something it would have to lie directly on your tongue,
in immediate contact with your organ of reception. The only
reality you would have any knowledge of would be that which
was directly on your tongue—a pretty limited perception of
the universe.

But you know, as a creature possessing five senses, that it is possible for you to be aware of things that do not contact you directly. Imagine now that you have the power of smell as well as taste. Your area of awareness increases. You can detect roses several yards away or smoke from a forest fire miles from your receptors.

With the addition of hearing, your world becomes even larger. The sound of a siren, a jet, chapel bells, informs you of the existence of things even farther from your perceiving organs.

Once you add touch, your world becomes greater again. You can feel heat from the sun millions of miles away. Even without vision, you *know* of the sun's existence because you can *feel* it.

With the addition of your last primary sense, sight, you can see the stars. You *know* of an existence light-years from your body.

All this knowledge comes to you without your budging an inch. Without your traveling one millimicron through space. All this awareness is possible from one stationary position. There is no travel, only awakening.

But, you may ask, what of the galaxies, the universes, the realities beyond mine? What of the worlds beyond the range of my strongest sense, vision? Most people would argue that you must travel through space to perceive them. You must get closer. While it is true that space travel could thus enlighten you, there is another way.

Sensory expansion.

It is possible for you to have knowledge of the existence of *all* things without traveling an inch through space. Just as the unfolding of taste, smell, sound, touch, and sight revealed ever greater knowledge, there is an infinite number of senses beyond your primary five that you can develop to encompass ever more knowledge.

In time you will see that space itself is an illusion. Your concept of space is directly proportional to the range of your senses. What does space mean to a creature who knows reality only through taste?

You can expand your perception *within* each sense or *beyond* your five senses. What is the sense beyond vision? You will learn that knowledge of the sixth sense comes from a fuller understanding of your first five.

One thing is certain. With the development of a sixth sense your world will grow again. You will "see" far beyond your present universe. Call this sense telepathy, precognition, or whatever. It will vastly extend your knowledge of "reality." And the impact it will have on you will be every bit as great as when vision became an actualized part of the sensorium.

You are embarking on a *journey out of space*; a journey of unfolding consciousness. Entering a reality that doesn't know the illusion of time, space, or motion. An "extraordinary reality" beyond your present sensory limitations.

The Negative Hallucination

Your journey to this extraordinary reality began with your development of profound relaxation. Your point of entry is the negative hallucination. As I explained in Chapter 3, you negatively hallucinate when you don't perceive something that is "really" there. You have the power to shut out reality in any or all of your senses. Remarkably, as you come to shut out your ordinary five-sensory reality by negatively hallucinating it, an extrasensory extraordinary reality emerges. Clearing your consciousness of ordinary reality makes room to process new data. Consciousness never dies, it only changes.

Images are your vehicle for peeling away ordinary reality to uncover the higher knowledge that lies beyond the illusion of your five-sensory world. An image in which you negatively hallucinate and a reality in which you negatively hallucinate are equally real in that both imagery and reality are capable of producing the same result. For example, your imagining eating a lemon will produce the same amount of salivation as your eating a real one. Imagining holding your hand in ice will produce numbness just as if you held your physical hand in physical ice. An imaginary fire will give you a blister every bit as real as a real fire. Negatively hallucinating senses in five-sensory images will reveal as great a truth about what lies beyond the "real" world of your five senses as negatively hallucinating your senses in reality.

What holds true in your reality also holds true in your imagery. You can expand one or more of your senses in reality by directing more of your attention there. A common example is the blind man who has better than normal hearing, "expanded" hearing, because he has directed more attention to that particular sense. His lack of negative hallucination of sight leaves him more room to process his remaining senses, all of which become heightened or expanded as a result. The surprising thing is that if you direct your attention to certain senses in images you will become more sensitive to them in reality. For example, if you repeatedly work at recalling images involving smells, you will find that you will become more sensitive to smells in reality. Images involving your negatively hallucinating your various senses enable you to focus more on, and thus expand, your senses that remain. This effect generalizes to reality.

As your power of imagery increases, so does your control over everything else. We are just beginning to tap the power of the mind and its relation to our bodies and physical reality.

Woods Scene

You continue your journey into sensory expansion, becoming more sensitive to the positive, and shutting out the negative aspects of your reality, by practicing the first image in this book, the *Woods Scene*. This image further deepens the concentration and profound relaxation you learned to create in Chapter 1, using the hypnotic clearing procedure.

I usually advise my patients to practice each image in this book three times a day for four days before going on to their

next image. Do the hypnotic clearing procedure first to free
your mind of distraction. Then go right into the image. When
you reach the end, say to yourself, just as you did to bring
yourself out of your hypnotic state, "I am now going to count
to three. At the count of three, I will open my eyes, I will be
completely relaxed, totally refreshed. One ... two ... three."

You may read this book through in its entirety before going
back to practice the images, or you may do the imagery exercises as you go—whichever you prefer. Some people like to
tape the images and play them back for practice. However, as
I advised you in Chapter 2, if you use a tape, it's preferable to
alternate your tape-guided sessions with sessions where you
do your image from memory. The tape allows you more freedom to concentrate on creating the sensations called for in
your image, while doing the image from memory permits you
to linger over various parts of the image you may need additional time to master. I will explain the basis for this image's
construction and what you are to focus on while practicing it
after you have read it through.

Woods Scene

You are walking through a forest of pine trees on a beau-
tiful summer day. See that the sky above is brilliant blue. Feel
the warmth from the sun against your face. Hear the soft, low
rustle of the wind through the pine boughs. Blue jays fly from
branch to branch, sounding out in loud, high cackles.

Reach up and pick a pine needle. Break it in half. A drop
of fluid falls from the needle onto your palm. Sniff the drop.
It smells of bitter pine. Lick the drop. Taste the bitter flavor
of pine. Now you come to the edge of the forest. Pass into an
orchard of apples, brilliant red in the sunlight, against deep
green foliage. Pick an apple. Take a jackknife from your
pocket and slice the apple in half. Beads of apple juice sparkle
on the metal of the knife blade. Sniff the sweet scent of apple.
Carefully lick the juice. Sweet taste of apple. Next you pass
into a grove of lemon trees, yellow fruit in chartreuse leaves
gleaming in the summer sun. Pick a lemon. Peel it. Smell the

sour *lemony fragrance of the rind. Bite into the lemon. The sour lemon juice squirts into your mouth. Your cheeks pucker, the saliva flows, as you suck the sour lemon juice. And you continue walking.*

Come out of the lemon grove onto a sandy ocean beach. Dazzling turquoise water stretches as far as you can see. Smell the salt in the air. Lick your lips. You can taste the salt from the ocean spray.

Walk out onto the hot, dry sand. Move closer to the shimmering sea, standing where water has been splashed. Remove your shoes and socks. Feel the cold, wet sand beneath your bare feet.

Walk back up on the beach. Strip down to a bathing suit. Lie down in the warm sand. A gentle breeze begins covering you with sand. Feel it dry and light, coating your body. Feel the ever increasing pressure as the sand continues to cover you, dry, heavy sand. Safe, secure, protected, in a warm cocoon of sand.

Now the sun is setting on the ocean. The sky is a throbbing orange, *turning fiery red on the horizon. As the sun sinks into the water, you are enveloped in a deep violet twilight. Look up at the night sky. It's a brilliant starry night. The sound of the waves, the taste and smell of the salt, the sea, the sky, and you; and you feel yourself carried upward and outward into space, one with the universe.*

Sensory Recall

Your key to making your images vivid enough to positively change your reality and make a difference in your life is *sensory recall*. Every sensation that you've ever experienced is recorded forever. You have the power to recall those sensations as vividly as the first time you experienced them. This recall is an active process. You recall a sensation just as you would a date, address, or any other piece of information you want to retrieve.

Your reality comes to you through your five primary senses: sight, hearing, touch, taste, and smell. These five sense modalities comprise the ordinary world as you know it. Therefore, if you wish your imagery to be as "real" as your ordinary five-sense reality so that it can positively alter this reality, you should experience your images vividly in all five of your senses, through developing your powers of sensory recall.

Your reality is a function of physical processes such as light and sound impinging on your organs of reception, such as your eyes and ears. You'll recall that the field of psychophysics studies the effect of these processes on your perception of reality. Your sensory receptors are sensitive to various aspects of the physical processes they receive.

Your eyes are sensitive to light's aspects of *hue* and *lightness*. You therefore see colors between ultraviolet and infrared on the spectrum of light frequency, and you are able to detect changes in lightness or darkness of these colors. Your ears respond to sound waves' aspects of *pitch* and *volume*. You're aware of how high or low a sound is and how loud it seems to you. Your sense of touch is sensitive to three aspects of your sensory reality: *temperature, pressure,* and *liquidity.* You can feel whether something is hot or cold, light or heavy, wet or dry. Your senses of taste and smell respond to four aspects of your ordinary sensory reality: *salt, sour, sweet,* and *bitter.* Everything you taste and smell in your present common reality is comprised of various degrees and combinations of these four gustatory and olfactory aspects. If you create truly powerful, truly "real" images, they will be vivid in *all* sensory aspects appropriate to the image.

I've designed your *Woods Scene* so that it includes *all* aspects of the physical processes, to which *all* five of your senses are sensitive. This will enable you to create vivid, "real" images and prepare you to produce wonderful effects with them. None of your other images will be so inclusive in their sensory representation.

Your *Woods Scene* contains the total range of hues to which your eyes are sensitive: sky that is blue, violet, red, and orange; yellow sun; chartreuse and green leaves; turquoise water. It also covers all degrees of lightness. Your image begins in brilliant daylight and ends in velvet darkness.

All aspects of sound are represented in the *Woods Scene*. Wind through the pine boughs is soft and low; blue jays circle overhead with loud, high cackles.

Combinations of the three aspects of temperature, pressure, and liquidity are comprehensively included. The beach sand is hot and dry, becoming hot and wet as you near the shoreline. As the breeze blows the sand to cover you, the sand first feels dry and light, till finally you experience it as dry and heavy, protecting you in a warm cocoon.

Your *Woods Scene* also has all four aspects to which your senses of taste and smell are sensitive: salt, sour, sweet, and bitter. The pine needle is bitter; apple is sweet; lemon is sour; ocean spray is salty.

After practicing this image you will have a solid foundation in recalling the gamut of sensations that comprise your ordinary reality. Now let's look at some of the reactions and benefits people have reported from practicing this image, so that you may know what positive results you also can expect from the *Woods Scene*.

Imagery-Created Relaxation Makes You More Sensitive to the Positive

You will find that combining your image with the hypnotic procedure gives you an even deeper state of relaxation than the hypnosis alone. You are never so relaxed that you can't be more relaxed, and the effect is divine. This relaxation lowers your positive sensory thresholds, and your sensitivity to pleasure increases.

"At the end I felt this major rush come over me," said a former patient the first time I gave her the *Woods Scene*. "Then I felt even more relaxed. I felt like I was sinking into the couch. All my muscles just went limp. I felt totally relaxed. It was like a wave, I don't know what it was. Like my head would go to the side, like I couldn't control my neck muscles. I especially felt it in my arms. This is great!"

"I felt really gone completely," reacted a man in his mid-thirties. "The colors were incredible. Sight was the strongest."

"I felt like I was just everywhere," smiled a fifty-two-year-old woman. "It was total peace. I could taste the salt. I was so relaxed."

"I could even feel the heat," said Cliff, a forty-seven-year-old auditor working on stress reduction. "I've never done an image in all five senses. It's the beginning of another dimension, that's what it is."

Imagery this strong inevitably makes a positive change in your reality. "I noticed a change of color when I walked out of your office last time," said Edward, thirty-two, describing the effect the *Woods Scene* had on him. "The sky was a different color. Sort of a total color. I can't describe it. I noticed an awareness of the color. Like feeling the color. More saturated. More intense. Like a drop of color. Like going from a clear glass to one with color. Quite a difference!" You too will find your senses expanding, your awareness of beauty increasing, as you begin practicing your imagery.

Sergio, a thirty-eight-year-old high school math teacher, complained of severe job burnout. "I just can't stand it anymore," he said. "I used to love teaching. Now I actually hate it. The daily routine is driving me nuts. I'm sick of the paperwork, the unruly kids, the noise, the parents, the staff, the evaluations—everything!"

I asked Sergio what he used to love about his work and he thought a moment. "Working with the kids was great. I used to get such a kick out of thinking I was helping somebody, that I could make a difference in the outcome of a young person's future. If one of my students got a new insight or solved a problem they'd been stuck on, it made my day. A smile or a thank you lit up my life." "What happened to change all that?" I asked. "I think the grim reality of life just finally wore me down."

"You know what I think?" I answered. "I think you *made* your reality grim by focusing on the negative. You were too stressed out to even recognize the positive elements of your job, which were all around you."

I asked Sergio to practice the *Woods Scene* for a week,

learning to create the profound relaxation that would put him back in tune with the positive facets of his reality. "I can't believe it," he said. "It wasn't the job. It was me. I was completely ignoring all the super things happening to me every day. The kids were still smiling and thanking me. I just wasn't noticing. My head was too full of garbage to see anything else. When I finally learned to relax, I once again saw what a great job I really have."

Mindy, eighteen, a college freshman suffering from anorexia, was down to skin and bones at the weight of eighty-five pounds. "I hate to eat," she revealed. "Just the thought of it makes me want to run. I was overweight as a kid and my mother was always on my case about it. The kids at school made fun of me. I remember being really depressed when puberty came and no guy would date me. I was so lonely. Then my senior year a miracle happened. I started losing weight. I reached a weight where I looked good, but I wanted more. I couldn't be *too* thin. I continued losing weight with a vengeance. Food was now my enemy and I hated it. I realize now that I have a problem. I can't make enemies with something I need to live."

I suggested that Mindy work on creating relaxation with the *Woods Scene* until she felt it deeply enough to make herself more sensitive to the wonderful taste and aroma of good food. She needed to counter the anxiety that was making her insensitive to the joys of eating. Mindy practiced the *Woods Scene* for a month before she noticed an improvement. "I felt more relaxed right away," she said, "but it took a few weeks before food started looking good to me again. It was strange, like waking up from a bad dream. I couldn't understand how I'd ever gotten into such a state. I'm happy to say that I like food now."

You can also use imagery-created relaxation to increase your sensitivity to your body. This can be especially beneficial in athletics. Marian, sixty-seven, a retired businesswoman, wanted badly to be a better golfer and help her team win their annual tournament at their club. "It's such a drag always getting the worst score," she said. "I know we say we play for fun and companionship, but I feel like I'm a burden. I wouldn't want someone on my team who played as poorly as me. But, I don't want to give the sport up. I love golf. I love the people I play with. Everything about it is great; the fresh air, the exercise, the beauty of the course. I even enjoy chasing that stupid ball all over the place!"

I learned that, according to Marian's friends and coach, her main problem was in her swing. She didn't keep her left arm straight. "It sure *feels* straight to me," she insisted. "I don't think they know what they're talking about." I suspected, however, that these people were correct, but Marian just wasn't kinesthetically aware enough to know the position of her body during her golf swing. The anxiety she generated by worrying about whether she'd make a good shot was making her less sensitive to the very thing she needed to focus upon: where she felt her left arm to be.

I asked Marian to practice the *Woods Scene* every time she was about to go golfing, to lower her general anxiety level and make her more sensitive to the positive cues her body would be giving her on the course. "It's amazing," she reported in less than a week. "I *was* bending my arm during my swing. I wonder why it took me so long to catch on to it?" Once Marian was able to recognize her error, she could correct it. It's simple to say that everyone performs better when they are relaxed, but it helps to know *why*. Relaxation makes you more sensitive to the positive cues and feedback you need to discriminate in order to give a good performance.

Imagery-Created Relaxation Makes You Less Sensitive to the Negative

The deep relaxation you will create using the *Woods Scene* not only makes you more sensitive to pleasure, it makes you less sensitive to the stimuli in your reality that you perceive as painful. Buster, a sixty-nine-year-old retired trucker, suffered excruciating pain from a cancer that had metastasized throughout his body. His condition was inoperable, and he had finished his course in radiation therapy. There was nothing more anyone could do, and he was dying. By listening daily to a tape of the *Woods Scene* Buster was able to raise his pain threshold, becoming less sensitive to his discomfort while expanding and potentiating the positive effects of the pain medication he was on.

Relaxation from the *Woods Scene* will make you less sensitive to emotional as well as physical pain. Maria, a single, thirty-year-old jewelry store clerk, was never able to make her relationships work. "I can't stay in a relationship for more than a few months," she said. "And most of that time I'm in pain. It seems like the man is always doing something to upset me. It's so draining I have to get out of it in order to save my health. But I want a relationship. I want a family. I feel the pressure of the biological clock. For a long time I blamed men, but I know now they can't be wrong all the time. Other women have lasting relationships with men. Some of the problem has to be me." Maria's anxiety in a relationship made her more sensitive to its negative elements and less aware of its positive. She was overreacting to the slightest negative thing.

I taught Maria to reverse this process by asking her to practice the *Woods Scene* once a day while she was in a relationship. With this practice she was able to create a general calm that made her much less sensitive to the slights, misunderstandings, and disagreements that are an inevitable product of even the best relationship. "It's surprising how much such a simple thing as relaxation could change my perception of my relationships," she confided. "Most of the time I was getting upset over nothing, nothing *worth* getting upset over at least." Maria's present relationship has lasted a year and she reports they're talking of marriage.

You can use imagery-created relaxation to make yourself less sensitive to the pain of a past relationship as well as to that of a present one. Rex, a twenty-six-year-old systems analyst, was devastated when Kelly, twenty-four, a drummer in an all-girl band, left him for another man. He lost his job, couldn't concentrate, dropped ten pounds, and had no motivation to go on living. "I think of her all the time," he said.

"Everything reminds me of her . . . a song . . . a streetsign . . . a perfume . . . even the trees and sky make me think of her. It's driving me crazy. I imagine her in bed with this other guy. He's not even as good-looking as me. Why is she with him? I can't stand it!"

Rex was in a state of acute anxiety and that only made his thoughts of Kelly more painful. I taught him to create relaxation using the *Woods Scene* in order to make him less sensitive to his painful memories of Kelly. In a state of truly profound relaxation, a negative thought can have no effect on you at all. You can transcend your pain threshold completely, become totally impervious to it, just as the early martyrs were able to laugh as flames engulfed them when they were burned at the stake, feeling no pain, only ecstasy.

Becoming less sensitive to negativity is a matter of degree, and Rex was able to raise his tolerance to a level where thoughts of Kelly no longer bothered him. "I have to admit it," he said. "The more relaxed I get, the more stupid the whole thing seems—agonizing over a girl who doesn't even want me anymore. Relaxation is a great tonic." If you have trouble in love, you may find, like Rex, that imagery-created relaxation is a universal antidote.

Sensory Expansion with the Negative Hallucination

Relaxation is not the only phenomenon you can use to lower your positive sensory thresholds and expand your senses. You can also use the negative hallucination to intensify your senses and extend your sensory range, thereby adding new knowledge and power to your experiencing of your reality.

When you negatively hallucinate or shut out a sense from your experiencing of reality, *the senses that remain are expanded*. This is because you can process only so much information at one time. Dropping one sense from your perception of reality allows you to concentrate more fully on your remaining senses. Directing your attention to a sense intensifies it. I've already mentioned how the painter, musician, sculptor, perfumer, and gourmet have respectively developed their senses of sight, hearing, touch, smell, and taste by directing their focus to these particular senses.

You can benefit practically from using the negative hallucination by shutting out negative stimuli from your reality and expanding the positive. It is not enough, however, that you learn to simply shut out a whole sense in your experiencing of reality. In order to make practical use of this phenomenon you need to develop a finer discrimination. By this I mean it would help you to be able to *selectively* shut out elements of your reality in a given sense or senses.

For example, let's say you get nervous in front of a large audience and have trouble making a speech. You want to be able to be less aware of and visually shut out your audience— to create a visual negative hallucination—but you don't want to negatively hallucinate your entire visual reality. You want to see your lecture notes and the podium before you, but not the people who are listening to you. You may need to selectively shut out your reality in one of, or a combination of, your five senses.

A selective negative audio hallucination may come in handy when you're reading a book and would like to tune out extraneous traffic noise, while still being aware if the phone rings or a baby cries. You might require a selective tactile negative hallucination to shut out the pain of a healing leg while still being able to hobble around on it, sensing its placement on the floor as you walk. A selective negative olfactory hallucination would be good in helping you shut out unwanted paint fumes from your sensorium while still leaving you open to smell the positive fragrances of a fresh breeze or flowers. Perhaps you're dieting and hate the nutritious foods you know you're supposed to eat, like cottage cheese, yogurt, or vegetables. You can use a selective negative gustatory hallucination to shut out the flavors you don't like while expanding the ones you do like, thus making dieting a much more enjoyable task.

To help you negatively hallucinate selectively within each

of your senses, I've used Aristotle's division of the world into the elements of fire, water, earth, and air. The images in this book teach you to negatively hallucinate water in each of your senses, leaving the fire, earth, and air portion of your world intact. Your result is that you will be able to shut out any facet of your reality you desire, in any sense you choose. In essence, you are learning to control your perceptual reality. Also remember that while your purpose may be to eliminate something negative, your very removal of this negative stimulus enhances the positive stimuli remaining by leaving you more room in your sensory channels to attend to them. You are thus moving ever closer to paradise, a marvelous extraordinary reality where the bad is eliminated and the good expanded.

Expanding the Woods Scene with Negative Hallucinations

I've designed two exercises for you that will begin giving you an experiential understanding of the negative hallucination. I want you to discover how valuable this phenomenon can be to you for expanding your senses, both in your imagery and your reality.

For your first exercise, please practice the *Woods Scene* three times a day, for four days, with one modification. Change the second paragraph as follows:

Reach up and pick a pine needle. Break it in half. A drop of fluid falls from the needle onto your palm. Sniff the drop. It has no smell. Lick the drop. Taste the bitter flavor of pine. Now you come to the edge of the forest. Pass into an orchard of apples, brilliant red in the sunlight against deep green foliage. Pick an apple. Take a jackknife from your pocket and slice the apple in half. Beads of apple juice sparkle on the metal of the knife blade. Sniff. They have no smell. Carefully lick the juice. Sweet taste of apple. Next you pass into a grove of lemon trees, yellow fruit in chartreuse leaves gleaming in the summer sun. Pick a lemon. Peel it. Sniff the rind. It has no smell. Bite into the lemon. The sour lemon juice squirts into your mouth. Your cheeks pucker, the saliva flows, as you suck the sour lemon juice. And you continue walking.

You'll find that eliminating smell from your experiencing of liquid in the above exercise will enhance the remainder of the image because you are concentrating more on the remaining portions. "I sure tasted the orange that time," said Harold, a thirty-two-year-old photojournalist. "Before, when I practiced the *Woods Scene* in all my senses, my recall of taste was really poor. It was more of a memory than an experience." "This time I drooled," laughed Emma, forty-eight, reacting to this exercise. "I had a faint sense of the lemon when I recalled it without the negative hallucination. But this time the taste of it made me salivate." Concentration on the taste of lemon, to the exclusion of smell, heightened Emma's recall of taste, with her resulting physical manifestation of salivation. Using a negative hallucination in imagery had enabled her to produce a physical effect in reality. You too will discover that you can effectively use the negative hallucination to intensify portions of your imagery, thus potentiating their effects in your reality.

For your second exercise, I'd like you to practice the *Woods Scene,* three times a day for four days, negatively hallucinating taste from your experiencing of liquids. Try modifying the second paragraph as follows:

Reach up and pick a pine needle. Break it in half. A drop of fluid falls from the needle onto your palm. Sniff the drop. Bitter smell of pine. Lick the drop. It has no taste. Now you come to the edge of the forest. Pass into an orchard of apples, brilliant red in the sunlight. Take a jackknife from your pocket and slice the apple in half. Beads of apple juice sparkle on the metal of the knife blade. Sniff. Sweet scent of apple. Carefully lick the juice. Taste nothing. Next you pass into a grove of lemon trees, yellow fruit in chartreuse leaves gleaming in the summer sun. Pick a lemon. Peel it. Smell the sour lemony fragrance of the rind. Bite into the lemon. Taste nothing. You continue walking.

Again, you'll be pleased to discover that the remainder of your image is more vivid because of the addition of a negative hallucination to make more room for focusing on that which is left. "That was the sweetest-smelling apple I've ever seen," said Ida, a twenty-two-year-old stenographer. "The smells of everything were much more intense when I didn't have to concentrate on recalling taste as well. It was wonderful." "The sky even looked bluer," reported Mike, a thirty-year-old construction foreman. "Isn't that strange? Not tasting a lemon can make for a bluer sky. It's great. I love it!" You too will experience that removing your experiencing in one sense will enhance your experience in *all* of your other senses.

Benefits of Using the Negative Hallucination to Make You More Sensitive to Positive

What you do in imagery manifests in reality. If you imagine making perfect basketball free throws, in time you will actually make better free throws in reality. If you imagine that your hand is hot and over a fire, soon blood will be diverted there and your hand will actually warm up. If you imagine eating a lemon, you'll actually salivate. If you heighten your remaining senses in imagery by shutting others out, these same remaining senses will be heightened in reality.

Justin, a thirty-two-year-old insurance underwriter, practiced the above exercises to improve his eyesight. "The more vividly I *see* in my images, the better I'm able to see in reality. It's incredible. I was getting terribly nearsighted. Too much eyestrain with paperwork I guess. Now I have moments when I can see almost as well without my glasses as with them on." The more you heighten your senses, the better you can function.

Tony, fifty-two, a renowned plastic surgeon, complained that he was losing his touch, performing with difficulty even the surgical techniques that he was most familiar with. "I feel like I'm doing surgery with mittens," he said. "I'm all thumbs. I just don't have the sensitivity I used to. There doesn't seem to be any sensation left in my fingers. I guess I'm just worn out." Tony experienced a noticeable return of his tactile sensation after practicing negatively hallucinating smell and taste in the *Woods Scene.* "I'm delighted," he said. "My hands are actually starting to feel again."

Not only can you use the negative hallucination to bring your weaker senses up to par, you can expand these senses beyond their "normal" range to acquire higher knowledge. Andrea, a thirty-one-year-old spiritual healer, practiced the above exercises to make her more sensitive to her patients. Her results were remarkable. "I can see auras now," she smiled. "I know there's been a lot of talk about energy fields and auric readings in the media lately, but I never believed in any of it. But as I continued working with imagery to expand my senses I began noticing a change in my reality immediately after I finished doing an image. The air looked kind of filmy, like looking through heat waves on a hot pavement. Next I noticed there was a mild kind of white light around objects, a kind of milky halo. It wasn't very pronounced and I might have discounted it at first if I hadn't been specifically looking for perceptual changes. I see that white energy field around objects almost all the time now and lately I've begun seeing colored sparks. I'm taking copious notes to correlate what I see in these fields with the conditions of my patients."

Benefits of Using the Negative Hallucination to Shut Out Negative

In addition to expanding your remaining senses of sight, hearing, and touch, your above exercises with the negative hallucination will teach you to shut out unpleasant tastes and smells.

Claire, a twenty-six-year-old loan officer, had a difficult time driving in city traffic because the smell of fumes from diesel fuel made her nauseous. "If a bus gets in front of me, I have to pull over," she explained. "You don't know how incapacitating it is to drive in rush-hour traffic with the restriction that you can't breathe any diesel fumes. I've thought of moving to a smaller city, but I like my job, and there's no guarantee I won't still have the same problem there. Every city is bound to grow and get more traffic." As Claire learned to shut out smell in her imagery, she was also able to do it in reality. After a few weeks of practice where she concentrated on negatively hallucinating smell in the *Woods Scene*, Claire was able to negatively hallucinate the smell of diesel fuel in reality.

Shipyards Scene

Now that you have developed a facility for negatively hallucinating your senses of smell and taste, you will learn to negatively hallucinate your sense of touch selectively. I've designed the *Shipyards Scene* expressly to help you to achieve that purpose.

Shipyards Scene

You are dry and warm, wearing a wool coat and muffler. You are walking along a deep blue river in the shipyards on a late foggy afternoon. Hear the fog horns. It's getting darker as the sun sets. Smell wet wood and algae from the pilings of the docks and embankments. Hear the water lapping against the pier. Suck in the air. It has a musky taste. Walk to the water's edge.

Wade into the water. See your clothes getting wet. You have no feeling of wetness. Feel warm and dry. Smell the wet wool. Jump into the water, totally immersing yourself. You still feel dry. Leave the river. Hear the sound of dripping water. Smell the wet cloth.

Enter a pub. The smell of ale is strong in the air. Sit down by a wooden table in front of a glass of golden ale. Smell its aroma. Put the glass to your lips. Drink with loud guzzling sounds. Taste the strong flavor. You have no sensation of wetness or coolness. You cannot feel the ale as it goes down your throat and into your stomach. It tastes, smells, looks, and sounds like ale, but it feels like air.

A sense of euphoria overtakes you as you drink another glass, and then another. Beside you is a blazing fireplace. Feel its warmth. Hear the crackling logs. The stuffed animal heads on the wall begin to blur. The room is spinning. Lie your head on your arms. Drift away.

Reactions

"It seemed strange wading into the water, seeing my clothes get wet, and still feeling dry," said Richard, a forty-eight-year-old plumber. "Somehow it seemed to make the smell of the wet wool and the sound of the dripping water stronger." Carrie, a twenty-nine-year-old airline stewardess, responded, "That was the strongest-tasting ale I've ever had, but it looked beautiful. It glittered gold, brilliant. I could see it so clearly." You too will experience how selectively removing touch from your image will intensify the remaining senses.

Benefits from Heightening Positive Senses

Laura, a forty-five-year-old artist specializing in oil paintings done in a classical style that required over a hundred coats of glazes per canvas, had perfect vision but needed to improve her discrimination within that perfect 20/20 range. "I see fine," she said, "and I'm not color blind, but I need to be able to discriminate colors better. You know how important nuances of shading and tone are to a painting. I've been told that my colors clash, that they aren't harmonious. I can't seem

to tell if a brown has too much green in it, or a beige is too
pink, or a gray too yellow."

I asked Laura to practice negatively hallucinating touch
in the *Shipyards Scene* in order to enhance the remaining
senses, including vision. "It's amazing," she reported. "Once
I was able to heighten the blue river and golden ale in my
image, I noticed I was also becoming more aware of colors in
reality. With that awareness came a growing appreciation of
the differences and degrees of color. My art is improving. I
can see the difference as contrasted with my older work. My
clients are commenting favorably too. Even the critics have
picked up on it! Instead of 'clashing,' they now say my colors
'glow.' That's because now I can tell which colors to lay next
to each other, what shades will bring out other shades."

Monty, fifty-six, a lighting technician for the movie stu-
dios, had been deaf for five years, ever since he overheard his
wife making love to another man behind a locked bathroom
door while they were at a party. He was diagnosed with "hys-
terical deafness," a term used to denote hearing loss brought
on by psychological causes with no underlying organic im-
pairment. Even though there was nothing physically wrong
with Monty, he had literally refused to hear another sound
since the trauma he'd experienced with his wife.

Monty practiced the *Shipyards Scene* for about a month,
whereupon his hearing suddenly returned. "It was the strangest thing," he happily reported. "I worked on this image every
day and nothing seemed to be happening. I was still deaf as
a doornail. Then one morning, I suddenly heard the phone
ring. I've been able to hear ever since." Monty's negatively
hallucinating touch heightened his other senses, including
his hearing.

Melanie, a forty-year-old cashier for a sporting goods store,
wanted to enhance her sense of taste. "You know how people
always complain that they gain weight when they stop smoking because their sense of taste comes back and everything
tastes so great?" she asked me. "Well I stopped smoking two
years ago and I still can't taste a thing. Food is as dull as
cardboard. That was one of the reasons I quit smoking, so I

could enjoy eating again." Melanie was able to intensify her sense of taste by negatively hallucinating touch in the *Shipyards Scene*. "When that ale started tasting good in my image, food started tasting good in reality," she said. Taking her attention off the touch of ale, by negatively hallucinating it, focused more attention on the ale's taste and heightened it.

Benefits from Eliminating Negative Senses

In addition to heightening the positive senses that remain, learning to negatively hallucinate touch is also beneficial to you in that it teaches you how to eliminate any tactile sensation that feels unpleasant or painful.

Clark, a twenty-four-year-old furniture craftsman, developed a severe case of shingles. The sores, which covered nearly the whole length of his back, were extremely painful. By learning to negatively hallucinate touch in the *Shipyards Scene* he was able also to negatively hallucinate the tactile sense of his shingles.

Donald, fifty-three, an executive for a medical supply house, had smoked over three packs of cigarettes a day for thirty years. I asked him what the big attraction was. "It's not the taste," he said reflectively. "I could say it gave me something to do with my hands, but then I guess I could substitute a fake cigarette and get the same result, couldn't I? When I was a kid I thought it made me look cool to smoke, but that sure isn't it anymore. Some people say a cigarette relaxes them, but not me. Others say it gives them energy, but I have to pass on that one too. You know what it really is? There's a feeling in my lungs that they should be full. There's a feeling that only cigarette smoke can satisfy."

After Donald practiced the *Shipyards Scene* for a week he told me, "I found that once I could truly imagine immersing myself in water and not feeling wet, I could imagine not feeling all sorts of sensations, including that sense of clawing emptiness in my lungs. Once I could vividly imagine it, truly conceive of it, I was able to do it in reality. Now, if that feeling of emptiness in my lungs ever raises its head, I negatively hallucinate it."

A sensation similar to the one reported by Donald was recounted to me by Viveca, a twenty-one-year-old college physics major who was trying to lose fifteen pounds. "It's not really that I'm hungry," she explained. "And I wouldn't call it a compulsion like so many of my friends say their overweight problem is. It's a hollow feeling in my stomach, and I just can't resist filling up the hollow. It's like my stomach won't leave me alone for a second until I put something in it." I hear complaints of that "hollow feeling" quite often from chronic overeaters.

I asked Viveca to imagine shutting out her sense of touch by practicing the *Shipyards Scene* for a week. Then, whenever she experienced that undesired hollow feeling that made her overeat, she was to imagine herself without the feeling. Her not feeling water in the *Shipyards Scene* prepared her to do this. If she could imagine negatively hallucinating one element tactilely, such as water, she could also imagine negatively hallucinating any other stimulus tactilely, such as her stomach's hollow feeling. In a few weeks she was able to become what she imagined, a woman without a hollow feeling in her stomach, and her weight problem was licked.

A Voyage Out of Space

Around the turn of the century, the Germans did some fascinating research with vision. They found that if you wear prismatic glasses that make your world look upside-down, in a few days your world will look upright again, even though you are still wearing the glasses. Then if you remove your glasses, your world will look upside-down. In a similar way, your reality changes when you practice imagery. You will soon notice that real colors and sounds become more vivid; your sensations become more fully experienced. Your body hasn't changed any more than it would have if you'd worn prismatic glasses. What has changed is your *way of perceiving.*

Think of your images as serving much the same function as prismatic glasses. They allow you to perceive the world in a different manner. They change your perception without changing your receptors. Your ears, skin, nose, tongue, and eyes all remain the same, but they process information differently. Just as in time the glasses are not necessary to maintain the new perception, so in time your images will not be necessary to maintain your new perception. You will throw them away, for they will have served their purpose. Like prismatic glasses, they will have enabled you to modify your perception, to open up areas you could not have navigated without them. Your present imagery state will then be your "normal" state and your "imagery" state will be a level of awareness far surpassing anything you have experienced today.

The images that I will be giving you in the following pages may sometimes seem repetitive to you. That is good because it shows you are learning. Repetition is the key to all conditioning. You usually don't achieve a perceptual change from one experience, but from repeated experiences. Your wearing prismatic glasses just long enough for you to view the world upside-down for a moment won't alter your perception; you need to wear your imagogic glasses for a few days. It is for this reason that I've included certain sensations over and over as you progress with these images and certain lessons are imprinted on your consciousness.

As a function of your practicing the twenty-nine images in this book, "reality" will begin to look different to you. Your positive senses will be expanded, negativity will be eliminated, and you will experience a wondrous new world you never before knew existed.

You are beginning a voyage out of space, a journey into infinite levels of ever-expanding consciousness. I trust that your journey will be a joyous one; discovery is exhilarating.

In the course of your journey I hope to teach you to develop the power of your sensorium in ways you never dreamed possible; ways that will lead you into higher realms of healing, knowledge, and power.

five

Universal Love and Rejuvenation

There is a loving force that permeates all creation. In this chapter you'll learn to raise your energy higher by feeling this universal love from all things, animate and inanimate; although as time progresses you'll come to realize that there is no dichotomy to existence. The line between animate and inanimate, life and death, you and the cosmos, is an illusion.

Séance Scene

Love is a great energizer. Your next image, the *Séance Scene*, teaches you not only to negatively hallucinate sound, it also gives you an emotional understanding of what it feels like to be loved by the elements of nature, in this case water. You need never feel alone. You are loved by all creation. A giant tidal wave lovingly enfolds you while whispering the beautiful affirmation, "We love you. You are home at last."

Séance Scene

It's Sunday afternoon. You are in a house in the country, lying in bed on your back reading. It's raining. See the rain pounding against the window and on the skylight above you. See the drops of clear water dash and splash against the glass overhead. There is no sound. The rain is silent. Outside there is a square and a road of cobblestones leading into a great deep green forest.

Now there comes to your ears the faint sound of organ music. You get up and follow it downstairs. The sound grows ever louder as you come into a parlor, dank and dark. It smells musty. Candles are lit. Smell the wax. A woman in her late thirties with her blond hair pulled back in a pug sits at the organ. You sit at a large round table covered with a lace tablecloth. Now other people enter the room. They also sit at the table. You all hold hands. Feel the warmth and blood pressure in the hands of the people on either side of you. There is silence as the rain pounds against the window glass.

You get up. Walk outside to the ocean. Waves are high and there is much wind. Taste and smell the salt air. The wind is strong, cool, and stinging. Gulls are screaming. The waves are silent, the wind is howling. You see a giant wall of water, a tidal wave approaching, silently and steadily. Listen . . . listen . . . it's speaking . . . listen . . . It says, 'We love you. You are

home at last,' as it engulfs you. You are one with the sea,
rocked eternally in the cradle of the deep.

We Love You

The first time that I became aware of a loving, helping force existing in creation was also the first time I ever had anyone or anything in an image issue an affirmation. I was working with Anne, a thirty-three-year-old legal secretary married six years to David, thirty-three, a computer programmer. Anne had come to me on heavy doses of medication seeking treatment for chronic fatigue, menstrual pain, itchy and tender vaginal warts, and headaches. She was also diabetic and required two insulin shots in the stomach every day.

I had just finished giving Anne an image involving her negatively hallucinating fire tactilely, called the *Plantation Scene* (which I describe in my book *Creative Imagery*), when I suddenly had a strong impulse to have someone or something speak to Anne in a future image and say, "You've been here before. You'll be here again. Don't you know who I am? Why did you take so long to come?" I'd never had anyone speaking to anybody in any of the images I'd used before and I didn't have any intention of adding this feature to future images I had already planned. It seemed like an odd idea, and I wondered where it had come from.

The day of Anne's next session she came in with a typewritten copy of a dream she had had the night before. Her dream was the identical setting as the image I'd planned for her that day; I was both delighted and amazed, and not sure what to make of it. There was only one difference between her dream and my image. Both scenarios involved a brown rock breakwater on a secluded beach, but while there were no people in mine, Anne's included a young man and woman walking together on the sand.

I started giving Anne the image I had planned, but in the middle I had a sudden impulse to add the man and woman from her dream. I suggested that Anne see the young man and woman approaching her from the breakwater. Then I was seized by an impulse to have the woman ask Anne the questions that had come to me after her image, the *Plantation Scene*. It seemed like a perfectly natural thing to do at the time, although in my entire working life I had never spontaneously altered an image before in the course of giving it.

I'll never forget Anne's reaction when I asked her, "Don't you know who I am?" Her body arched and she gasped loudly, relaxing as a joyous smile illuminated her tear-streaked face. "At first I didn't recognize the two people in the image," she said when it was over. "But as soon as the woman asked me if I knew who she was, I knew it was my grandmother. She died when I was thirteen. We'd always been so close. The man was my grandfather." Tears of joy wet her cheeks as she continued, "I can feel my grandmother's love. It's everywhere." She paused a moment and said, "I've just experienced infinity."

I remained silent, transfixed by her experience, waiting for her to go on. "Do you see what I see?" she gasped suddenly, her eyes wide with astonishment as they rapidly surveyed the room, appearing to be observing some great activity in the air. "There are flowers blooming," she laughed in childish delight, "unfolding all over. They're deep red."

I didn't feel love everywhere or see flowers unfolding in the air as Anne had, but as I drove home from work that evening my mind was filled with urgent, unsolicited voices giving me messages, messages *as if* they had come from Anne's grandmother and I was to relay them to Anne. I thought it was ridiculous. The people in Anne's image couldn't be talking to me. By the time I reached home the voices were so insistent I wrote their messages down in hopes it would help to clear my mind. Here is what I wrote:

> Direct your attention to the water.
> You are over eighty percent water.

> Don't presuppose that death reveals the universal or ultimate truth. You've died before.
> Don't blow it this time.

Do not assume that our state is inferior or superior to yours.

You are on the brink of a realization greater than we have ever experienced. We want you to reach it.

Don't assume that all people are in the same state or level of awareness after death.

The levels after and before your state are infinite.

Death is but a change in levels, and not necessarily an enlightenment.

You have been chosen. You have been selected. At this point in time you are special.

As soon as the messages were put to paper, the voices inside my head stopped. I examined what I had written. The force generated by the image was not only loving, it was helpful. It wanted to help Anne reach a wonderful new realization, one so profound it involved the mysteries of life and death. It seemed that the force wanted to help Anne learn to break the reincarnational cycle, navigate without her body, literally go to paradise!

However, by the time of Anne's next session, I'd returned to my "normal" senses and the ideas of reincarnation and navigating without a body in the next dimension seemed preposterous. Even in the heart of my experience, when I truly believed the messages I had written, I never thought the information had come from Anne's disincarnate grandmother, but rather from the ether, the interface between this dimension and the next, or possibly simply from a higher state of my own consciousness. I had decided not to give her the messages.

Anne said she had heard her grandmother's voice since her last session. "Last night she asked me to reevaluate my feelings about death, to listen to someone who would explain death to me." I felt compelled to give her the messages.

"That's amazing," Anne responded. "For years I've been preoccupied with the concept of the ultimate realization of truth in death. At one time I even thought about taking my life, not because I was depressed, but just to discover this truth. Now I see that knowledge comes from living, not dying." She thought a moment. "I had another past life regression since our last session. I was doing the *Surf Scene* [described in *Creative Imagery*] and I saw myself burned at the stake as a witch. I think it was in Salem. It's like I've had several lives where I'm getting close to this great metaphysical realization before death stops my progress; once as an Egyptian high priestess, once as a witch, who knows how many other times?

"Does my grandmother saying, 'Don't blow it this time, direct your attention to the water, you are over eighty percent water,' mean that through an understanding of the physical and chemical properties of water I'll gain an understanding of what constitutes me, of what is life? An answer to the questions: Where do I come from? What am I? Where am I going?"

I was glad it was time to give Anne her next image, because I wasn't able to answer any of her questions. The scene called for her to negatively hallucinate water gustatorily, and when it was over she said, "I feel very strange . . . All my body water has just been replaced by the water from the well. I feel like I have to hold myself down mentally . . . feels light . . . really spooky . . . I'm afraid to move . . . everything is tingling, absolutely everything. I really feel that peace. I'm immune to everything."

Everything tingling pointed to her rising energy, her increased vibratory rate before scaling a new dimension. Although she mentally held herself down during her session, she let herself go soon thereafter. "I was driving home the night after my last session with you," she told me the day I was to give her the *Shipyards Scene*. "A John Denver tape was playing on my tape deck. He was singing, 'Lady, my sweet lady, do the tears belong to me? I'm as close as I can be. I swear our time has just begun.'

"Suddenly something snapped, something like a click. It was no longer John Denver singing. It was Christ. And the words were no longer sung, but spoken. I began to cry. Then I saw in front of me, on the road, a huge head of Christ. My mind blows up with the experience. I drove into his head. The car vanished and I saw myself in blue with dark hair, crying. Words of comfort came to me from Christ as if I were his mother. I was very frightened. I tried to deny it and said to myself, 'You're going to be Napoleon next.' It was like two realities coexisting, both equally real. I was always simultaneously aware of both the road and the Christ image."

I suddenly understood. Anne *was* the mother of Christ. She was the mother of all things. We are all the mother of all things. We all create our own realities, including our own selves. Her experience was an emotional understanding of the power of creation within her. It was also a lesson in love, for doesn't the creator love his creation? Love yourself and the world. You created both.

"Then today," Anne went on, "driving to session, I had a sensation like butterflies in my stomach, like crackling energy that filled me with a greater joy than I've ever known. It moved out of my stomach and floated up to eye level. It was a white light like crackling electricity."

I like to think of this crackling white energy as what the Hindus term *prakriti,* the undifferentiated stuff of creation; the primal force that you channel into any form you choose. Such creation from raw energy takes concentration; it takes concentration to hold any energy configuration together. The images in the progression that you are beginning will help you to develop that concentration needed to mold the energy, the undifferentiated stuff of creation called *prakriti,* into any form you focus upon.

"I felt incredible energy and joy as the wave approached," Anne said, describing her reaction to the *Séance Scene.* "I heard the wave say, 'We love you,' before you said it." Whether this phenomenon was telepathy (she read my mind as to what I was going to say next) or precognition (she was actually seeing a tiny time particle into the future), it is not an uncommon one for me to see. Patients often report knowing ahead of time what I'm going to tell them in an image.

Your working with the phenomenon of the negative hallucination is particularly conducive to your developing extrasensory powers. When you take your attention off one of your senses—i.e., you negatively hallucinate it—that leaves more room in your channels to process additional data. The result is that your senses that remain are intensified, making you more sensitive in these modalities and thus raising your sex energy; plus, extra senses begin developing.

What pleased me most about Anne's reaction to the *Séance Scene* was her response of emotional communion with the element of water. We, in our present state of matter, are the elements. Self-transformation is in essence alchemy. Anne's learning to navigate outside her body, or any out-of-body experience, is an elemental transformation involving energy, as is any alchemical transformation.

All creation is crying to transcend the state of matter. *The Sacred Tarot,* by C. C. Zain, refers to matter as "spirit in equilibrium." Equilibrium is static, based upon a balance between two poles. To grow spiritually you need to transcend polarity, rise above the static equilibrium that is matter to achieve spirit. To do this, energy is necessary, just as energy is necessary to change any state to a higher form. *Lower* means giving up energy. *Higher* means taking it on. The greater the configuration, the more concentration required to maintain it. Paradise is a higher energy configuration. You get there by developing your concentration.

Positive builds energy and concentration. Negative depletes it. Love is positive energy. It builds. It charges. It takes you to paradise. Love of yourself and your creation, the world you live in, gets you higher. That love includes everything—the rocks, the plants, the animals, the people, the fire, water, earth, and air of your creation. The mother and father you created, as well as the enemies you created. Love the rocks, love the trees, love your parents, love your enemies. Positive feelings can only take you higher.

This knowledge is embodied in the words of Christ when

he said, "And I give unto you the greatest commandment, that you love your neighbor as yourself." You *are* your neighbor. You are your creation. All creation is you. There are no barriers, no compartments. Separateness is an illusion. There is only One. As the Upanishads so aptly put it, "He who sees the separateness and not the One wanders on from death to death." When you love yourself you are loved by all creation.

Listen. Direct your attention to the water. The elements have things to tell you. We call alchemy the mental transformation of elements and psychology the mental transformation of people, but we are One.

Anne

Before examining other people's reactions to the *Séance Scene,* I'd like to take a little time to give you more background information on Anne, because her case so well illustrates the benefits that you too can expect from practicing imagery: profound relaxation, growing energy, lowered positive sensory thresholds, vivid childhood memories, time distortion, and pain control. Here is how she recounted what followed after one of her early sessions:

"As I made my way down the hall to the elevator, I felt my energy grow. By the time I reached the ground floor I had an incredible sense of alertness, focus. I remember walking out onto Wilshire Boulevard and hearing what I considered a deafening gobbling sound above me. I looked up and was amazed to discover this clamor was nothing more than the cooing of two doves on the fourth-floor windowledge. It didn't seem possible birds could sound so loud. By the time I crossed Wilshire I was flooded with a sea of childhood memories. I vividly recalled my mother telling me stories around a campfire, how I used to eat the petunias in her flower bed, all sorts of crazy, happy childish antics I used to delight in.

"Suddenly I realized I was no longer walking. I glanced at my watch and saw I'd been standing there on Linden Street over fifteen minutes looking at the sun set through the trees.

I swore I couldn't have been there over a minute. Then I realized something else, with a joy that took my breath away. My pain was gone!

"I got into my car and headed homeward, driving into the setting sun. I don't know how long I'd been in motion, but I remember becoming gradually aware of a humming around my car. The sound was loud and all around me. It was more exciting than frightening. I was aroused by it. It was kind of sexual, but more electrical, like a surge of adrenaline. Then I noticed a rhythm to it as if it were somehow in pace with the car, like the car's life force.

"The sea of car lights around me appeared as rubies and diamonds, a molten strand of jewels flowing to and from the sunset. My arousal intensified and I felt powerfully female, perspiring heavily, melting into a living ribbon of highway, charged by the heat of the pavement. My energy soared. I felt omnipotent, all-powerful. I owned the buildings, the cars, the road. I was hot and wet and charged and nothing else mattered. I was about to discover America!"

Two sessions after the above incident, Anne reported a telepathic experience. "My mother phoned and told me Dad had made a ghost with a pumpkin head for Halloween. And I said, 'Yeah, I know.' It's amazing. I really knew that before she told me. Is the hypnosis doing that to me?"

Anne next reported that after practicing time expansion on her own at home, she had an exhilarating experience during which her perception changed. "I was driving home from work one evening when suddenly my eyes felt two yards wide. I blinked tight and then opened them slowly. The headlights of oncoming cars looked like snowflakes. They pulsated. In fact they were pulsating in time with the car blinkers. My time expansion is sure getting better too because this seemed to go on for several minutes, but when I looked back at my watch, the whole episode had only been a matter of seconds."

Two days after Anne's perceptual alteration of the car headlights she had the following experience, which illustrates how changing your time sense leads to alterations in your senses of space and motion as well: "David and I went to a swap meet.

It was a beautiful day and we were having a great time. We were rummaging through some old stuff being marketed by one of the vendors when I found myself becoming transfixed by the carved figure of a snake on an obelisk. I don't know why I found it so fascinating, because I'm deathly afraid of snakes, but I couldn't take my attention off it. Suddenly the figure began to grow. It got bigger and bigger, coming toward me, till it was all that existed in my view. Then suddenly everything went back to normal, except for one thing. I'm no longer afraid of snakes. Isn't that amazing?"

Once Anne learned to use imagery to create anesthesia using the glove anesthesia technique I taught you in Chapter 3, her headaches were gone and she had no more menstrual pain. Her vaginal warts, which numbered over 160 when I first saw her, had gradually diminished over the course of our sessions together and had now cleared up completely. I had never given Anne an affirmation related to the warts, and attributed her success in ridding herself of them primarily to the deep relaxation she was able to induce through the images she practiced.

Stress reduction and profound relaxation alone can eliminate many a problem. In fact, Anne told me that her endocrinologist said she might be able to relax herself right out of her diabetes. She reported digging ditches in her garden with no insulin reaction, and her doctor reduced her insulin dosage. Also, her energy level was phenomenal, light-years from the chronic fatigue she had complained of the first day she entered my office.

Anne continued seeing me after she became problem-free in order to keep on growing, since she was feeling so good from practicing her imagery and experiencing such wonderful new sensations. "Do you hear a ringing?" Anne asked me, opening her eyes after I had given her an image of a sand pit in a forest. Her question startled me. I did hear a humming, ringing sound. I thought back, trying to figure out why we should both be hearing a humming. Then I understood. The image described a hush coming over a forest at the end. It's common to experience a ringing in your ears during total silence, and as I always go into the image with my patients, we had both evidently done exceptionally well this time. We'd created an image so vivid, we were both still feeling its effects, the hum of our mutually imagined silence.

Three sessions later we once again had an extraordinary mutual experience. I had just finished giving Anne an image involving dissociation, set four thousand years ago in a torch-lit limestone chamber in ancient Athens. Her lids were just fluttering open when, without thinking, I asked, "Why did you make it Egypt when it was supposed to be Athens? And why did you put all that gold and treasure there and make it a tomb?"

"I was an Egyptian priestess," she said with an ethereal smile, "lying in my tomb surrounded by treasure. I know I lived that life before." It wasn't till then that I realized I'd seen the contents of her image without her telling me. It felt so natural to me at the moment, I took the experience as a matter of course. I didn't know how to explain it. Anne didn't even comment on it. The only thing I was sure of at that time was the energy present during her experience. It was riveting. She was positively charged beyond anything I had ever witnessed. I could *feel* the energy in the silken quality of the air. I could see it in her eyes.

A week later she described the following experience: "I was at home," she said, "in the den practicing dissociation by imagining that I was outside my body in the room where I was actually lying [an imagery technique for producing dissociation that I described in Chapter 3]. Then I heard a jangling of keys and was certain that you had entered the room. You said to me, 'That's wonderful. That's fantastic. You've finally got it. Keep on. I'll see you soon.' Then I heard the keys jangle a second time and I came out of my image.

"I looked for you thirty to forty-five minutes afterward. I was sure you'd really been there. I checked all around the house and yard. The experience was so real. I told David about my experience and he admitted that he entered the room while I was in my image and that he accidentally jangled his keys. But he says he only made noise with them once. I distinctly heard them on two separate occasions, once when you came into the room and once when you left. I just know you were there. Weren't you really?"

Anne's power to imagine was growing rapidly. Her image had induced an audio hallucination so vivid she couldn't distinguish it from reality. Imagery was now impinging on reality, the two merging. Strangely enough, her imagery also began impinging on mine, for, as I have already described, ten days later I was to give Anne the *Plantation Scene* (two images in the progression before the start of this book), and have the impulse to have someone speak to her in her imagery. You will see, as we progress, where this energy was to lead her.

Other Reactions to the Séance Scene

While I have never had another patient write out an entire scene beforehand as Anne did with the image of the beach and the brown breakwater, I did have a somewhat similar experience with another patient and the *Séance Scene*. Judith, a fifty-six-year-old manicurist working on eliminating the pain of a divorce, told me the day that I planned to give her this image, "Something in my head tells me there's an affirmation that you need to give me. I don't know where it came from, but it wouldn't leave me alone. Here it is," she said, handing me a slip of paper. I looked at what she had written: "We love you," was all it said. Judith may not have been precognitive for the image, but she certainly had a preview of its message.

As the images progress, their effects become more profound. Sensations of relaxation and heaviness become especially pronounced. "At the end I didn't want to get up," sighed a woman in her twenties. "I feel limp," said a young man working on concentration for his college studies.

This image is also often emotionally evocative, creating a kind of bittersweet longing. "I thought of the Cornwall coast," said Raymond, a thirty-one-year-old police officer. "I've always been fascinated with the sea. It's haunting." "Part of it made me feel stoned—like the rain splashing and no sound," said Grant, a forty-two-year-old architect. "Also standing above the sea—I see myself standing in wind often by the sea and crying. That emotion goes with that image. Weird. I felt really deep. When you said you were going to count three I felt like I was dreaming, like I was going to wake up from a dream."

Sometimes people comment on the difficulty or bizarreness of the imagery. "It's hard not to hear the rain," said Clarita, twenty-five, a free-lance writer, "but I certainly am relaxed." "My mind is blown," smiled Neil, a thirty-four-year-old real estate broker. "My feet are asleep. My poor mind."

Benefits

In addition to making you feel loved by the elements of creation, the *Séance Scene* is excellent for giving you a beautiful, calming sense of serenity. Mark, a thirty-one-year-old stockbroker, reported, "Whenever things get hectic on the floor of the exchange and I feel anxiety approaching, I just heave a deep sigh and see myself in the eye of that tidal wave, clear water and calm. The hubbub around me is replaced by stillness."

The *Séance Scene* also teaches you to negatively hallucinate sound. What you can do in imagery you can do in reality. Hal, twenty-nine, a junior associate in a prestigious Century City law firm, complained that although the offices were plush, he couldn't concentrate on his work because of the continual sound of sirens on the busy streets below. "I can't stand it," he said. "Everyone keeps saying I'll get used to it, but I don't. I've been there four years and some days I swear I'm going to jump out the window. It doesn't bother me if I'm just talking with a client, but if there is an important document I have to prepare and a siren interrupts me, I'm lost. I just sit there waiting for it to sound again."

I asked Hal to practice the *Séance Scene* for a week, imagining silent waves and raindrops. Then I asked him to imagine himself happily preparing a document in his office, with silent ambulances and police cars traveling the streets beneath his window. Next, he was to hold this image while he was actually working in his office. In time, his image overrode reality and Hal no longer heard the sirens. "It's great," he said, "I hear everything else just fine, but if an ambulance shrieks past the building, it just doesn't register."

Learning to negatively hallucinate sound not only enables you to shut out unpleasant auditory stimuli, it leads to the enhancement of the positive senses that remain. Diane, twenty-three, a clerk in the perfume department of a major store, said that her sense of smell was so poor she was about to lose her job. "I can't tell Giorgio from Seagram's," she said. "It's embarrassing. People ask me to recommend fragrances and I haven't a clue. It's particularly bad if they ask me to guess what scents they're wearing. I'm never able to recognize it and it makes me look like I don't know my business. I know the name of every perfume made. I just can't tell one from the other. It's terrible!"

The first time that I gave Diane the *Séance Scene* she commented on how strongly she was able to smell the salt air as the tidal wave approached, so I knew I had a good candidate for sensory expansion. After she practiced the image a week she noticed she was developing a heightened sensitivity to smell. "It's incredible," she said. "At first I only noticed an increased facility for smell in my imagery. Then gradually I started seeing a difference in reality as well. First, smells just seemed stronger. But then they seemed richer, more developed. I could spot nuances, differences I'd never experienced before. I could also note differences in perfumes that I'd been blind to before. The more I practice my image, the better I get. I can even tell some of the floral derivations in my perfumes now, whether the base is rose or lilac or lily or whatever. It's wonderful!" Whenever you wish to enhance one sense it always helps to practice an image where one or more of the other senses are negatively hallucinated.

Bath Scene

The purpose of your next image, the *Bath Scene,* in addition to teaching you to negatively hallucinate sight, is to enable you to feel loved by all humanity. It involves your experiencing being made love to by many people at one time and is usually reported as a more sexual experience than the *Séance Scene,* where you are loved by the elements of the cosmos.

The important lesson to be learned here is that, whether sexual or nonsexual, love is positive. In this image the people you are intimate with *really* love you. That is the exercise. I've found that it is usually more difficult for most people to view love as positive when it is sexual than when it is nonsexual. One of the goals of this image is to help you to overcome that limitation. Negative perception of any kind can only restrict you. All is good in the direction you are moving.

Bath Scene

You are walking down a long hall of mirrored walls and red light past room after room after room. Come to a large basin around which are tall Greek columns. In the basin are nude men/women [sex to which you are attracted]. Stand beside the basin. Feel steam, wet and warm, but the air is crystal clear. There does not appear to be water in the basin. Walk down the steps leading into the basin. It feels like walking into hot water. Sit. Feel the motion of water against your body like a whirlpool. Feel wet moisture on your face. Wipe your forehead with your hand. Look at your hand. It looks dry but feels wet and warm.

Now you feel a man's/woman's leg against you. Feel the softness, the warmth of his/her body against yours. His/her hands run along your neck, down your chest, and between your thighs. Another man/woman on the other side of you begins to caress your legs and runs his/her mouth over your *nipples. Feel an increase in heat, in pressure . . . throbbing, aching . . . in your thighs. They whisper, "We love you."*

Walk out of the basin and into a room with mosaic walls. It feels like hot water shooting on you, running down your body. Smell chlorine. See nothing but an empty room. Leave this area. Enter a large, dark, carpeted chamber. Nude male/ female bodies embrace you. They are young, strong, supple. They feel you with passion. Lie down on a huge bed. Bodies massage you. Caress you. Make love to you.

Reactions

Again, all the effects you have thus far been able to create with imagery will intensify as you continue this progression. "My legs are rocks," said Quincy, sixty-two, who ran his own design company. "I could barely move my hand."

"It was really strange when I opened my eyes," said Elizabeth, a thirty-six-year-old nurse. "I saw an afterimage of the scene, in dark blue." The probability of your achieving amnesia with this scene also increases. "I didn't hear one word," said Joyce, a forty-one-year-old public defender.

Jane, a twenty-seven-year-old social worker coming to me for stress reduction, was disturbed by the *Bath Scene*. She said, "I have a cold chill running down my back. I'm so cold . . . like I knew what responses I should have and wasn't having them. Scary. It was a trapped feeling. There was a malevolent overtone to the men like, 'We wish you no well.' All the men's eyes were on me. They were all of one mind. I had no place to look."

Jane's was a case where her present feelings were being colored by her past experiences. She perceived the men in her image as malevolent due to a history of bad encounters with males. It was time to turn her negative perception around. "When the sea said, 'We love you,'" I pointed out, "you felt great joy, but when men said, 'We love you,' you felt afraid and victimized. You'll gladly open yourself to the sea, the sky, the earth, the fire, the universe and become one with them, why won't you open yourself to man? Because man can hurt you? So can fire, water, earth, and air. You can be free with the elements, why not your fellow man?"

When Jane said she felt the men were "all of one mind" she unfortunately perceived this mind to be negative rather than positive. I asked her to continue practicing the *Bath Scene* until she could conceive of the men truly loving her rather than wishing her ill. At this point she said, "I realize now how much other people's hatred and hostility is really a function of my own perception. If I don't expect, if I don't open myself to be loved, I'll never feel loved no matter how loving the people I meet really are."

The men and/or women in this image *really* love you. That is the image. That is your affirmation. This is not to encourage promiscuity, but to allow feelings of love, be they sexual or platonic, to exist for mankind. Open yourself to loving feelings from others and you will feel freer and more loving than ever before. Allow yourself to feel a positive sexual response in this image. A good feeling is positive, whether sexual or nonsexual. Allow others to share your good feelings and express theirs to you. Allow yourself to love and be loved.

Benefits

Practicing the visual negative hallucinations in the *Bath Scene* prepares you to eliminate unwanted visual stimuli from reality. A well-known actress needed to improve her concentration in front of the camera. "There are so many distractions on a set," she said. "Even if the crew is quiet during filming, I can still see them. I find myself wondering about what they think of my performance rather than focusing on my character. I need to be able to blot out all the production people so I can really get into my scene."

I asked her to practice the *Bath Scene* for a week. Then I explained, "Just as you can imagine a basin and shower with invisible water, you can also imagine a set with invisible production people. They're there. They get the work done. You just don't see them." I suggested the actress next spend a week imagining herself concentrating beautifully in her scenes before the camera while the production crew was invisible. She was then to hold that image simultaneously with her actual filming. "I thought the image would distract me," she later reported, "but it didn't. It peacefully coexisted with me and my fellow actors and I was completely oblivious to anyone else on the set." When your image is vivid enough, it becomes your reality.

You will also be happy to find that the *Bath Scene* can be a boon to your interpersonal relationships, as demonstrated by Gloria, a twenty-six-year-old cosmetician who was using imagery to improve her lovemaking with her boyfriend Tom, twenty-five, a mechanic for the airlines. "It didn't give me as much of a sexual reaction as the regular sexy images you've given me," she said. "It's a different kind of feeling, more than just sex. My skin feels so funny, it's tingling. Come to think of it, it did give me a nice morning in bed with Tom. I think I just liked him more as a person, not just sexually. I think I resented his sexuality before. That image got me over it. It made me feel that someone can love me and want sex from me at the same time. I can love him for his sexuality now."

After practicing the *Bath Scene* for five days, John, a twenty-five-year-old clerk for a video-store chain, got a promotion to manager. "My boss said he liked my positive attitude," he smiled. "I think that image of everybody making love to me made me feel like loving everybody back. It sure improved my relationship with the customers."

Sand Scene

Your third image in this chapter, *Sand Scene,* teaches you to expand your senses of sight, sound, and touch by negatively hallucinating smell and taste. This is the first time that you remove two senses rather than one, in your imagery. Your remaining three senses are thus vastly heightened because more of your attention is directed to them. What you can accomplish in imagery will also manifest in reality.

Your *Sand Scene* is also a "rejuvenation" image in which you feel as if the aging process has been reversed. Your skin becomes firm. Wrinkles smooth and a youthful glow returns. You can take years off your physical appearance; your muscles relax, shadows vanish, and lines fade. As you learn to further control your blood flow, your skin becomes radiant and glowing.

Mental techniques have long been used to slow or reverse the aging process, including "rebirthing," as popularized by Leonard Orr in San Francisco, and Kriya Yoga, taught by Self-Realization Fellowship in the Pacific Palisades, California, and Yogoda Satsanga Society of India. The great avatar and proponent of Kriya Yoga, Babaji, is reported to have maintained the youthful body of a twenty-five-year-old for centuries, possibly millennia.

Paramahansa Yogananda, the yogi credited for bringing yoga to the West, in easily one of the greatest books I've ever read, *Autobiography of a Yogi,* says, "Only one reason, therefore, motivates Babaji in maintaining his physical form from century to century: the desire to furnish humanity with a concrete example of its own possibilities. Were man never vouchsafed a glimpse of Divinity in the flesh, he would remain oppressed by the heavy mayic delusion that he cannot transcend his mortality."

Sand Scene

You are standing on a salmon sand dune against a crimson sky with orange sun. Desert stretches as far as your eye can see. Miles of fine, rippling sand. It's scorching hot. Heat waves rise off the dunes, wavering like spirits. Begin walking through the hot, loose sand. Hours pass. Come to a vast expanse of salt flats, shining, shimmering white in the desert sun. Smell the salt. Lick it from your lips as the wind blows it by your mouth. Begin crossing the flats.

Suddenly before you is a great sea. Take off your clothes.
Go into the salty water. Drink the water. It has no taste or
smell. Come out of the water. Salt cakes on your body in the
sun. Your skin becomes golden tan. Hair bleaches blond like
corn silk. Walk into the desert. Hours pass. Once again the
sea stretches before you. You have been going in circles. With
a great roar the waters part. Walk on wet sand bound on either
side by a great wall of water. The water is without odor. The
spray is without taste.

Reach the far side of the sea. Find yourself in a fertile delta
area of cypress trees and raging river. Walk along the river.
Come to rice paddies. Walk in the thick mud. Cover your body
with mud. It has no smell. The mud cakes and peels off your
body, leaving your skin young, fresh, and smooth like a
baby's.

Next, you come into vineyards of purple grapes, lush,
round, and ripe. There is a great pit of grapes. Jump into the
pit, squashing the grapes beneath your feet, knee-deep in
grape juice. Drink the juice. It is warm and wet, but has no
taste. Sniff the juice. It has no smell.

From the vineyard you go into a grove of castor-oil bushes.
There are great vats of castor oil. Sniff the oil. No smell. Swallow the oil. No taste. It feels thick and oily, clinging to the
insides of your mouth. Dive into one of the vats of oil and bathe
in it. Your body becomes golden, supple, young, glowing, in
the castor oil.

Leave the oil. Enter a grove of date palms. Pluck a date.
Eat it. Taste it. Your hunger satisfied, you lie down. Sleep to
the sound of wind in the date palms.

Reactions

Common reactions to the *Sand Scene* refer to how good
it makes people feel or how interesting all the activities are
that comprise it. I often hear comments such as, "I could
keep on going, it felt so good," or "My foot is really asleep.
There was so much in that image," or "I've always wanted
to squeeze grapes with my feet," or "It was kind of funny

opening the Red Sea. I saw Yul Brynner. That scene cost a million dollars."

Benefits

The *Sand Scene* prepares you to eliminate unwanted stimuli in two sense modalities from reality. If, for example, you are trying to build your body's iron supply by eating the right foods and you loathe the taste and smell of liver, you may wish to develop your facility for creating negative gustatory and olfactory hallucinations. By imagining shutting out taste and smell in the *Sand Scene,* you are able to shut these two senses out in reality.

Removing two senses from your experiencing results in even more attention being directed to those senses remaining. All positive sensations will thus continue to intensify. Colors will be brighter, music more melodious, touch more ecstatic.

Practicing this image will also make you feel younger. Laurel, a thirty-six-year-old marriage and family counselor suffering from job burnout reported the following amazing experience using the *Sand Scene:* "My technique was to practice late at night when everything was quiet," she explained. "I'd sit Indian-style, naked, in front of my mirrored closet door. I'd light candles and maybe even float some flowers in a bowl of water that I'd put by me for atmosphere.

"Then I'd close my eyes and take a couple of deep breaths, induce self-hypnosis, and do the *Sand Scene.* When I got to the part where I was in the castor oil and my body was becoming young and glowing, I'd linger until I really felt it, until I was convinced that if I opened my eyes and looked at myself in the mirror I really would look about twenty-one. The first time that I opened my eyes after this image and saw myself in the mirror I closed them again almost immediately. My eyes were open only long enough to get an impression. There really wasn't time to register lines or shadows in my face, plus the candlelight helped a lot to make what I saw momentarily look good.

"I must have done this same routine on and off for over a month, always closing my eyes again the moment I saw my reflection in the mirror. Then one night something strange happened. I felt different by the end of the image. I don't know, deeper I guess. Something clicked. I felt like I had melted into the floor. This time when I opened my eyes before the mirror I was transfixed, suspended, riveted to my reflection. I was definitely in an altered state. My mind was totally clear, completely fixated on my mirror image. It seemed effortless, automatic, and yet there was a tremendous amount of energy involved. It was like the energy focused me, held me together in that state.

"For a long time I just stared at myself in the mirror. The reflected image I saw on that mercurial surface was so beautiful. The light was so beautiful. I looked like an angel. My face glowed. I couldn't have been twelve inches from the glass, but it was like viewing myself through a soft lens. I was brightly, blearily, hazily shimmering. My blond hair was dazzling, my skin luminous beyond anything I'd ever seen. I wished that I had a camera. I wanted to take pictures to prove I could really look like this.

"Then I looked closer, thinking maybe all the light that was emitting in that candlelit room was blinding my vision. I got so close that my nose touched the mirror, but there was not one line on my body. The hollows around my eyes were plumped out. My skin was blemishless, firm, and radiant. I told myself I must be hallucinating, I was still in an altered state. It was my perception, not my body, that had changed, but as long as I looked in the mirror I was ageless. Finally I went to bed.

"In the morning everything was back to normal. I looked energetic, but thirty-six. I doubted I would ever have a similar experience again, but I tried that night. And it happened again! I wished there was someone there to see me, to tell me if my features were really changing. I considered inviting a friend over, but I was afraid they'd distract me and I wouldn't be able to generate the energy and concentration necessary to achieve this incredible transformation. I continued getting these results for about a couple of weeks, looking twenty-one in the mirror every night and waking up thirty-six.

"Then one Saturday morning I awoke, still feeling in the same altered state as I'd created the night before. Could it be I still looked the same? Did I dare look at myself in broad daylight? I went to the bathroom mirror where the sun was pouring in and looked. It was the same face I'd seen last night, not a line, not a shadow. I had plans to attend a seminar on child abuse that day, and I wondered if I'd be able to maintain my state till I got with other people. Was I just delusional? Would I look twenty-one to a stranger? Why hadn't sleep broken this wonderful state of mind? I wondered. Was it because I'd kept my head clear even while asleep? If so, how could I get ready and drive through traffic, still maintaining this beatific state of mind?

"It was two hours before I got out of my car in front of the building where the seminar was to be held. I felt like I had still maintained the state, but I wasn't sure. I'd refrained from looking at myself in a mirror since I'd seen my unchanged reflection in the bathroom. I had to find out. I took my mirror from my purse and looked at my forehead. Not a furrow, not a line. I couldn't believe it. Hurriedly, I went inside.

"The lecture hadn't started yet and people were milling everywhere. I flitted from person to person, like a butterfly, introducing myself and asking them to guess my age. I made up a story that the question had to do with some research I was doing on social reactions to aging. Of the five or six people I managed to ask before the seminar got under way, not one guessed me to be over twenty-three. I was in heaven. If this was a hallucination, it was a mass one. Everyone there was seeing the same face as I." Laurel and the yogis are right. There is a state of mind that produces rejuvenation and bodily immortality. Go for it! See what you can do.

Tahiti Scene

Your last image in this chapter, the *Tahiti Scene,* teaches you to expand your senses of sight, sound, and taste by negatively hallucinating smell and touch. As a result, your daily work goes better, you become more aware of and seize opportunities, people react to you more favorably, creativity emerges and flourishes. A desire to write, paint, build, discover, will nourish you.

Tahiti Scene

You are standing before a great waterfall in the jungles of Tahiti, surrounded by wet, sparkling ferns. The light's reflection off the water creates a dazzling rainbow of brilliant color. Hear the water thundering down upon the black rocks creating a great splashing. At the base of the falls is a still lagoon. Bend down and drink the water. It tastes sweet like honey. Sniff the water. It has no smell. Now you stand. Approach the waterfall. Walk through it. You cannot feel or smell the water. See water running down your body. See wet grass and leaves and skin. But the air is odorless and you feel dry.

Jump feet-first into the lagoon. Surface dive. Swim underwater. There is no sensation of wetness or coolness, only the sensation of movement and the sight of your body shooting through water. There is a ringing in your ears from the water pressure. Hear the water passing by your body. You surface. Leave the lagoon. Come into a giant field of pineapple. There is a knife on the ground before you. Use it to slice a fresh pineapple into sections, golden and juicy. Sniff the fruit. There is no smell. Eat. The fruit tastes sweet and rich. Your mouth feels dry. Suck the juice from the pineapple. There is no sensation of wetness or coolness. It feels like sucking pineapple-flavored cotton.

Cross the pineapple field. Enter a grove of coconut palms.

Crack a coconut with a rock. Pour the liquid into your mouth.
No sensation of wetness. Taste the sweet, milky coconut juice.
Cover your body with juice. It has no smell. It becomes rich,
warm coconut oil in the tropic sun, sinking into your skin,
making your body smooth and supple. Lie in the grove of
coconut palms covered with oil. You drift ... you sleep ... you
dream.

Reactions

As the images progress they require more concentration
from you, and this added energy takes you into new dimensions of awareness. "That was really hard," said Paula, a
thirty-one-year-old pediatric resident, "one of the two or three
hardest ever. Tasting but not feeling was difficult. My mind
is completely warped." "I lost awareness of the place," said
Ken, a man in his mid-twenties. "I didn't know where I was."
Sydney, a thirty-year-old TV repairman, gained a better self-
image from the positive feelings he was able to generate from
the *Tahiti Scene*. "I'm not here a lot till you say three. I'm so
relaxed. For the first time I'm glad to be me."

As your concentration increases, your energy builds. You
may sense this growing energy in the form of motion, vibration, or even shaking. Lonnie, a twenty-two-year-old bartender, related, "I felt a real shaking all over my body at the
beginning of the image. Then it stopped. How strange." Most
commonly, you'll notice that the senses remaining in the image—in this case, sight, sound, and taste—are more vivid than
you are normally able to conjure. Ben, an engineer in his mid-
forties, said, "It's getting harder and harder to come back. The
oil was out of sight. When you remove some properties the
others become so wildly defined."

Benefits

Heightened senses in imagery will lead to heightened senses in reality. You will become more aware of what is going on around you and be more alert to opportunities. People will pick up on your higher positive energy and react more favorably to you. They will like you more without even realizing why. Your life at both work and play will go better.

As you tune more in to your senses you will also become more sensitive to the feelings of others. You'll become more compassionate. After practicing the *Tahiti Scene* for a week, Barry, twenty-six, a court reporter, said, "The world is infinitely more lovable now because of its frailties."

The more in touch you become with the sensory aspects of reality, the more childlike your perception becomes. The younger you are, the more sensorially oriented you are and the less deadened you are by the competing stimuli of negative thought and memories. Rebecca, a stressed-out thirty-four-year-old fifth-grade teacher, said, after practicing the *Tahiti Scene* for four days, "My perception is becoming as childlike as my students'. I'm getting back to basics. My husband noticed that I'm sitting in and assuming juvenile postures. I unconsciously squatted ten minutes to smell a rose and didn't even feel cramped. Normally I'd bring the rose up to my nose or at least sit on the ground to admire its fragrance."

You'll be delighted to discover that as you are able to take in more of the world, greater creativity will emerge and flourish. Anne reported, "I'm writing more and more poetry now, an art I always loved. I'm exchanging my poems over the telephone with my boss's little girl who's also into composing poetry."

In addition to reaping the benefits of a heightened five-sensory reality, you may experience gains in the extrasensory department as well. Using negative hallucinations to take your attention off one group of senses and put it on another leaves more room in your sensory channels to process new senses as well as the old ones remaining. Anne said that more and more she felt that she and David could read each other's minds and knew what the other was thinking.

I couldn't argue with her, because a similar form of telepathy occurred between her and me just a couple of days later. I had been browsing through a secondhand bookstore and ran across a volume containing the artwork of Maxfield Parrish, one of the greatest and best-loved artists of the early twentieth century. It was my first encounter with Parrish, and I marveled at his splendid gardens, exquisite buildings, and misty mountaintops; a shimmering never-never land of dreamlike beauty that reminded me very much of some of the images in her progression. I bought the book and brought it to Anne's next session, thinking she would enjoy seeing the similarity between Parrish's artistic visions and her imagery experiences.

"Have you ever seen this book of pictures by Maxfield Parrish?" I asked her, showing her the volume of Parrish prints. Her eyes widened. "I just finished looking at it," she said, smiling. "Someone at work last week said she thought I'd like Parrish so I looked him up in the library this morning!"

I was glad to see Anne smiling at the continued development of her powers. Although she had eagerly embraced all of her metaphysical experiences at the time of their occurrence, she had later attempted to deny some of her reincarnational ones, thinking she was crazy for having them. "Maybe I am only 'being' these people I'm reincarnated as and there really isn't déjà vu," she had rationalized. She had been especially reluctant to later accept her vision of Christ on the freeway, waking up that same night screaming, "No! It isn't possible!"

Anne's experience was telling her that she, like all of us, was the mother, the creator, of all things. Don't deny the power of creation, the Christ consciousness, within you. It is your way to love, rebirth, and eternal life. In the words of Sri Yukteswar, the guru of Paramahansa Yogananda, "The Son of God is the Christ or Divine Consciousness in man." You reach the One, the Kingdom of God within you, bliss, paradise, through the door that is your power to create.

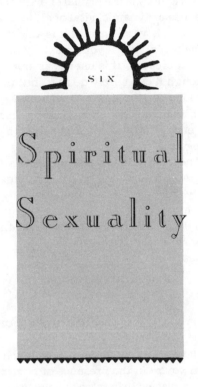

six

Spiritual Sexuality

As you continue clearing your sensory channels via the exercises for creating negative hallucinations contained in the images that follow, you will find that your senses are also heightened in reality. With your enhanced sensuality and sensory expansion comes the benefit of rising sexuality, and what I call sex energy. This energy can be both healing and uplifting. Anything you can do to increase your level of sexual energy makes you generally more powerful. When you use your sex energy to take you to new heights of healing, positive knowledge, and experience, it becomes "spiritual sexuality."

Sex energy is the primal energy of creation. It is the purest, most basic, dynamic, vital of all forces. It is the energy of life, from which we all spring. It is also the most accessible energy in the beginning of your mastery of reality. Your prime purpose in creating this energy is not to enhance your sex life, although it can surely do that, but to use it as the generating force in the attainment of whatever goals you have. You will learn to create sex energy using imagery, and you will use this energy for healing and achieving higher knowledge and experience.

The images in Chapter 6, *Windmills Scene* and *Fan Scene*, will teach you to combine sensory expansion with your sexuality, fueling further the sex energy that will take you to ever higher levels of knowledge and awareness. All energy, including sex energy, transcends the illusion of your five-sensory world. It reveals to you a truth uncolored by your senses.

Windmills Scene

Have you ever noticed how much higher your energy is when you're in the presence of someone to whom you're sexually attracted? There's a charge, an electricity that isn't there normally. Have you also ever noticed how much your enjoyment of life is dependent on your energy level? When your energy is high, you feel motivated. You want to explore, discover. Life is an exciting, effortless adventure. In addition to expanding your senses of smell and sound, the *Windmills Scene* helps you to raise your sex energy by visualizing a wonderful adventure with a person to whom you are powerfully sexually attracted. Sensory expansion plus sexual attraction produces powerful energy!

Windmills Scene

It's late at night. You are standing in a kitchen staring at a sink of pots and pans. A rusty faucet is dripping water on a pan. The drops are silent. Drop after drop... after drop... after drop... Sniff the rusty water near the faucet. The water has no smell. On the counter beside the sink is a cup of hot coffee. Sniff it. No smell. Drink the coffee with a slurping action of your lips. The slurp is silent. The coffee creates no sound. Taste the bitter sweetness of the coffee.

Walk down three carpeted steps into a sunken living room. The living room is all glass on one side, letting in the blueness of the night. Lie on a white satin couch. The satin has a bluish sheen. Stare at the deep azure sky through the glass. As you continue staring into the night, the forms of mountains and rivers manifest themselves. You are suddenly on a raft riding down churning rapids of white froth. Feel the water beneath you. Feel it splash, ice-cold, against your body, cold, wet, and tingling. The river is silent. Lining the river are tall fir trees and lonesome pine.

The raft comes up on shore and you begin walking along trails through the pine. Come upon a beautiful naked man/ woman [whichever sex you are attracted to] lying in a bed of pine needles. Feel yourself instantly and powerfully sexually attracted to him/her. Suddenly he/she stirs from his/her slumber, opening his/her eyes to smile at you with mutual attraction. He/she takes you lovingly by your hand and leads you through the woods.

Flowers fill the forest: daisies, columbine, tiger lilies. Turn a bend. Come to a whole valley of yellow daffodils. Smell their sweetness. Canals run through the fields of yellow. Take off your clothes. Wade into the canals till the water is neck-deep. Walk along the fine, sandy bottom. The daffodils are now replaced by deep purple crocuses which are at your eye level. Come out of the canal into a patch of soft, furry pussy willows. Walk through the pussy willows. You are dried by their softness.

A great field of red and yellow and white tulips, waxy in the sunlight, lies ahead. Scattered throughout the tulip fields are windmills spinning in the wind. Huge fluffy clouds float in a vast light-blue sky. They form a castle in the sky. It begins to rain, a light, silent rain. The water is warm and wet against your skin. It has no smell. The sun continues to shine, producing a mammoth rainbow encircling the castle. Stand there together in the rain, in the sun, looking up at the rainbow in the sky.

Reactions

Your feelings of relaxation, anesthesia, tingling, vibration, and motion will continue to become more pronounced. "I went real deep," sighed Royce, a thirty-one-year-old executive. "It was fine, very relaxed." "My finger got so numb it was almost painful," said Mary, a thirty-three-year-old physician. "My chest cavity feels tingling and cool," reported Sheryl, a twenty-six-year-old hair stylist. "My face started to tingle as soon as I went into the image," said Ray, a thirty-five-year-old department-store buyer. "I was feeling a vibration, a motion."

Collette, a forty-two-year-old engineer, said she found it worked better to put any specific affirmations she was working on after the image, rather than between the self-hypnosis procedure and image as I usually suggest. It's good to experiment and see what works best for you. Collette also said she experienced a perceptual change after coming out of the image. The light looked yellower when she first opened her eyes. "I can see quieter," she said, referring to a mellowing effect that the imagery had on her perception of reality. "I wanted to go back to Holland," she continued. "They have a sky like no other because they are below sea level. It's interesting when you put one image in another, living room to forest."

Benefits

Raising sex energy can heighten your sex drive and improve your love life. "This was a perfect image for me," said Ginny, a twenty-five-year-old landscape artist who had been sexually unfeeling since her father had sexually abused her regularly between the ages of ten and twelve. "I liked the idea of being attracted to a man, being naked with him, but still not having sex. I found that very arousing. Maybe because it seemed safe, and the sex act still frightens me."

As Ginny continued to practice the *Windmills Scene,* her libido, which had been repressed by past sexual trauma, was energized sufficiently to make itself felt, and as her sex drive became ever stronger, it finally overpowered the fear that had been repressing it. The dominant feeling prevails, and raising sex energy through the *Windmills Scene* empowered sex to dominate over fear in Ginny's case. "Once I actually started feeling sexy, I wasn't afraid of anything," she said. "But as long as fear kept these feelings down, I was dead. It's good to be back among the living!"

Raising sex energy can also lead you to higher knowledge and experience. After practicing the *Windmills Scene* for three days, Anne raised so much energy it propelled her out of body. She related the following experience: "This morning, when I was driving to work, it suddenly seemed as if my car stopped moving. I was by this beautiful tree in the middle of an open field. Then I felt like I was going out of the car.

"I just floated up. I had a gut feeling that I was suspended above the car. Then I had a feeling like someone was gripping me around my waist to wake me up. I kept shaking my head and I felt like someone was shaking me. Then this was replaced by a feeling, 'Brace yourself. Something big is going to happen.' By the time I got to the freeway ramp, I felt myself float back into the car. I got that same feeling on my way here tonight: 'Something's coming big. Keep your foundation firm and stable.' All I know for sure is it sure made me horny. I haven't had sex this much with David since we were married seven years ago."

As your senses heighten from sensory expansion, so will your sexuality. Your resulting sex energy will then take you to experiences beyond the realm of your five-sensory world. Anne's growing sex energy took her momentarily out of body, free of carnal limitations, free to perceive past the veil of a physical sensorium.

Raising your sex energy will manifest itself in beneficial ways other than making you aware of an increased sex drive. You will feel much more energetic in general. In fact, you may not even be conscious of a rising libido. You'll simply feel stronger, healthier, more motivated. JoAnne, a sixty-two-year-old retired librarian, had difficulty regaining her strength after a traumatic car accident in which she received a head injury and her best friend was killed. Then her mother, with whom she was living, became ill and JoAnne, still weak from the trauma of the accident, found herself unable to take care of her sick mother, who was the world to her.

"It broke my heart to put Mom in a convalescent home," she said. "She didn't want to go, but I was just too weak to cook and buy groceries for her." Then JoAnne discovered that the home where she'd put her mother wasn't taking care of her properly. They'd allowed the woman to dehydrate and strapped her to her bed to make her more manageable. JoAnne used her last bit of energy getting her mother transferred to another facility, but she was too late. Her mother died less than a week after entering the new establishment. JoAnne had a total collapse. "It was all my fault," she cried. "If I'd kept Mother at home with me, none of this would have happened. I keep seeing that poor, painful face pleading with me to get her out of that terrible place. They murdered her, that's what they did."

For over a year JoAnne was so debilitated from this series of traumas that she left her apartment only to buy food, and she'd have to rest up several days to muster the energy to do that. "I'd be so weak when I got back from the store," she said, "I'd have to rest a few hours before I was able to put the gro-

ceries away. It would be days before I'd be strong enough to
go shopping again." Gradually JoAnne was able to build herself up somewhat by experimenting with various vitamins,
minerals, and nutrition preparations. It was then that she had
the strength to come and see me.

I knew immediately that what JoAnne needed was a fast
way to generate energy. I asked her to practice the *Windmills
Scene* three times a day. In two weeks she reported, "I'm feeling stronger. I really am. I'm not into any of that sex stuff. I
haven't dated in twenty years, but I can appreciate a good-
looking guy when I see one. It's not that the image even
aroused me really. It just sort of perked me up, added a spark."
Any time you are feeling low and your energy is down, you
can use the *Windmills Scene* to generate sex energy and pick
yourself up.

Raising sex energy also yields increased motivation that
can show up in your job performance. Samuel, a thirty-eight-
year-old medical technician, lost interest and suffered burnout
in his profession after his mother and father died. "They had
some sort of fight and my mother had a stroke," he said. "My
dad said he couldn't deal with disease and I had to take care
of everything. I got Mother into the ward where I worked so
I could take care of her. It was strange, she just became one
of my patients. That's how I dealt with it. When she died I
didn't feel grief or cry. I just handled it efficiently and made
the necessary arrangements. A few weeks later when my dad
said he wasn't feeling well, I didn't believe him. But sure
enough, in a few days he was in the same ward where Mother
had died. The staff cried when they saw me bring him in, they
felt so sorry for me. When Dad died, I once again handled it
like one of my patients. I dissociated myself from the situation,
but now, for some reason I hate my work. I can't deal with
the patients anymore. It's funny, I used my role as a medical
professional to distance myself from my parents' dying, but
now my profession reminds me of it."

The emotional distancing that Samuel did in order to escape the pain of his parents' death cost him a great deal of
psychic energy. First he needed to get in touch with his feel-

ings of grief surrounding his parents' death, which we were able to accomplish after several months of therapy. Then we needed to find a way to restore his depleted energy supply, to motivate him once again to be enthusiastic about his work. I suggested he practice the *Windmills Scene,* and in less than three weeks Samuel said he was feeling better about his job. "I can enjoy helping people again," he said. "That image gave me some oomph, an added push that I needed to get back in the swing of things. I wouldn't say it made me horny, but it certainly made me feel more energetic and like going to work." You too will discover that boosting your sex energy heightens your motivation for work and improves job performance.

Sondra, a thirty-three-year-old executive secretary, came to me saying she needed help in making a career change. "I've had twenty jobs in the last ten years," she said, "and they're all boring, boring, boring. Help me find something that will make me happy." After a couple more sessions it became apparent to me that Sondra was never happy no matter what she did. She'd tried acting, writing, painting, teaching, secretarial, clerking, and several other occupations, and been bored by them all. Finally I said, "Sondra, I think you need to take responsibility for your own boredom. It may be you, not the job, that needs changing."

Feeling energetic is never boring, and when you have energy you feel like doing almost anything. I therefore asked Sondra to practice the *Windmills Scene* so that she could learn to become more energetic by raising her sex energy. After a week of practicing, she said, "It really surprised me. I never thought sexy imagery could make me like my job more, but work suddenly seems more interesting. I'm more into it. I concentrate more on what I'm doing and that makes me get more involved. When I'm involved I like what I'm doing. I guess all I needed was more energy. If it had to come from my sex drive, then so be it!"

Fan Scene

By practicing your next image, the *Fan Scene*, you continue to merge your growing sensuality from sensory expansion with sexual eroticism to produce greater sex energy. In this image you negatively hallucinate smell and sight while being seduced by a lover one sultry, rainy night in the tropics. While it is patently arousing, the image allows you to take it where you wish sexually, not necessarily ending in actual lovemaking or climaxing, but certainly going a step further sexually than you did in the *Windmills Scene*. Your result will be a wildly defined sensory impression that is both expanded and erotic, charged and energizing.

Fan Scene

It's night. You are lying in bed on your back staring at a rotating fan on the ceiling. You are in the tropics. The room has bamboo shutters and wicker furniture. Slow, sultry blues music is playing. It's hot, sticky, humid. Hear the sound of rain against the window. The shutters are banging. Get up and go outside. The wind is blowing hard. Palms and ferns are swaying. Your face becomes wet. The taste of rainwater comes to your mouth. Look up at the sky and open your mouth. It feels like water pouring into your mouth, wet and cool, running down your face and body. Your hair feels wet. See no rain. Smell no rain.

Walk into a bar. The place is deserted except for a lone piano player. Hear the sound of rain upon the roof and against the windows. It looks clear outside. There is an empty crystal glass on the bar. Approach it. Put it to your lips. Sniff. There is no smell. Tilt the glass. It feels like liquid pouring into your mouth. Tastes like whiskey. Keep drinking. A feeling of intoxication comes over you.

Suddenly the wind blows the door open! Hear the sound of

*water trickling on the floor. Your skin feels wet. There is the
heavy scent of sandalwood. The alcohol produces a spinning
sensation. A sailor/painted woman [whichever you are sexually attracted to] enters. He/she takes you sensually by your
arm to the back of the bar. All is oblivion.*

Reactions

As your energy rises, whether it be sex energy or any other
form of energy, so does your concentration. Concentration is,
in effect, your ability to *maintain* focused energy. As a result
of your growing energy and concentration, your images will
take on an increasing richness of detail. "It reminded me of
a bar in Ensenada I went to many, many years ago," said
Adam, a fifty-four-year-old high school teacher. "It's incredible the detail with which I was able to see that place. I could
even read the labels on the bottles over the bar."

"In the *Windmills Scene* I could only see the rusty faucet,"
said Mercedes, a twenty-eight-year-old pilot, "but I had the
whole set from *Rain* as soon as you said ceiling fan. I can't
believe how clearly I saw every part of it."

You may also notice that as you reach higher states of
being, your perception of light changes. In fact, all creation
may be perceived as expressions of changing light, as you
shed the limitations of your physical body to reveal the astral
body. "When you said you were going to count to three my
eyes lit up like sunlight," smiled a woman in her early thirties.
"Golden light just covered the inside of my eyes, my whole
panorama of vision. It lasted at least five seconds. I didn't want
it to leave." The yogis speak of three "bodies" or encasements
that cage the soul or Bird of Paradise. They call these bodies:
physical, astral, and causal. It takes energy to break free of
these cages and fly. A change in your perception of light is a
clue that you are on your way!

Benefits

You definitely will enjoy sex more by this stage in your imagery progression. "I'm sexually irresistible now," Anne laughed after practicing the *Fan Scene* for five days. "David kidded me that I'm getting to be too much to handle. When we first met, seven years ago, there was a strong sexual attraction from the beginning. He proposed on the second date, which consisted of four consecutive days in bed. He called our early days of marriage my 'seventeen going on twenty days,' because I climaxed seventeen times in one five-hour period. But with the advent of my headaches and warts, our lovemaking went down to only once every three months by our fourth year of marriage. It was on the rise again since I started seeing you, and we were averaging twice a week, but since the *Fan Scene,* we've had sex every day. I love it!"

Sex energy, like all energy, will make you more alert. Being alert helps you function better in all areas of endeavor, at work, home, or play. It is especially beneficial in fighting off narcolepsy, a condition characterized by brief attacks of deep sleep. Christopher, a twenty-six-year-old art-gallery curator, hit a dog with his car and killed it when he suddenly fell asleep at the wheel while driving. "It was one o'clock in the afternoon," he said, "broad daylight. I was wide awake. I don't know what happened. Suddenly I was out like a light.

"I've had trouble like this before, but I guess I've been lucky. I never did any damage before. A couple of times I caught myself starting to drift off while driving, but the shock of discovering it always pulled me back. This last time I wasn't so lucky. I sure am sorry about that dog. I need to do something before I hurt myself or another person. I'm terrified to drive now, but it's the only way I have to get to work."

I told Christopher that he could become more alert by raising his sex energy. At first he protested that he didn't want to be sexually aroused all the time, and I explained that just because he was using sex energy, that didn't necessarily mean he'd feel sexual. It would depend on how he channeled his sex energy as to whether or not he'd feel sexually aroused. It was possible to use his libidinal energy in the service of maintaining wakefulness and concentration without becoming distractedly aroused in the process.

He agreed to give it a try and practiced the *Fan Scene* three times a day for a week before resorting to the following strategy: Whenever he was in a situation where he absolutely needed to remain alert, such as driving or dealing with an important problem at work, he was to flash onto the image of the *Fan Scene* and say to himself, "Fan." Saying the image's title to himself served as a trigger to cue the effects of the image he had spent a week practicing. Once Christopher began using a trigger word to cue sex energy in situations where he needed to be alert, he found he no longer had attacks of sudden sleep. You too can use the image's title, or a word that represents it in your mind, to cue sex energy and keep you alert, once you've practiced the image at least a week.

It is common practice among athletic coaches to forbid their athletes sexual activity while they are in training, in the assumption that their dammed-up sexual energies will be sublimated or redirected in the direction of athletic excellence. Unfortunately, this repression of sex energy often leads to its extinction, and there is nothing there to divert when the big game or performance occurs.

You may therefore find it beneficial to use sex-energy-generating imagery to ensure that you have energy to sublimate or channel when you wish to direct sex energy into achieving maximum athletic performance. John, a twenty-four-year-old professional football player, said, "You know the expression, 'If you don't use it, you lose it'? Well I find if I don't have sex for a long time I just lose interest in everything, not just sex, but football too. This sublimation shit doesn't work for me. Problem is, if I break training and have lots of sex, that can poop me out too. Can't you hypnotize me into having tons of energy and being able to party too?"

"John," I said, smiling, "it's up to you what you use your sex energy for, winning the game or having a great orgasm.

I can, however, show you how to refrain from sex and not lose interest in football, along with being sure you'll have plenty of energy there when you need it for a touchdown."

I advised John to practice the *Fan Scene* for a week, until he got the knack of creating sex energy with imagery. Then I suggested, "Right before a game I want you to take some time by yourself and rehearse the *Fan Scene,* making it as real as possible in all five senses. If the image makes you horny or aroused, that's okay. You're going to spend that arousal on playing football, not having a climax. If the image simply charges you and makes you more energetic, that's fine too. Whatever the energy you create from practicing the *Fan Scene* feels like, you're going to channel it into playing the sport. The important thing is that you have energy to channel!" John followed my suggestions and his game vastly improved. If you need more energy for sports, try generating sex energy and channeling it into your athletic performance the same way I suggested to John. You'll find it can be very effective.

Raising sex energy is also excellent for lifting depression and apathy, as well as restoring faith. You cannot be depressed and energetic at the same time. They are incompatible responses. The low-energy state we call depression vanishes with the addition of more energy, until it finally becomes the high-energy state we call joy. A joyous state such as this often takes on religious and/or mystical proportions.

Julie, a fifty-six-year-old telephone operator, said that when her husband Ned, a fifty-five-year-old systems analyst, died of a sudden heart attack, she lost her faith in everything and fell into deep despair. "I didn't want to go on living," she said. "I hated Ned for leaving me, and I didn't want to spend the rest of my life alone. Plus I didn't want to have to keep working. Ned left me with nothing but bills. I hated everybody, even God. I said no god would treat someone like I'd been treated so I decided there couldn't be a god. But all I accomplished with that attitude was to get more depressed. I considered suicide, but I didn't have the guts. If I couldn't kill myself and I couldn't stand my present state, there was only one other option: get out of my depression."

I taught Julie to create sex energy using the *Fan Scene*. She practiced diligently and soon found that her general energy level began to rise concomitantly with the falling away of her depression. "The world looks different to me now," she said. "The more energy I feel, the more love I feel. I've gone back to church. I've gone back to God." Without energy there is despair. With energy, you can feel only joy.

You can also use heightened sex energy to strengthen your immune system to help you fight disease. "I had that stupid flu virus that's been going around," said Kathy, a twenty-two-year-old nutritionist, "but I handled it much better than I normally would. Ordinarily, I'd be down for a week, but I was well in three days. I practiced the *Fan Scene* throughout my illness and was psychologically up through the whole thing. I think it was 'cause I was so horny. I had sex twice while I was still sick in bed and even found myself giggling before it."

Why is it that two people can be exposed to the same germ-infested conditions, and one contracts the illness while the other doesn't? As surgeon Bernie Siegel observes in *Love, Medicine, & Miracles,* "Our state of consciousness and disease are inseparable. . . . Do not close your eyes to acts or events that are not always measurable. They happen by means of an inner energy available to all of us."

Negativity, the unpleasant state of mind associated with dour images and loss of energy, encourages the development of illness, allowing you to slip into a vulnerable state where your defenses to disease are down. Positivity, the pleasant state of mind associated with positive images and rising energy, strengthens your defenses and keeps you healthy.

As your energy from sensory expansion and sex imagery increases, you, like Kathy, will be able to handle sickness better than you normally would. May the healing energy of spiritual sexuality be with you.

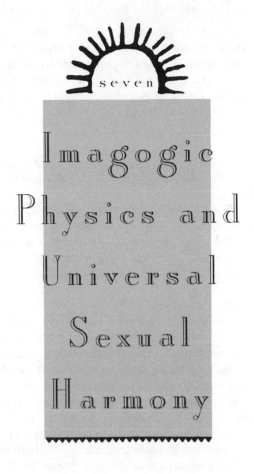

seven

Imagogic Physics and Universal Sexual Harmony

The seven images in this chapter, *Yellowstone Scene, Giants Scene, Enchanted Isle Scene, Topanga Scene, Africa Scene, Taj Mahal Scene,* and *Cathedral Scene,* are designed to give you an emotional understanding that your body and the universe are not separate, but one. In the following images your senses remain intact, but you negatively hallucinate the physical properties that constitute your reality. Your senses don't change, the world does. In essence, however, there is no difference. While common belief holds that your senses belong to you and properties belong to that which is independent of you, outside of you, this is not so. Your senses create the properties in the first place. The properties are a function of your senses. You cannot alter one without altering the other. With this realization you gain control of your reality. As you will soon experience.

Intuitive vs. Rational Knowledge

You can spend a lifetime trying to "figure" things out. You can read every book ever written on a subject, take every class, attend every seminar, and still not really know or grasp your area of pursuit. True knowledge is more than just a collection of facts or an extensive data base. It is also a product of intuition, direct cognition without rational thought and inference.

Knowledge that is in accordance with inferences reasonably drawn from events or circumstances gives you an intellectual understanding. It makes sense. It agrees with everything we've all accepted to be true. You can use it mechanically to start a lawnmower or drive your car. Knowledge that you accept simply because it *feels* right provides you an emotional understanding. This kind of immediate apprehension or cognition may not make sense to you. It violates logic and deductive reason, which insist truth must come from an observable data base. You may not be able to build a space shuttle using only your powers of intuition, but then you may not need a physical craft at all to travel if you rely on intuitive rather than rational understanding to effect change in your life.

Mechanical vs. Metaphysical Principles

With rational knowledge you can master mechanical operations. You can effect physical changes in matter. You can carry a chair across the room or build a tree house. With intuitive knowledge you can master metaphysical operations. You can effect changes beyond the physical. You can leave your body and travel to a plane beyond the physical realm.

To truly understand metaphysics, you must first understand physics. *Meta* means beyond or after. *Metaphysics* literally means beyond or after physics. Just as calculus comes beyond or after arithmetic, so metaphysics comes after physics. In both cases it helps to have mastered the first before advancing to the second.

Physics is the science that deals with matter and energy and their interactions in the fields of mechanics, acoustics, optics, heat, electricity, magnetism, radiation, atomic structure, and nuclear phenomena. By *truly* understanding this science, I mean your attainment of the knowledge of physics intuitively as well as rationally. With an intuitive knowledge of physics you will be able to transcend the mechanical principles limited to the use of the rational mind alone, and effect change in reality directly. No hammers, saws, or screwdrivers will be necessary to transform the matter of your creation. The images in this chapter are designed to give you an intuitive, emotional understanding of the physical qualities comprising reality. With this knowledge you transcend traditional mechanical processes and effect change directly.

Six Physical Properties of Reality

A primary property of reality, the world as you know it, is *mass,* the amount of matter in a body. Reality is composed of matter. One of the most fundamental attributes of this matter comprising reality is *inertia.* This is the tendency for any object to stay at rest if it is at rest now, or—if it is in motion— to continue moving as it is now. When your car starts out suddenly from a stop, you fall back in your seat. Nothing actually pushed you backward, your body just tried to stay as it originally was, at rest. If you then jam on the brakes, your body lurches forward, trying to persist in its previous motion.

A body shows a greater inertia the more weight it has. What we call the weight of a body is the amount of the pull of *gravity* on it. Gravity is the accelerating attraction between any two free pieces of matter. This attraction between any two bodies in the universe is directly proportional to their masses and inversely proportional to the square of their distance apart.

Another property you may have noticed in reality is that of *centrifugal force,* the force that tends to impel mass outward from a center of rotation. If this mass then hits other mass, it is bent back or returned, exhibiting the property of *reflection.* When ripples traveling on water strike a wide obstacle, such as a floating board, you can see a new set of ripples starting back from the obstacle. Similarly, sound waves may be reflected from walls, mountains, the ground, etc. A long "rolling" of thunder is usually due to successive reflections from clouds and ground surfaces.

The mass or matter comprising your reality can take three forms: solid, liquid, and gas. A property of the solid and liquid forms of matter is *constant volume.* Volume is the amount of space occupied by matter. Regardless of what shape they take, solid and liquid matter always occupy the same amount of space. You can pour a cup of water or sand on the ground and it will still only fill as much space as it did when it was in the cup. Such is not the case with a gas, which will fill whatever space it is given.

Negatively Hallucinating the Physical Properties of Reality

You gain an emotional understanding of the physical properties comprising reality by *experiencing* them. Once again, you will use the phenomenon of the negative hallucination to heighten your experiencing.

As you learn progressively to negatively hallucinate each of the physical properties comprising reality, the properties that remain will be vastly intensified. Just as directing your attention to remaining senses energized or empowered them, so directing your attention to remaining properties energizes them also. This heightening of your energy will also automatically heighten your sex drive, unless you deliberately block the energy from taking this form. Your sex drive *is* energy.

Concentration

Concentration is the key to creation. Taking your concentration off one property leaves more room to process other properties. Concentration also raises energy. Whether you direct your concentration to a sense or property only determines the *form* the energy of your concentration takes. Senses and properties are only concepts that the energy of your concentration materializes by crystallizing around the thought form that is the concept. Forms differ only in terms of their configurations, the arrangement of the energy comprising their parts. They are all energy. Concentration determines the arrangement or configuration of that energy.

Your mind gives energy form through the power of your concentration. That is the power of creation. You don't create the energy, you create the form. The energy is infinite, and comes from the Infinite, One, or Uncreated.

To truly appreciate the power of your concentration you may need a paradigm shift in terms of the way you view creation. Ask yourself, "In this creative process of concentration am I taking in or projecting out?" Are you clearing space in your sensory channels to process more of independent reality (taking in), or are you directing more of your energy reserve to create more of this aspect of reality (projecting out)?

You may argue that the results in either case are the same. However, the way you act, depending upon your interpretation of reality, may be completely different. In the former you are primarily a victim of reality; in the latter you are the creator. You go from a finite system to an infinite one and your possibilities with this emotional understanding are suddenly, immediately, and irrevocably limitless!

Opponents could call your using imagery to achieve an emotional understanding that reality is a function of your consciousness projected outward, a case of your being hypnotized into belief, but what of the power of belief? Is not absolute, unequivocal belief the key to all manifestation? Did not Christ say, "All things are possible to him that believeth." Did he not also say, "For verily I say unto you; that whosoever shall say unto this mountain, Be thou removed, and be thou cast into the sea; and shall not doubt in his heart, but shall believe that those things which he saith shall come to pass; he shall have whatsoever he saith."

The key to mastery is refusing to entertain any thought other than the one you wish to manifest. Your belief in your power of creation is truly the point of entry into the realm of limitless possibilities. Do you want to believe you are a finite, limited, mortal person, or do you want to believe you are an infinite, limitless, immortal energy form? Whichever you believe, you are right. You *are* what you believe yourself to be. You truly are your own creator.

The following images will give you an emotional understanding of yourself as creator. Controlling your reception of an independent reality may not make you realize that this reality cannot exist independently of you, but directly changing this reality will surely emotionally convince you that it is a function of you, and not vice versa. It is a wonderful dawning to know you are so close to your creator. You are as close as you can be. You are truly One.

Yellowstone Scene

The *Yellowstone Scene* is the first image where you deal with what I term "imagogic physics," imaginally adding or removing physical properties from your reality. In this image you learn to negatively hallucinate mass, the amount of matter in a body. In order to develop a fine discrimination and control you continue to restrict the negative hallucination to the element of water. You experience water as if it had no density.

Without density or mass, water would have no weight and exert no pressure; it would also offer no resistance. It would feel like air. You could pass your hand through it without resistance. In the following image water tastes and smells sweet like honey, feels cool and wet, looks and sounds like water, but has no weight and offers no resistance; it has no mass.

In your prior images you negatively hallucinated your ability to sense reality. Here you negatively hallucinate reality itself. Before you altered the perceiver. Now you alter the perceived. Both strategies will take you to the same place, the profound realization that you are what you perceive. The perceived and the perceiver are One.

Yellowstone Scene

You are standing before a large lake of crystal-clear water surrounded by pine trees and rocky mountains. The snow-capped peaks are mirrored in the still surface of the lake. A hundred yards of sandy shore stretches in front of you, leading to the water. Begin running toward the lake through the soft, loose sand. Going faster . . . and faster . . . and faster. Hit the water with a great splashing sound! It feels like cold, wet air. There are ripples where the water breaks into bits of light. Feel no pressure. The water offers no resistance. It feels cold and wet. Sniff. It smells sweet like honey. Drink. It tastes sweet like honey. Attempt to swim. The water will not support your body. It gives no sensation of buoyancy.

Go deeper and deeper. You are now in water up to your neck. Once again you try to swim. It's like flogging in air. Run through the water at neck-depth at great speed. The water offers no resistance. Take a deep breath. Submerge. Crawl along the lake bottom. There are brightly colored fish and

*seaweed. Feel no water pressure. There is no ringing in your
ears. Hear birds chirping overhead above the water as clearly
as if you were on dry land. Look up at the murky water above.
See a faint yellow light filtering down from the water's surface.*

*Stand above the water line. You can breathe again. Take a
deep breath. Begin walking to shore. Leave the lake. Come to
a geyser of hot, gushing water. Stand over the geyser. Feel
the heat, the wetness. There is no sense of pressure.*

*Next you come to a great waterfall on black rock. Hyacinths
bloom around the water. Smell their fragrance. Walk to the
center of the falling water. Feel its coldness, its wetness, but
no sense of pressure.*

*Leave the waterfall. Find a bed of lilies of the valley. Lie in
the bed of lilies. It begins to rain a warm rain without pressure.
The sun is still bright. See a rainbow in each drop of water.*

Reactions

Your most likely reaction will continue to be an incredible
sense of relaxation. "I feel like a zombie," said a young man
after the *Yellowstone Scene.* "When I practice it on my own it
sometimes takes half an hour to pop out. I'll feel really foggy,
like I've been sleeping and just woke up."

You will also find that this new reality devoid of properties
that you are used to is somewhat strange. It may take time
for you to imagine it. "I had trouble walking on the bottom of
the lake without bobbing up," reported a woman in her forties.

This image requires even greater concentration on your
part than the prior ones, and as your imagery becomes more
intense, the imagery process may blend into reality. Sensory
impressions in any sense modality may appear outside of the
circumscribed imagery session. "I saw a cat in the corner of
the room," smiled Tom, a thirty-two-year-old accountant, "the
moment I opened my eyes. Then it was gone."

These leftover thought forms usually last only a moment,
and you will probably be the only one who will be able to sense
them. I say "probably" because Tom's reaction reminds me of

a singularly odd case that I used to tell about mainly to get a laugh, although it seems especially appropriate here. Ed, a fifty-four-year-old attorney, presented me with the following problem: "Sometimes, when I climbed the steps to the courthouse, I used to hallucinate that a rabid skunk would bite me in the ankle. I was able to slough it off by examining my leg and seeing that no damage had been done, and telling myself that I had imagined the incident. Then one day, while I was driving in my car, I heard that a rabid skunk had been seen in the area of the courthouse. I had thought I'd been bitten that morning and had passed it off as a hallucination, but the radio announcement made me look at my leg more carefully. There were two red marks like bites on my shin. I want to be hypnotized to determine whether or not I was really bitten."

I told Ed that if he had hallucinated the skunk, reexperiencing it under hypnosis still wouldn't determine whether the skunk was real or not. If he hadn't known then, he still wouldn't under hypnotic recall. Ed begged me to give it a try, however, and so we proceeded. I hypnotically regressed Ed to revivify the incident with the skunk on the courthouse steps. As predicted, Ed clearly saw the skunk, but was unable to say whether it was real or hallucinated. About five minutes after Ed left I saw a wisp of black light with a white stripe down the middle run across my carpet. "My gosh," I thought. "I just exorcised a skunk." Then I passed it off as an overactive imagination on my part. Two days later I was talking to the cleaning lady for my building and she said, "You'll never believe this, but I thought I saw a skunk in your office the other night." This imagogic residue sure had a long shelf life!

Benefits

You may find that as you begin imagining reality without mass, the world seems less restrictive to you. It offers less resistance. It is easier to get around and navigate in. Clark, a twenty-two-year-old economics major, reported that practicing the *Yellowstone Scene* helped him make his college swimming team. "It's great," he beamed. "I used to get winded in the last couple laps of the butterfly. Now it's a piece of cake. It feels almost like I'm swimming in air. I can sure go a lot easier and faster when I imagine the water has no mass." If you tire easily just moving through the day I think you'll find that practicing the *Yellowstone Scene* will make life easier. It will at least enable you to conceive of passing through reality without resistance. The thought is the father to the deed.

Removing mass from reality tends to make it more dream-like, and as this occurs the frequency of your dreaming may increase. It's as though the two states of mind are attempting to merge. The quality as well as frequency of your dreams is often altered. Your dreams become more reality-oriented, take on more of an informative or problem-solving nature than they normally have. This is excellent. You are integrating self, getting in closer touch with the vast storehouse of knowledge that comprises your subconscious. As reality becomes more dreamlike, dreams become more lifelike. Your goal is a complete union. Then all things will be known to you.

But don't be discouraged if this doesn't happen right away. Take your time to enjoy the benefits of the images I'm giving you. If removing mass from reality seems a difficult task at first, don't worry about it. You'll get it in time. You have forever.

Giants Scene

Your mastery of imagogic physics continues with the *Giants Scene,* where you remove from your body, via the negative hallucination, the property of centrifugal force, the force that tends to impel mass outward from a center of rotation. This image is a primer for a more advanced series of images, and is the only one in this chapter where the negative hallucination is not restricted to water. In addition, this scene engenders a wonderful feeling of being part of the cosmos, being basic and in harmony with one great energy force.

Giants Scene

It's a hot summer day. You are climbing upward over purple rocks and orange sand by an aqua-blue river, winding higher and higher toward a mountain peak. As you walk, people join you one at a time till finally there are nine of you in all. Climb past the clouds. You are above the clouds.

At the summit is a long, slender, silver pole with a golden orb at the top. Around the orb is a ring to which are attached nine silver chains with handles at their bottoms. You each grab a handle and start going round and round the pole. The rings to which the chains are attached revolve with you such that the chains do not intertwine or wrap around the pole. Go faster and faster . . . and faster.

Your feet leave the earth and the nine of you revolve around the pole holding to the chains. Now the chains begin to grow. They get longer and longer, extending far, far out into space. The chain of the person next to you stops growing. Your chain stops growing. And so it goes progressively down the line, each one of you stopping a bit further from the pole. The revolution continues to pick up speed, gaining in momentum, faster and faster. The chains snap!

Keep going round and round, in orbit around the golden orb. Flowers grow out of your body, white Madonna lilies. Smell them. The orb turns red. The sky turns red. The orb progressively becomes black, in portions. It is night. Stars fill the sky. The orb reappears, first red and then golden. The sky is blue.

Reactions

The *Giants Scene* engenders feelings of being an integral, supportive part of cosmic creation; a feeling of being basic, nurturing, and in harmony with one great energy force. You and your companions become planets revolving around the sun. You become Earth. You support and sustain life as plants grow from your nourishment. When the silver chain snaps, you remain in orbit around your axis, the silver pole, because you have removed the property of centrifugal force from your body.

People often see symbology in the *Giants Scene*. "It was like a maypole," said Arlene, a twenty-eight-year-old office administrator. "A phallic symbol," Marv, a thirty-year-old yacht broker, reacted, "You must read fantasy. That was Venus, the goddess of Beauty. Lilies are the ultimate destination." Personally, I see this image as a good metaphor for staying centered and keeping your sanity in a changing world. When attachments break (the chain snaps) through the loss of a loved one, a job, a home, you remain in harmonious emotional equilibrium (continue orbiting your center).

"That image made me feel very warm," said Greg, a thirty-nine-year-old nurse. As you remove properties, less energy is needed to maintain the configuration called reality, and this energy can then manifest itself in its pure form. You very often will experience this form as heat.

Benefits

"I use the *Giants Scene* to help me with my morning jogging," said Wendel, a fifty-two-year-old restaurant owner. "I used to slip or turn my ankle rounding curves at my health spa track, but no more. I hold the image of staying in perfect orbit around my central point, never flying off a degree, and presto! I stay on perfect course circling my track."

The *Giants Scene* will give you an intense awareness of the love that is all around you. The first time that Anne experienced this image she said, "It was so logical. I was a step ahead of you all the way through. I knew the chains were going to snap and the flowers were going to grow out of my body before you said so. The other people became like dim lights. Now that it's over I have a sense of self-contained floating. I feel so loved."

The next time I saw her, after three days of practice with the *Giants Scene,* she was breathless. "The last two and a half hours have been electric. I'm totally convinced that if I ever have a crucial need it will be satisfied. I was driving home from work before coming to see you. The brilliance of the clouds intensified. They became a bright iridescent white.

"When I got home I felt an overwhelming impulse of love toward David. I shook him violently and shouted, 'Damn, I love you.' He was stunned, but delighted. Then I left and drove off to see you. The car felt like it was flying. As I drove through the countryside I felt I had my arm around the mountains. There was an intense, powerful feeling, 'Something's coming.' I'm starting to listen to images from my inner mind, moving on pure impulse. And my sex drive is enormously strong. It's as good as it was when we first married. I've heard that women are capable of climaxes three minutes apart. I know that I can always manage just one more."

As a function of the vividness and brilliancy of Anne's hypnotic imagery, sensations from the external world were now becoming intensified. Whites were iridescent and the very landscape was exuding love. In past images the sea and humanity were loving. Today, in reality, Anne had felt as if the mountains loved her and she embraced them, putting her arms around them. She was shaken with a love for her husband. Love was all around her. What begins as a sensation in your hypnotic image becomes a sensation in reality. Hypnosis can wonderfully change your creation of reality.

Enchanted Isle Scene

By the time you finish practicing the *Enchanted Isle Scene*, where you negatively hallucinate the property of gravity—the accelerating attraction between any two free pieces of matter—you will feel a strong, constant sexual power. Your removing properties from reality has the same effect as your negatively hallucinating in various senses. It allows you greater room to process additional data, and that data translates into heightened sensuality and sexual energy.

Enchanted Isle Scene

You are on an enchanted island. You've always been there. You'll always be there. The island has always been there and will always be there. You belong together. There are miles of white, sandy beaches and aqua-blue water. The sun is orange, the sky azure. You are young and will be forever. Run through the shallow water along shore splashing water. The water sails up into the sky against the orange sun, going up forever, never coming down. Wade deeper into water up to your waist. Splashing. Splashing. Water never comes down.

Leave the sea. Go inland along canals lined with palms, and ferns, and vines. Come to a great spring of clear, sweet water shooting up into the sky, never coming down. There are thousands of springs of water shooting into the sky; countless rainbows reflected in the water and crisscrossing.

Walk through the garden of springs to a pool of deep emerald-green lime water. Smell the lime. Gargle the lime water. Taste it. Spit out the lime water. It goes straight ahead, neither up nor down, never stopping. Huge avocado trees surround the pool. Lie in their shade drifting to the smell of lime.

A New Purple

A most interesting phenomenon that I have observed in people whose concentration and energy reaches a certain level is their perception of a purple of such brilliance and beauty that it outshines any other colors they have ever known. It is as though they are seeing beyond the normally visible range of the spectrum into the area of ultraviolet, a light frequency that certain species of ants are reportedly able to perceive. "When you mentioned the rainbows, they became purple," said Allan, a twenty-six-year-old ticketing agent. "Then they became pinwheels. They intertwined like a solar prominence, light lavender against a deep purple. When I looked at the pool it was deep purple."

You can only see 1/30,000 of an inch of the entire spectrum of electromagnetic waves, which range from gamma rays with a length less than a hundred billionth of an inch to electric waves extending beyond one thousand miles. The magnitude of the limitations to what we can know through our present five senses boggles the mind. So much lies beyond our present range of perception it seems fair to say that the bulk of creation is unknown to us. However, your knowledge is now increasing. As your senses expand, your bandwidth of perception widens. You sense light in the ultraviolet range, beyond the violet end of your heretofore visible spectrum. A new purple is a signal that the invisible is becoming visible!

Benefits

In addition to expanding your awareness of creation, the *Enchanted Isle Scene* can make you feel light on your feet, unimpeded by the strictures of gravity. Clint, a sixty-seven-year-old retired upholsterer, complained of feeling useless and decrepit. "There's nothing really wrong with me," he said. "I just can't seem to get around like I used to. I hobble when I walk. I move so slowly. It's like I'm carrying a sack of rocks on my back. If I could move better I'd go back to work. It keeps me busy and makes me feel worthwhile."

After practicing the *Enchanted Isle Scene* for a week, Clint said, "I imagined that my body water had no gravity. We're 80 percent water, you know. The image made me feel so light. Soon I found myself bouncing around like I was thirty. Moving like an old man was a state of mind." Feel free to do like Clint and modify these images to meet your own needs. You'll discover many benefits to feeling unencumbered by gravity.

Tara, a twenty-six-year-old dancer, successfully used the *Enchanted Isle Scene* to improve her movements. She too imagined that her body fluids were free from gravitational pull. "It was wonderful," she said. "I felt light as a feather. My jumps were amazing. I literally soared through the air.

Nothing stopped me. Steps that normally were laborious became effortless."

Daryl, an overweight thirty-one-year-old refrigeration technician, was able to change his self-image and drop forty pounds using the *Enchanted Isle Scene.* "It's so depressing to know you're fat," he told me our first session together. "When I think of myself as fat I hate myself and when I hate myself I eat more. It's a vicious circle. How am I ever going to lose weight if I won't stop eating unless I like myself and I won't like myself unless I weigh less?" "Why don't you begin by *thinking* of yourself as weighing less?" I suggested. "That way you'll like yourself more, be better to yourself, and stop gorging."

Daryl practiced the *Enchanted Isle Scene* for a week, imagining water free from the confines of gravity. Then he imagined that the water comprising his body was free of gravitational attraction and he suddenly felt like he weighed a great deal less. "I really did feel lighter using this kind of imagery," he said. "The lighter I felt, the better I felt about myself and the more energy I had to stay on my diet." If you wish to lose weight, begin by thinking of yourself weighing less. Prepare for this by practicing the *Enchanted Isle Scene* for about a week and then imagine that the water comprising your body is weightless, free of gravity's force.

Sexual Harmony

The session after the one where I gave Anne the *Enchanted Isle Scene* was emotionally charged and lasted two hours. She wore a dress of green brocade with long sparkling earrings. "I'm quite a woman," she began almost defiantly, as if issuing a challenge. "The *Bath Scene* finally caught up with me. I have a constant hum in the groin area that never goes away. I got laid by another man, Carson. He's young, handsome, black. I met him at work. I seduced him to a beachside motel. The experience was ecstatic. I didn't get home till ten o'clock that night. David didn't say anything. He took the attitude that it's my life to live as I please.

"David and I made love five times on Saturday. Then on Sunday David came six times and I came fifteen. I still could have managed one more. I'm so superalive. I feel young, vibrant, beautiful. It's like a big chunk of programming has chunked off my body. I've been incredibly heady ever since. Work is going incredible. It's as if I'm in another world. I've maintained this euphoric state for four days running. I'm going to milk every second, like electricity! My love for David is boundless. I feel so sage with him. I'm enthralled by the possibility of exploring the facets of his personality that I never dreamed existed before. We're becoming soulmates. I want to know him more and more till we become of one mind as well as one body.

"I told David about Carson on Sunday night. He was totally understanding and said he was for anything that made me happy. I think it would be delightful if he had someone else too. I could cry, he was so understanding. I feel closer to him now. I see him as much more together than I had imagined."

It was April 30, 1974, that Anne said these words. A year later I completed the first draft of this book and gave it to her to read. She wrote comments in red ink throughout. Here is what she wrote regarding David's reaction of unconditional understanding: "I now fully realize what 'grace,' love, and courage David showed—what *patience,* understanding and faith in 'our' future he exhibited. I have proven, I know, since then and without words—that I truly can be worthy of his grace and love. He has shown me in many ways that he is happy." In reference to her stated desire that David see other women, she wrote, "a bald-faced self-delusionary falsehood— Besides, no one can say a thing like that until they have experienced it—I went from the 'ridiculous,' to the 'ridiculous,' didn't I!" Relating to their weekend sexual marathon, she wrote: "I now believe this was a function of guilt—because it was *after* this romping that I finally told him about Carson."

I was pleased to see that Anne's sex energy was growing,

but I was concerned knowing that she still needed to learn how to channel it. For the moment it was sweeping her away, as evidenced by how she viewed these experiences a year later. That same session, she went on to recount a dream she had. "I dreamed once more of the Enchanted Isle. This time, instead of you and your beach-city accoutrements, Carson was on the beach drinking orangeade. I asked myself, 'Where's the other guy?' referring to you. Then you came and sat down beside me."

Anne's dream was openly seductive. She'd had sex with Carson and now it was my turn. "I think a doctor-patient relationship is ridiculous," she went on, not waiting for me to interpret the dream. "We should be on an equal basis. Our relationship cannot continue as it is. You're being hard, insensitive, and unsupportive."

Anne had made a tremendous leap forward with her creation of sex energy. However, every level change requires an adjustment; the greater the change, the greater the adjustment. I was tremendously pleased by her increased feelings of self-worth and love for her husband, but I was concerned by her affair, not simply because she had been unfaithful, but because she held the *Bath Scene* responsible for it. She wasn't taking responsibility for her own actions. The purpose of the *Bath Scene* is to create love for humanity, not promiscuity. The problem with infidelity is not sex per se, but the breaking of a contract, a mutual trust.

I gave Anne support and promised to be more understanding in the future. She needed time to adjust; there was no point confronting her with interpretations. When she read this account a year later she wrote in reference to her demand to be on an equal basis, "I'm sorry I was so hard on you—I can look back on this session and see it so differently. You were sensitive, supportive, and—especially—kind to me. And let's not leave out PATIENCE. I'm deeply in debt to you spiritually—I really am!" Finally, regarding my concern that she held the *Bath Scene* responsible for her affair with Carson, she wrote, "It wasn't at all. It was worth the benefits. Poor, *blind,* child—well, the fog is lifting—as I increase my sensitivity and depth, I begin to recognize yours. That is an entirely new and enchanting experience in human relationships. Thank you!"

In Chapters 9 and 10 you will learn to accomplish a sex-energy transfer, a technique that redirects your sex energy, channeling it into a manifestation other than arousal, one of pure energy. As your sexuality increases, so should your power to control it. You will become adept at turning it on and off at will. In reference to this last statement, Anne wrote, "I am. It comes only when I want it now." This is truly sexual harmony.

Topanga Scene

In the *Topanga Scene* you remove the influence of centrifugal force, the force that tends to impel mass outward from a center of rotation, from water. This is in contrast to the *Giants Scene,* where you removed the effects of centrifugal force from your own body. You imagine a rotating sprinkler and hose where water coming out the ends falls straight down rather than flying off as it would if the property of centrifugal force were acting upon it.

Topanga Scene

It is a dark night. The stars are shining, but there is no moon. You have been walking miles up a winding path on an old dirt road in a canyon of sycamore trees. There is a sense of magic in the air, as if something mystical will happen. Come to a wood ranch house. Go in. There is no heat except for the fire in the fireplace. Smell the smoke. A young man and woman sit in front of the fire. The girl plays a flute. Clear tones fill the room and float out into the canyon. They get up and the three of you go outside into a large yard.

In the center of the yard is a massive oak tree with a swing.

Next to it is a gigantic twenty-foot-high sprinkler. It has five tubes like spokes of a wheel revolving; water is coming out the end of each of the five tubes, forming a perfect ring of water twenty feet in the air. The water does not fly out from the revolving tubes, but falls straight down, creating a hollow cylinder of water. Walk through the water to the center where the support for the sprinkler is. You are surrounded by water. Smell the wet grass.

Walk out of the water cylinder into a meadow. Before you on the ground is a garden hose that is squirting water. Pick it up and begin spinning wildly in circles, creating a perfect ring of falling water around you. Whirl to the sound of the flute music echoing among the canyon walls. The man and woman dance around the outside of the water ring while you spin within.

Drop the hose. The three of you walk to a great grove of cottonwood trees. Lie down together, listening to the wind in the cottonwoods.

Magic

The extraordinary events that you imagine in the course of negatively hallucinating the physical properties of matter will give you a sense of magic. You will feel as though you possess supernormal powers, which you do, but which are of value to you only if you believe in them and put them to use. The *Topanga Scene* helps instill an emotional understanding and belief in the magical powers you possessed all along. "I was very numb all over," said Katy, a thirty-two-year-old receptionist for a record company. "Most of all in my brain. Magic—I had the feeling I had when I still believed in fairy tales." When you are able to clear and quiet your mind, when your brain is "numb," you are ready to perform magic; the earth is ready to be planted with the seed of imagogic creation.

Benefits

Picturing yourself with a calm, still center, while liquid energy orbits all around you, not flying off in chaos, is an excellent image for inducing the alpha waves conducive to sleep. "It seems like the outside of my body is moving and the inside is still," said Kevin, a thirty-year-old court reporter with severe insomnia, the first time I gave him the *Topanga Scene*. After a week's practice he said, "It's great. At night I feel so calm inside. I drift right off to sleep."

There are not only benefits to eliminating properties, there are also benefits to heightening them. Just as you reaped benefits from both removing and intensifying senses, you will now be pleasantly surprised to find advantages to removing and intensifying the properties that constitute your physical reality. It is the properties remaining that intensify, due to your giving them more attention, more room to process in your consciousness. Therefore, through practicing the *Topanga Scene,* you may expect any or all of the properties comprising reality, *excluding* centrifugal force, to become more prominent. You thus progress from sensory expansion to property expansion.

Malcolm, a twenty-five-year-old taxi driver, was thinking of changing occupations because his job continually took him into bad areas of town and he was afraid of getting beaten up. "I'm taking boxing lessons," he said, "but I'm still scared. My dad used to call me a sissy when I was growing up. The kids would lay for me after school and I'd run all the way home. I was too frightened to fight. There wasn't a guy in class that couldn't cream me. Even the girls used to pound on me. The thing is I know how to fight now, after all these boxing lessons, and I'm still scared shitless. I feel like such a wimp."

After Malcolm practiced the *Topanga Scene* for a week, his sense of mass changed. "It's amazing," he said elatedly. "I feel more solid, impenetrable. I'm not afraid to have someone take a swipe at me. If they hit me I won't break. I'm beginning to feel like a brick shithouse. It's great!" Taking his attention off of the property of centrifugal force heightened Malcolm's sense of mass because it allowed him to direct more of his attention to this remaining property.

Glenda, a thirty-one-year-old physical therapist, said she had trouble getting through her workday. "I keep slowing down and getting a backlog of patients," she said. "Then I have to force myself to catch up. It's really draining. It's obvious that I can work faster or I wouldn't be able to get back on schedule. I don't know why I can't hold on to my momentum once I get going." She practiced the *Topanga Scene* a week and found that it heightened her sense of inertia while she was in motion. "That image really helped me keep the ball rolling," she reported. "Once I get into my work I keep on moving a whole lot longer than I used to." Heightening your sense of inertia will keep you in motion, once you are in motion, for a much longer period of time. You can use this benefit productively to get more things done in your life.

"That image sure helped me improve my tennis serve," said Natalie, a twenty-nine-year-old interior designer, referring to the *Topanga Scene*. "Every time I serve, this image flashed through my mind of whacking the ball straight down with a loud smack, like it's hitting harder than ever, like it weighs a ton or is under the influence of supergravity. And it *does* come down harder. My opponents run away from, instead of into, my serves. I love it." Natalie benefited from an expanded sense of gravity through eliminating the property of centrifugal force. The image she described using on the tennis court came to her automatically as a function of her practicing the *Topanga Scene*. You too will discover that images relating to imagogic physics will spontaneously pop into your own mind in situations where they are useful.

Africa Scene

The property you learn to negatively hallucinate in the *Africa Scene* is inertia, the tendency for any object to stay at rest if it is at rest now, or—if it is in motion—to continue moving as it is now. Water does not splash in this image because there is no inertia to keep it in motion. When water is forced through holes in a dam under great pressure, or through an elephant's trunk, or when you spit, it falls straight down because there is no inertia to keep it moving forward in a straight line. Likewise, since there is no inertia to keep water at rest remaining that way, liquid moves spontaneously without the aid of an external force. Waves go forward, backward, and sideways at the same time without a wind to set them in motion, and pineapple juice swirls spontaneously in your cup and stomach! Have fun with it. Changing reality spells a good time.

Africa Scene

You are in deepest Africa, standing before a great waterfall that stretches as far as you can see on either side and is over one mile high. Hear the thunderous roar of the crashing water. The water does not splash. It is perfectly still at the base of the falls. Take off your clothes. Swim downriver. Millions of vanda orchids, white, lavender, and pink, line the river bank. Come to a great dam. There are holes in the dam. Water shoots straight out only one inch, then falls straight down. It does not go out any farther in spite of the great pressure that was behind it.

Take a big gulp of water. Spit it out with all your might. The water falls straight down. It does not go forward. Immersed in water waist-deep you race your hands along the water's surface. You cannot make the water splash. The water will not go up. You can cup it in your hands and let it fall but you cannot splash it up.

Wade closer to the dam. Find a small stream leading sideways to a pond. The roar of an elephant's trumpet comes to your ears. A herd of the gigantic animals comes crashing through the jungle to the pond. They suck water from the pond up into their trunks, force water with a great force outward. The water falls straight down as soon as it clears the trunk. It will not go up once it leaves its pressure source. Now currents of water appear sporadically in the pond. Water moves forward and backward spontaneously. There is no wind. Waves are going in and out at the same time. When the waves meet they form larger waves going sideways.

Leave the pond. Walk into the depths of the jungle. Night is falling. Shrill animal sounds pierce the tropic darkness. A native village comes into view. There are thatched huts in a circle. The natives are having a tremendous feast and celebration. They give you a cup of pineapple juice. The juice moves in the cup spontaneously. The cup is still. The juice rolls and swirls. Drink. Taste the sweetness of the pineapple. Feel it swirling and sloshing in your stomach.

Next you are given a cup of rum. Drink. It's strong. A feeling of intoxication overtakes you as you continue to drink. The natives dance a primitive, wild movement, contorting around a fire. Take your rum cup and join them in the ritual. Jump up and down to the beat of the drums. The rum will not come out of the cup. It will not splash up, but it will pour out. The beat gets stronger and stronger, pulsating, vibrating rhythm. Collapse in the dust. Drift to the beat of the drums.

Reactions

Most people have a really good time with this image and laugh when it's over. "I got the biggest kick out of the elephants," said a woman in her fifties. "They were so funny. They expected water to squirt as I did." As the imagery becomes more vivid it is common to embellish it, giving it an added richness. Curtis, a fifty-year-old film producer, said, "I smelled cow dung. They use it for building. They drink cow blood. It's silly to think of water going out one inch and falling down."

Sometimes people alter the image in order to make it easier to do—like Winston, a twenty-four-year-old law student. "Neat. This big ole wall there. I didn't picture it as water though. I made the water dense cause I couldn't picture water not splashing up. Especially if it dropped from my hand and I patted it and it wouldn't come up. I made it heavy water." It's fine to use a strategy such as Winston's as a step to mastering this image, but change it only as a means to an end. Ultimately your goal is to imagine regular, not heavy, water without the property of inertia.

Benefits

Removing inertia from reality will give you get-up-and-go and eliminate procrastination. Darla, a divorced forty-year-old tax consultant with three boys, aged seven, nine, and twelve, complained of being exhausted from the rigors of single parenthood. "I'm up at six A.M. I'm never home before seven P.M. I try to get dinner for the boys right away, but if I sit down to rest first, I'm dead. If I'm lucky enough to feed the kids before I plop in front of the TV, I'll put off getting ready for bed so late I don't get enough sleep and I'm beat all the next day at the office."

I asked Darla to practice the *Africa Scene* for a week, imagining the still pond water beginning to move easily, effortlessly, spontaneously, without the application of any external force. Then I suggested that the next time she found herself immobilized, inert as a rock, plopped in her chair putting off fixing dinner, she should envision herself manifesting that same kind of effortless, spontaneous motion. "At first I thought your idea was a crock," Darla said after she had practiced the *Africa Scene* for two weeks, "but I did it anyway just to see what would happen. In the beginning it was just as I figured. Nothing happened. Then in the first half of my second week I freaked out. I collapsed in my chair as usual, but I was nearly catapulted out of it, like I'd sat on hot coals. I was in the kitchen before I knew it. It was like the scene finally kicked in and gave me a boost the moment I sat in that chair." It may take you some time to condition the response you want, but when it finally takes, your results can be amazingly abrupt.

You may also benefit from certain of the remaining properties that are expanded. Brent, a seventeen-year-old high school student and track enthusiast, was delighted with the effect practicing the *Africa Scene* had on his discus throwing. "It's incredible. I do my spin and then when I let go that baby takes off like a bat out of hell. I've never seen anything like it. I expect to see sparks when it releases from my hand. It's like it has a power of its own." Brent enjoyed the benefits of heightened centrifugal force by taking his attention off inertia. He, as the discus thrower, was the center of rotation, and when he released the discus it was impelled outward with amazing force. You'll find that imagogic physics will improve all phases of your athletic endeavors. All the exercises comprising sports are a function of the properties of physical reality. As you grow to master these properties, by expanding or eliminating them, you come to master athletics.

Wrestling is another sport you can improve upon through practicing the *Africa Scene*. Sadie, a thirty-year-old professional wrestler, was worried that she was getting too old to keep up with her younger competition. "I just don't have any bounce anymore," she said. "My opponent throws me and I hit that floor like a wet dishrag. It nearly kills me every time I take a fall, and that's a lot of times in the course of one match. You have to spring back like a rubber ball when you hit the mat, not break like a load of dishes. I'm turning into a real clod. My fans are noticing, too. They boo and hiss and heckle. I can't take it anymore." After practicing the *Africa Scene* for a week she said, "It's wonderful. I'm getting my old bounce back. When I hit the mat I don't lie there like a dead fish. I spring back." Sadie was enjoying the benefits of expanding reflection, the property of reality that causes mass to be bent back or returned when it hits other mass.

Property expansion includes a heightened awareness of the property, which gives you an intuitive, emotional understanding of its place in creation. After practicing the *Africa Scene* for three days, Jean Paul, a thirty-four-year-old clothier, experienced the following incident: "I was sitting by the pool of my hotel, having a drink. Someone called out to me and I turned quickly, spilling the glass. I turned back and was suddenly transfixed by the puddle of liquid on the glass tabletop. It was as if the entire contents of my drink were suspended before me. I could barely discern the glass supporting it. Maybe it was the sunlight passing through the liquid that held my eye. I don't know. I only know I was so aware at that moment. I thought, That's odd. It shouldn't do that. There should be more water now. It has more space to fill. It's free now. It doesn't have to be this way. I can change it. It seemed like a lucid dream. I really felt that I could make the water do anything I wanted it to then, as if it were part of my dream and I had control of it. Then somebody yelled by the pool and the spell was broken, but it left me with the strangest sense of the arbitrariness, the capriciousness of creation. Like there's really nothing sacred at all about water retaining its volume or falling on the floor when you tip your glass. There's really an infinite number of other ways that reality could work. This is just one of them. The only thing special about this one is it's where we are now." Expanded in Jean Paul's consciousness was water's property of occupying the same amount of space regardless of its container, its constant volume.

Taj Mahal Scene

Your sensuality and sex energy will continue to grow as you clear your sensory channels by negatively hallucinating the property of reflection, bending back, in the *Taj Mahal Scene*.

Here water doesn't splash because it doesn't reflect on impact with another body. In your *Africa Scene* water was reflected but you didn't imagine it as splashing because there was no inertia to maintain its motion once it was turned back from an object. Its change of course would not be visible without inertia to continue its action. In contrast to the *Africa Scene*, water in the *Taj Mahal Scene* is able to shoot out in streams, but once it hits your body it doesn't rebound. It simply runs off, obeying the law of gravity.

Taj Mahal Scene

It is night. You are gazing at a great, long pool at the end of which is a domed, marble temple with many high towers. The marble dazzles, luminescent in the moonlight. Smell sandalwood. Remove your clothes. Wade into the pool, gliding through waxy white water lilies. It begins to rain a fine, light rain. The drops do not splash. They cause ripples in the pool, but they do not reflect or bounce from the pool's surface. The rain hits your body and remains on your skin to run off. It does not splash off your flesh.

Swim to the temple and inside as the pool extends to the interior. Above you is an enormous vaulted azure ceiling, glowing with a brilliant blue luminosity. Come to a great sea. High cliffs surround you. Waves hit the rock and immediately dissolve and run down the cliff side. They do not splash. Leave the water, walking up rock cliffs toward the top of the ceiling.

Approach a waterfall, water falling on hard rock. There is no splashing. Walk through the waterfall. Enter a cavern filled with blue light. Streams of water shoot out the cavern walls with great force at given points on your body. Feel a water jet against your forehead, arms, legs, thighs. The water does not reflect off your skin; it hits the flesh and runs straight off.

Climb a spiraling path bordered on each side by rock walls with shooting jets of water. Reach the top, the middle of the dome over the sea. Hang from the apex of the dome. Let go. Fall. Hit the surface of the sea. There is no splash. Shoot down through the water. Fall deeper . . . and deeper . . . and deeper.

Reactions

Positive feelings you've learned to create continue to intensify. These include profound relaxation to the point of feeling drugged, vivid embellishment, amnesia, motion, precognition, and emergence of a new supersaturated purple. "I got a funny feeling going down into that water like that," said Sandie, a thirty-year-old airline stewardess. "I'm just lying here feeling all those sensations. It's hard to get up." "I was really gone," sighed Florence, a forty-year-old teacher. "I heard you say three. And when you said to undress I took off an elaborate costume—beads and things. An Indian costume. I feel drugged." "I had a strange feeling at the end," said Roy, a thirty-five-year-old electrician. "A strange feeling through my legs. Like on an elevator going down." "I anticipated the domed temple before you said it," said Mel, a forty-five-year-old carpet salesman. "I saw a deep blue-purple. Fourteen rivers of lava. Then a lot of red got in. I saw the ceiling in red filigree like a Chinese dish. I knew there'd be lilies in the lily pond." The fact that Mel saw the purple before I even specified the dome told me that he had reached an exceptional depth.

The Uncreated

"You do go deeper," said Maurine, forty-five, after the *Taj Mahal Scene*. "Wow . . . I don't get the same profound feeling I used to. It's more now a feeling of nothing . . . no pain . . . just gets more and more nothing. Just more and more nothing." You need to start blank, clear, before beginning vibratory creation as stimulated by the images. The approximately 250 words comprising the images are the vibration causing creation. Out of the Uncreated comes the vibratory creation of the image.

What Marissa understood, and what you too will now be beginning to comprehend, is that the images can also serve to *create* the blank, the void, the Uncreated. You stop the vibration of creation using the negative hallucination. The negative hallucination eliminated the vibration *caused* by your focusing on a property or sense. New creation, paradise, begins by first eliminating the old, imperfect one via the negative hallucination, recreating the Uncreated.

Benefits

As you continue to remove properties from reality, peeling away the illusion of matter to arrive at pure energy, your energy, including your sex energy, grows. This added energy makes you feel better about yourself, and your self-image improves dramatically.

Celia, a fifty-year-old caterer, married to Mort, fifty-five, an investment counselor, was delighted by this stage in her progression of images. "I'm feeling more and thinking less," she told me. "I feel incredible energy. Work is going great. I'm so mellow with customers it's unbelievable. I'm even beginning to draw Mort out. I used to get so impatient with him. All he did was work. Never gave me a compliment. I always felt unappreciated and like he was putting me down. Now that I feel so much better about myself, I feel good with him. My sex life is better. After intercourse one night, Mort looked at me lovingly and said, 'I think you're beautiful.' That's not like the old Mort at all. When I changed for the better, so did he."

Skeeter, twenty-six, a defensive tackle for a professional football team, derived exceptional benefit from his acquired ability to negatively hallucinate reflection. The first time I saw him, he said, "I just can't seem to hold on to my opponents. They keep shaking me. I scatter like buckshot. My coach says I act like the guys on the other team are greased pigs. I'm forever letting them get by me." I asked Skeeter to practice the *Taj Mahal Scene* for a week. Then, the next time he was on the playing field, he was to imagine that the water comprising his body did not have the property of reflection. It stuck on contact. In two weeks Skeeter reported excellent progress. "I keep telling myself, 'Cling on contact,' whenever I go for a tackle. And when I hit that mother I stick like glue. No more reflection there!" The *Taj Mahal Scene* helped give Skeeter an emotional understanding of his affirmation, "Cling on contact," such that when he told himself the appropriate words, they meant something to him. The meaning then translated into manifestation on the football field. Skeeter is now considered one of the best tackles in the sport.

You will also find many uses arising from the heightening of the properties remaining. Cora, a forty-seven-year-old sculptor, found that her work improved not only because of her ability to remove reflection, but also due to her increased sense of gravity that came from her practicing the *Taj Mahal Scene*. "It's wonderful," she said. "I've always had so much trouble chiseling in stone, and I love that medium so. What is more beautiful than Carrara marble? I always wanted to work with the same materials as Michelangelo, but when my mallet hit the irresistible surface of my metal chisel firmly planted against rock, it would often bounce right off. My chisel would move and I'd end up fracturing the stone or whacking off a feature I'd spent weeks creating.

"By envisioning my body water free from reflection, I was able to get my hand to stay firmly grasped on the mallet when it impacted the chisel and there was no more wavering pressure to cause an accident. An extra bonus was that I also noticed more force in my stroke. It was as though there was more gravity acting on my chisel arm. With reflection removed and gravity intensified, I've easily doubled the speed of my production. I used to worry that I didn't have the strength to carve rock, but not anymore. With gravity on my side I can cut through anything!" If you want to improve your ability at hammering a nail, chiseling a rock, or chopping a tree, see what happens when you first envision the fluids in your body free from the property of reflection. You'll find you have a much steadier hand when the hammer, chisel, or ax makes impact. Prepare for this specific image by practicing the *Taj Mahal Scene* for a week, getting the knack of negatively hallucinating reflection from creation.

Daniel, a forty-four-year-old executive in the automobile industry, suffered debilitating anxiety attacks. "They can come upon me anytime," he said. "It's just an overwhelming, irrational fear. My heart starts to pound. I sweat. I shake. I feel like I'm going to crawl right out of my skin. I can't function. If I'm in the middle of a business meeting, I have to make a quick excuse and get out. It's embarrassing. It makes you look weak. I feel about so high," he gestured, indicating a tiny space between his right thumb and forefinger.

After Daniel practiced the *Taj Mahal Scene* for a few days, he discovered that it heightened his sense of centrifugal force. This provided a wonderful metaphor for reducing anxiety during a panic attack. "I flashed on the greatest image for unwinding," he said. "I picture myself wound up tight like a top, charged with tension. Then I envision myself rapidly, almost violently, unwinding, tension being thrown off in all directions, thrown off with even greater force than it would be according to the normal property of centrifugal force. It's fantastic! It leaves me limp as a wet noodle with no hint of anxiety." You never know for sure which property or properties will be expanded as a function of your removing others. In Daniel's case it happened to be centrifugal force. We all respond differently. That's what makes psychophysical exploration so exciting. Be adventuresome! Start playing with reality and see what happens. I'm sure you'll find many practical ways to beneficially use your results.

Many excellent spontaneous healing metaphors may crop up out of your imagery sessions on imagogic physics, just as the one did for Daniel. Sally, thirty-two, mother of four children, married to Doug, thirty-two, an electronics contractor, wasn't happy with her life. "I never seem to do what I want to do," she said. "Maybe I'm just too wishy-washy. I'll plan something like a movie with a friend and then something will come up with Doug or the kids and I'll cancel out and do what they want to. I don't mind doing this once in a while. That's part of a relationship—give and take. But it's beginning to seem like I do all the giving and they do all the taking. I don't want to be selfish. My family is the most important thing in the world to me and I love them with all my heart, but shouldn't I still be able to have some kind of independent identity? Sometimes Doug makes me feel like I'm crazy when I talk like this. 'Independent?' he asks me. 'What are you talking about? Who in the world is independent?' Yet I notice that his plans never get canceled. I've never seen him call off a fishing trip because I suddenly wanted to do something else." Sally was a product of what I call the Good Girl Syndrome, and I refer you to the book I co-authored by that title for strategies in asserting your independence from anyone who attempts to dominate you.

When Sally practiced the *Taj Mahal Scene* it gave her an expanded sense of mass, which in turn gave her a wonderful metaphor for asserting her independence. "I felt physically more solid after practicing that image," she said. "It made me think, 'My feet are firmly planted on the ground.' This affirmation, which included my newly acquired sense of increased physical mass, made me feel solid, stable, indestructible, and most of all, sane. I was able to stick up for myself with Doug because he could no longer make me feel crazy for not giving him what *he* wanted all the time." Sally had never really thought of herself as strong before. Her increased sense of mass made her feel powerful, immovable. She liked the feeling, and asserted herself in reality with her family to maintain it. If there are situations in your own life where you feel intimidated, dominated, overpowered by conditions or people, expanding the sense of your own mass can give you a solid center from which to withstand any opposition.

Cathedral Scene

The final property you learn to negatively hallucinate in this chapter, on your way to mastering your reality, is constant volume, the property of a liquid or solid to always occupy the same amount of space. You do this with the *Cathedral Scene*.

Cathedral Scene

You are in the middle of a great cathedral surrounded by massive stained-glass windows. Streams of brilliant colored light illuminate the interior. Before you is a large pool reflecting the light from the glass like a kaleidoscope. Statues of saints line the walls. There is a powerful fresco of the creation on the domed ceiling. The water smells of lilies. Take off your clothes. Glide into the water. Begin swimming and splashing the water. The water runs into your mouth. It tastes sweet like honey. It feels cool and refreshing.

Now you notice that the sides of the pool are beginning to close in. The water level does not rise. The water gets denser and thicker. It supports your body more and more as you feel more buoyant. Ooze in and out of the water. You can almost lie on the surface, but then you sink back in. You are oozing slower and slower. Finally you can lie on the water's surface without submerging. Stand. The water supports you. Feel the wetness beneath you on your feet. Begin walking. The sound of your footsteps splashing on water echoes and resounds through the cathedral like thunder.

A bolt of electric white lightning streaks through the air. The clouds on the ceiling fresco churn and billow. The sound of breathing comes from the statues, growing louder and louder. It starts to rain. The cathedral immediately fills to the top with infinitely expanding rainwater, taking you straight up with it. The pressure from the water blows out the dome. Shoot up into the sky with a great force.

Reactions

Increased concentration, a quiet mind, precognition, and a growing sense of heaviness are common reactions to the *Cathedral Scene.* "I feel quiet, sleepy, not really drugged, but quiet," reported Robin, a young mother of two girls. "I got the images before you said them," smiled a man in his fifties.

"It was raining before you said so. I was floating before you said so." "You ought to go there sometime—that's a lovely place—heaven is," said Larry, a thirty-five-year-old stressed-out airline pilot. "I can't lift my head." He had to use his hands to move his head. Taking his attention off constant volume had caused Larry's sense of inertia to expand. His physical body felt more at rest than normally.

Your sense of space and direction will also begin to alter at this point in your imagery progression. "I'm lethargic," said Stryker, a thirty-five-year-old mechanical engineer. "I have a strange feeling of moving in different directions at the same time." Direction is a spatial delusion, a delusion of the third dimension. Time, space, and motion are a function of limited perception. Direction does not exist out of space. As you strip away the illusion of physical properties operating in a continuum of time, space, and motion, the concept of direction loses its meaning. In an infinite system all things are possible and you truly can go all "directions" simultaneously.

Benefits

You can use the *Cathedral Scene* to decrease what you don't want in your life and increase what you do. Neither bad nor good elements need any longer remain constant. Contract the bad and expand the good. Tuck, a fifty-five-year-old ocean-ographer and recovering alcoholic, had been primarily dry for the last five years, a fact he attributed to the splendid help of AA. "I still go off the wagon once in a while, though," he said. "As soon as I start to feel the alcohol it seems to take off and have a mind of its own. Until that feeling, I have some control and can still stop. After that feeling, one drink leads to a two- or three-day bender, though I'm happy to say that these bend-ers are now few and far between."

I told Tuck to practice the *Cathedral Scene* for a week. Then I suggested, "If you ever find yourself taking another drink again, I want you to stop and imagine that the alcohol already in your system contracts smaller and smaller till finally it has no volume at all." It was several months before Tuck transgressed and could use this strategy, but when he did, he reported, "I was amazed. It sobered me up, got rid of that feeling that usually triggers a bender, and I was able to stop drinking." Imagining the elimination of alcohol from his system through negatively hallucinating its property of constant volume, and thus allowing it to shrink, had the same effect as if this were really occurring, a potent testimonial to the psychological component of inebriation. Naturally this technique only works so far. Past a certain level of consumption it loses its effect, but it is usually successful if you use it somewhere in the course of your *first* drink.

Diedre, a forty-five-year-old screenwriter, used the *Cathedral Scene* to raise her wealth-consciousness. "There's still something not right about the way I view money," she said in our first session together. "When I was younger I think I was poor out of guilt and all that religious conditioning that it's easier for a camel to go through the eye of a needle than a rich man to go to heaven. I equated money with being mean and stingy and selfish. Rather than deprive someone else of money, I'd deprive myself instead. That way I didn't have to feel guilty and could think of myself as an angel, self-sacrificing for the good of others. Then one day it finally dawned on me that my being poor really wasn't making anyone else wealthier or keeping anyone else from starving. So I went out and bought all the books I could find on positive thinking and getting out of your own way in the process of making money. These books helped to the degree where I don't think I feel guilty anymore striving to be rich, but I still can't seem to sell a script. I'm a good writer. I have a good agent. He helps me get my material to the right people. They love my projects. But they never buy anything. What am I doing wrong?"

Unlike many people, it wasn't Diedre's concept of herself that was blocking her from financial success. She truly had overcome her feelings of guilt and of being undeserving. It was her concept of money that needed changing. She saw money as finite, limited. In Diedre's mind there was only so much and definitely not enough to go around.

In order to help Diedre conceptualize wealth as infinite, I asked her to practice the *Cathedral Scene* for a week. Then I told her, "If you can expand water to infinity, you can expand anything else, including wealth, to infinity. I want you to place a hundred-dollar bill on your nightstand and give it your total concentration before retiring each evening. The moment you turn out the lights, envision that hundred-dollar bill expanding infinitely, no longer a victim of the property of constant volume that you yourself created by focusing on such a property or concept."

Three weeks later Diedre sold a script for a feature film for a price that went well over six figures. It was a script she had been trying over ten years to sell. Her concept of her product had not changed, but her concept of the wealth available in exchange for her product had altered infinitely. Good is infinite and without constant volume. If you want more wealth in your own life, practice the *Cathedral Scene* to change your concept of good from constantly limited to infinite!

You benefit not only from removing the limiting property of constant volume, but from expanding the properties that remain. After practicing the *Cathedral Scene* for a little over a week, Ariel, a twenty-three-year-old professional football player trying to develop his concentration for the game, reported the following benefit: "I always considered myself a pretty good defensive linebacker, but I also knew I had a lot of room for improvement. I let too many guys get by me, but I usually made excuses like, 'I'm doing as good as the next guy,' or 'I can be better if I just work on it.' But until now I never did work on it. It was just a way of fooling myself. But after that *Cathedral Scene* something really strange happened. Imagining removing the property of constant volume actually made me feel bigger. I know that sounds crazy, but it did. I now know that subconsciously I thought a lot about not being as big as other linebackers and that secretly undermined me and I acted like I was puny. I didn't go for it physically the way I do now that I think of myself as bigger.

What's even better, I got a bonus. I not only feel bigger, I feel denser, more solid, like I'm made of steel. Man, I'm downright indestructible, a real mean machine." Ariel's taking his attention off constant volume expanded his sense of mass. When he felt bigger and denser, he acted as if he were, and he *got results as if he were.* He was later voted his team's most valuable player.

Kristian, a thirty-year-old cosmetologist, was in deep depression over the breakup with her last boyfriend, Kiefer, a twenty-five-year-old graduate student in business education. She'd read my book *Breaking Free: 90 Ways to Leave Your Lover & Survive,* and had come to my Beverly Hills office from out of state for a crash course and more strategies for getting Kiefer out of her mind. "I thought what with all the people needing advice on relationships I'd have trouble getting to see you," she said. I smiled. "In my eighteen years of practice I've never been so full that I've had to refuse a prospective client," I answered.

"Good," she said, "'cause I need your help desperately. I truly am a woman who loves too much. I have a terrible need to be needed so I always pick a guy who has something wrong with him and can depend on me to fix him. Kiefer was heavy into cocaine when I met him. Then when the relationship, which is always doomed from the start, fails, I blame myself. 'What did I do wrong?' I ask myself, knowing full well I selected the wrong guy in the first place. Instead of learning from my mistakes and trying to create a healthier relationship with someone new, I launch into a full-scale depression that can last anywhere from a month to years. It's been two years since Kiefer left me. We were together less than six months. Isn't that crazy? More than two years to recover from a six-month relationship?"

I started Kristian on the imagery progression to improve her concentration and keep unwanted thoughts of Kiefer out of mind. After practicing the *Cathedral Scene* she said, "I kept getting flashes of myself bouncing around like a jumping jack saying, 'Bounce right back. Bounce right back.' I thought it was really nuts and totally worthless until I connected it to my relationships. My higher self was telling me to bounce right back from my bad relationships. The image of the jumping jack made me somehow feel like I really could."

Kristian's removing constant volume in the *Cathedral Scene* had served to expand her sense of the property of reflection, and that was manifested in the marvelous metaphor of the jumping jack affirming "Bounce right back." Expanding her reality's property of reflection made her feel more resilient in her relationships, more able to spring back into a new and better one. When she started to conceive of herself as resilient, capable of jumping right back into the emotional area of relationships, she was able to, and her depression lifted.

A Dramatic New Reality

The results of practicing your imagery progression will combine in many wonderful and unexpected ways to make your life healthier and more beautiful. Many of these results will be practical, like the ones you saw in the cases we just discussed. Others will be more profound, impacting you on a highly spiritual level. You can expect benefits at all levels, from acquiring skills as utilitarian as increasing your typing speed to floating out of body into a realm of different vibratory existence.

Anne's case is an excellent example of the wide range your benefits can cover. At this point in the progression, she was pleased to find the practical benefit that, if she urinated while she was imagining the *Cathedral Scene,* she no longer experienced the discomfort she had previously felt from her diabetes. She imagined the urine minus the property of constant volume, contracting to the point of being imperceptible to her sense organs. An even more dramatic practical benefit at this stage in her imagery was that she was able to reduce her injected insulin dosage by fifty percent, and felt she might be able to become diet-regulated or switch to oral insulin pills. She was presently self-administering two shots in the stomach a day. Positive feelings yield positive results.

Not only was her sex life now excellent, it was harmonious with the needs of her partner and she was developing a deeper, more dimensional love for David. "That constant hum is gone now," she said, "although I know I can bring it back at any time by recalling the *Bath Scene* or any other sexual image. I have no compunctions about having had a sexual episode with Carson. We are companionable friends now and can even discuss the 'act' occasionally without embarrassment. He was really surprised at David's understanding. He thought David was only giving it lip service and would blow a few weeks down the line, but David never did. I even confronted him with the fact that Carson was worried, and he seemed hurt by my lack of faith in him. He looked at me so tenderly and said, 'You can have honest trust in me.'

"Later, that night at dinner, I felt so close to him. After we'd eaten he took my hand in his and said with so much love, 'You are going to go through that therapy until you come to meet me. Then you'll know how great our relationship is.' It made my spine tingle. There was so much more for me to learn about David. As I grow I gain more ability to understand and appreciate him. For a long time, in the beginning of my therapy, I'd felt superior to David in many ways. As my imagery powers increased I was afraid that I might be outgrowing him. I wished that he would listen to my tapes and grow too. Now suddenly, abruptly, the tables are reversed. He's talking about me coming to meet him as if he is ahead and I'm behind. I'm asking myself, 'Who is this?'

"One night after we'd made love he did something that up till now was not like him. He looked me squarely in the eye and said, 'You know what? You are absolutely lovely.' It feels more like the beginning rather than having been at it fifteen years. It's like childhood wonder mixed with an adult maturity."

Don't be surprised if your wondrous expanded new perception seems odd to others, especially strangers who haven't had a chance to get used to the emerging revolutionary you. I remember the medical community's initial reaction to this expanded mode of perception as clearly as if it were this morning.

It was Saturday, May 18, 1974. I was participating in my first of what was to eventually become over two hundred seminars with my friend and partner, psychiatrist William S. Kroger, M.D. Dr. Kroger, then approaching seventy, was the greatest clinical hypnotist in the world, and at the age of twenty-eight, having been in practice less than two years, I considered it a great honor to be sharing the workshop with him and his two other eminent guests, Drs. Donald Schaeffer and Eric Wright, both highly respected men in the field of medical hypnosis.

I was particularly excited because I had a surprise for everyone: my fantastic new creation, Anne. I wanted everyone there to see what incredible things you could accomplish with hypnotic imagery. In 1974 imagery for self-healing was still a new frontier to conquer. Little had been written about it and few were practicing it. Clinical practitioners of hypnosis were still relying largely on suggestions, or affirmations, as the holistic health movement now calls them, to get their positive effects.

The seminar, sponsored by the Institute for Comprehensive Medicine, of which Dr. Kroger was president and I had been benevolently made a director, was scheduled for the weekend of May 18 and 19 at the Beverly Wilshire Hotel in Beverly Hills, at Rodeo Drive and Wilshire Boulevard, just four blocks east of my office where I still practice. I remember that I saw Anne for her regular one-o'clock appointment. I gave her the *Cathedral Scene,* and the two of us walked over to the seminar afterward in the glorious spring sunshine.

We arrived about 2:15. The Beverly Wilshire is an exquisitely beautiful and grand hotel and I felt inspired as Anne and I walked up the crimson stairway to the seminar room. It was jammed. There was a terrific turnout primarily of psychologists, psychiatrists, physicians, dentists, and related health professionals. Anne was to have an audience of some of the brightest minds in the field.

It was still an hour before we would come to her part of

the program, and as I took my place at the speaker's table, facing the audience, I couldn't help but notice how serenely, blessedly detached she looked next to the hubbub around her. Finally it was our turn. I gave a short speech about imagery and the phenomena it could produce. Then I introduced Anne. She glided up to the front and sat calmly posed on a chair before the crowd. Looking back, I realize she was still maintaining a residue of the imagogic state that she had created by doing the *Cathedral Scene* earlier that afternoon.

She went quickly into a deep hypnotic state using an abbreviated form of the hypnotic induction described on pages 59–63. I then gave her three images to create profound relaxation, glove anesthesia, and negative hallucinations. After each image she went still deeper. She answered the barrage of questions that came from the audience with a pleasant equanimity that was unrivaled. Her features displayed a perpetual, radiant smile, and she literally seemed to glow. She responded, but was untouched by the events around her. The accelerating relaxation from the rapid series of images that I gave her relaxed her vocal cords to the extent that her voice had a low, rasping resonance that was musically unearthly. She plainly looked and sounded not of this world. I thought she was super.

The bulk of the medical audience was as positively impressed as I; however, there was a handful who were outraged by what they had witnessed. They found the demonstration frighteningly sexual. Be it understood that there was nothing directly sexual in any of the images that I demonstrated. What these images truly were was *sensual,* and Anne's reaction was sensual, and that was what caused the furor. Many people, including doctors, are afraid to feel. They are much more comfortable with the brain's logical left side than the waters of intuitive, sometimes sexual, feelings brewing on the right. They equate logic and reason with safety and security, sensation and intuition with chaos and danger. They are wrong.

Dr. Kroger invited the people at the seminar over to his home afterward for refreshments and an opportunity to view his films, in which patients underwent surgery using hypnosis as an anesthetic. Anne had always wanted to see his mansion on Lexington Drive and was enjoying the attention she was receiving from the participants whom she had favorably impressed, so she eagerly accepted the invitation. Most of the guests had spilled out into the pool area, but I was still standing in the library, waiting for the movies to start downstairs in the ballroom. A doctor from the seminar approached me. "You ought to book her," he smiled, referring to Anne. "She's better than Sarah Bernhardt. I believed her at first, but you went too far. The drama of her reactions demeans your credibility."

Is only the undramatic credible? Have we thrown out the baby with the bathwater and gotten so entrenched in the reason of the scientific method that we've forgotten *why* we seek knowledge in the first place? What good is healing and knowledge without passion? What good is science if it doesn't lead to energy and joy and paradise? If the scientific method can't pave the way to ecstasy, who needs it?

Yes, Anne was dramatic. She was totally caught up in the drama of the universe, connected to the life force, in expanded touch with feelings and sensations out of the realms of the ordinary realities of most people, people who dismiss the exceptional with a shrug, passing it off as unconvincing. She was also real. This was Anne. This will also be you. People may not believe you at first. Your reality is now a different one than the one known to most. It is beautiful, vibrant, alive, and dramatic!

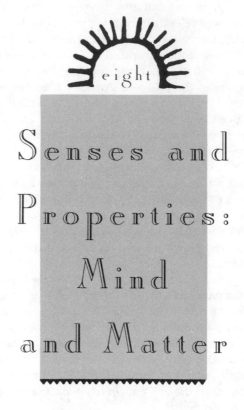

eight

Senses and Properties: Mind and Matter

The great French philosopher René Descartes spent much
of his life seeking a *simple, universal truth* on which to
build all knowledge. The renowned behavioral psychologist B. F. Skinner wanted a basic, elemental unit of behavior
on which to base the science of the prediction and control of
human behavior that we call psychology. Throughout history,
men have sought a pure, indivisible unit with which to build
a new, more perfect reality. Now it is your turn. You are about
to discover this primal unit for yourself. In order to arrive at
a basic unit for reconstructing a better reality, you are learn-

ing to attack reality from both angles, breaking down both
that which cannot exist independently of you, senses or mind,
and that which many say can, properties or matter.

As you strip away reality from both sides, negatively hallucinating senses and properties, you will discover that it is
energy that remains beyond the illusion of what the Hindus
call "maya," the magical power of creation by which limitations and divisions are apparently present in the Immeasur-
able and Inseparable. Energy is the basic building block of
reality. At the level of pure energy the dichotomy of senses
and properties is meaningless, as energy is the common de-
nominator for both. Senses and properties, mind and matter,
are equal and interchangeable in energy. A simple unit of
consciousness, mind, sensation, is pure energy. A simple unit
of matter, reality, properties, is pure energy. Senses are necessary to perceive the properties, and without properties there
is nothing to sense. They are equal. Senses *are* properties.
Properties *are* senses. There is no inside and no outside, only
one—energy. Mind and matter are ONE. Perception of sepa-
ration is illusion. From the illusion of duality you extract the
indivisible truth of unity. The following images are designed
to give you an emotional understanding of this axiom. They
will help you to internalize these concepts, make them a part
of you, so that you can *use* them, work with them, as they
truly are, extensions of yourself. Here lies your power.

Fantasia Scene

This is the first image in which you remove both a sense
and a physical property from your experiencing of water. Removal of a sense or senses will intensify your experience in
your other sense modalities. Removal of a physical property
or properties will give you a greater feeling for the essence of
matter. Both will give you greater control over your experiencing and heightened energy. You can choose both which
properties or attributes of the universe you wish to respond

to and in what sense you wish to experience them.

You may, for example, wish to experience reality *as if* there were no gravity only in one sense modality, touch. Everything, including your body, would feel light; the entire world would have a sense of weightlessness. You would, however, experience gravity visually. Objects would not appear to float, but would come down when thrown up. The following image removes the sense of smell and the physical property of mass from your experiencing of water.

Your experiencing of this scene also involves an image of an afterimage. Whenever you look at a bright color and then close your eyes, you will see its complementary color. Your imagogic reality is so developed at this level in your progression that when you imagine looking at a yellow sun, and then imagine closing your eyes, you will most likely see a purple sun, purple being the complementary color of yellow. Likewise, when you imagine looking at a red sun and then closing your eyes, you will see a green sun. The afterimage produces a color of brilliant intensity. Your focusing on green in the beginning of this image will intensify and enhance your experiencing of the red at the end. Green is the complementary color of red, and focusing on it will give you a brilliant red afterimage. Relying on this psychophysical phenomenon for its creation may very well give you your most visually brilliant image thus far.

Fantasia Scene

You are staring intently at a brilliant yellow sun against a clear, white sky. Keep looking. Your attention is riveted. Close your eyes. What do you see? Open your eyes. The sun is now blood-red against the clear, white sky. Direct your total attention to the redness, focusing with all your power. Close your eyes. What do you see? Open your eyes.

A white mist envelops you, a dense fog. Look into the fog. Forms take shape. All is becoming a lush green. There are bogs, twisted trees, and an infinite number of shades of green.

It's early afternoon. Very foggy. You are in wet marshlands. The water vapor is without odor. Cup the water in your hands. Sip it. Tastes rusty like iron. It feels cold and wet. Gargle it. It feels like a mouthful of cold, wet air. The water has no density.

Rain falls. It feels wet and cold, but exerts no pressure on your body. When it hits the pool of water it forms no ripples and does not splash. It is simply absorbed. There is a great, twisted tree hanging out over the pool. Crawl along it. Hang over the water. Wild grapes wind around the branches. You fall. Hit the water ... and then the pool bottom. The bottom is spongy. Bounce as if on a trampoline, up and down above and below the water's surface, passing through the water with no resistance.

Leave the pool. Come to a patch of wild strawberries. Look farther. See that the entire hillside is covered with wild strawberries. Climb to the top of the hill. Find a pool of wild strawberry juice. Sniff the juice. It has no smell. Go into the pool. It feels like pink air. Drink. It tastes like wet, cool, strawberry-flavored air. Walk through the pool. Hear the sound of liquid sloshing against your body.

The sun is setting. The sky is turning brilliant crimson. Look up. See a V-formation of silver-white geese. The lead goose leaves the formation and swoops down toward you. Mount his back. He rejoins the V. Fly on the silver down of a goose over a strawberry sea in a sky of crimson into the sunset.

Reactions

The most common reaction to the *Fantasia Scene* is the sense of brilliant color it produces. "It's so beautiful I don't want to come back," said Maxim, a twenty-seven-year-old record producer. "I got the afterimages. I went deeper than ever. It was the first time I could really see it, you know, seeing versus imagining. The red was living . . . a living, breathing, pulsating red like I was inside my body, inside my blood vessel. I wouldn't have gained ounce one from this two months ago." Maxim's last statement is a testimonial to the benefit of practice. Without the preceding imagery progression to pave your way, the *Fantasia Scene* may only seem like a pleasant, somewhat bizarre fantasy trip, rather than an exploration into living, breathing color.

The feelings that you can expect from this scene run the gamut from "glowing" to "blank," but in any event they are usually singularly outstanding, being quite different from what you are used to in your ordinary reality. "I feel very glowing," smiled Senta, a thirty-two-year-old private-duty nurse, "from my toes to my fingers." "Fascinating. Amazing," sighed Brian, a thirty-three-year-old bookstore manager. "You go deeper. It's really exciting. It's different from what I thought it was. A blanker feeling. A complete nothing. It becomes more and more blank. It doesn't sink or rise. It's blank, yes, that's the best I can do to describe it." When Brian first began imagery training he'd had sinking sensations like going down in an elevator and rising sensations like floating off the couch. These were now replaced by a deeper feeling, a sort of nondirectional blank.

Benefits

The *Fantasia Scene* prepares you for any instance in which it would be helpful for you to be able to remove smell and mass from reality. Roger, thirty-eight, owner of three broiler houses, was having trouble dealing with the ammonia fumes generated from the excretions of 75,000 chickens he was raising. "I'm over a barrel, Doc," he said. "I've got everything I own invested in these broiler chickens. I've got to stick with it, but the smell of that ammonia is making me sick. It's really bad when I'm doing hard labor in the houses, like when I have to shovel up the old litter after we ship out a batch. We keep the chickens nine and a half weeks. By then the wood shavings covering the floor are drenched in chicken droppings and shoveling it up really gets it flying. I've hired a high school basketball team to help me load the chickens out, but I still have to be there to pitch in."

I asked Roger to practice the *Fantasia Scene* for a week. Then I told him, "Just as you can remove smell and mass from your perception of water, you can also remove them from your perception of the wood shavings covering the floors of your chicken barns." I suggested he spend an additional week imagining shoveling the old wood shavings into a loading bin, and not smelling their ammonia fumes or feeling their weight. "The shavings have no smell, no mass." At this time he was to practice actually loading the shavings while imagining they were odorless and weightless. "I had more trouble imagining water without smell and mass in the *Fantasia Scene* than I did not smelling or feeling the actual shavings," he reported. "By the time I got around to the real situation, I was ready. As long as I concentrated it worked. I forgot all about the smell and the shovel felt lighter than ever. It sure made work a whole lot easier!"

You'll also benefit from the heightening of the senses and properties remaining in the *Fantasia Scene*. Lana, sixteen, wanted badly to make her high school girl's basketball team. She came to me to improve her concentration and athletic prowess. "My slam dunk really needs some help," she said. "I just don't seem to have enough power. When I go to shoot the ball into the net it just sort of thuds. I don't have a strong enough sense of my hand on the ball. It feels kind of dead. I want to be able to feel what I'm doing and drive that thing into the basket so hard the sound of it scares my opponents to the other side of the court!" Lana discovered that practicing the *Fantasia Scene* expanded her sense of touch as well as the property of gravity in her reality. "That ball went through the hoop so hard I thought it was made out of lead," she said. "And boy did I feel it! It was like every pore in my hand had been asleep, and then suddenly woke up. I had so much more control over the ball."

Negatively hallucinating a sense and property in your imagery doesn't necessarily heighten only one each of the senses and properties remaining. You may experience an expansion of any number or combination of the senses and properties that remain. Clearing her sensory channels by negatively hallucinating smell and mass in the *Fantasia Scene* made Kimberly, twenty-eight, a professional artist trying to expand her creativity, more sensitive to two senses, sight and touch, such that both her painting and sculpting improved dramatically. "My colors are living now," she explained. "And the clay beneath my fingers actually seems to be breathing." You can expect a surge of creativity from practicing these images that expand senses and properties. By using your power of creation you learn to heal and transcend this earthly plane.

Ballroom Scene

In the process of arriving at indivisible awareness, you continue to subtract senses and properties from your perception. The *Ballroom Scene*, in which you will learn to negatively hallucinate smell and centrifugal force from your experiencing of reality, ends with your being in a heady state of intoxication from your drinking from a moonlit fountain of champagne in a classical garden.

Ballroom Scene

It is a moonlit night. You are standing on a circular ballroom floor of shining silver surround by a six-foot wall of foam rubber. Beyond the wall is an immense garden with marble columns, garlands of flowers, and mammoth alabaster urns. In the center of the dance floor, hanging from a tree, is a crystal ball, prismatically reflecting all the colors of the rainbow.

Now the floor begins to turn, revolving like a turntable on a record player, going very slowly at first, gradually picking up momentum. Going faster and faster, round and round. Cling to the tree in the center of the floor to keep from flying off. Leaves fly wildly through the air.

It begins to rain. The rain has no smell. It falls straight

*down and lies motionless on the spinning silver surface. The
water gets deeper and deeper. It is perfectly still. You are up
to your neck in water. Let go of the tree! Fly off the ballroom
floor, skimming along the surface of the water till you hit the
rubber wall. Bounce back to the center. Sink into the water.
You are pulled through the water to the wall again. Bounce
back again to the center. The floor stops revolving. You are
standing in water up to your neck.*

*Leave the dance floor. Walk through marble columns to a
huge fountain of champagne sparkling in the moonlight.
Wade waist deep into the champagne fountain. Float in it. Sniff
the champagne. It has no smell. Drink. It is bubbly with a bite
like ginger. Keep drinking. Blood is getting hot ... hotter. At
the top of the fountain is a revolving sprinkler shooting champagne. The champagne does not fly off into the air, but falls
straight down forming a perfect hollow cylinder around you.
Intoxication overtakes you. Veins are pulsating. The moonlit
garden glimmers through a fine, wavering wall of champagne.*

Reactions

The frequency of evocation of archetypal symbology and
precognitive experiences increases as the images progress.
Kelvin, twenty-two, a newspaper reporter, said "I saw lots of
circles, Jungian archetypes for psychic wholeness." "After
you said 'ballroom' I saw it," reported Carol, a thirty-year-old
floral arranger. "I saw it before you described it."

People often react to an image in terms of how well they
think they did with it, i.e., how vivid or real it seemed to them.
"I didn't do too bad," laughed Kier, a forty-seven-year-old sales
manager. "It was so real I'm still tired from hanging onto that
foam-rubber wall." Stan, a thirty-two-year-old architect, had
slurred speech on coming out of this image. "I really got
drunk," he laughed. When he got up from the couch he stum-
bled. "Too much. I don't feel very graceful. My pulse feels so
strong I think it shows. My neck always gets red when I
drink." Sure enough, Stan's neck was red and his face was

flushed. You can produce warmth by recalling any point in time when you experienced this sensation, even if it was when you were intoxicated.

Benefits

Your imagining the heat of intoxication stealing over you at the end of the *Ballroom Scene* causes blood to flow to the surface of your skin just as it would if you were actually inebriated. This is the same kind of flush that Stan got, and you can use it to clear up dermatological disorders such as acne or psoriasis. Cliff, a nineteen-year-old college junior suffering from embarrassing runny eruptions on his chin and forehead, practiced the *Ballroom Scene* for a month, at which point his face was clear. "I'm so impressed," he said. "I never would have believed that imagining getting drunk would clean up my skin problem." If you're troubled by an oily and/ or blemished complexion, try practicing the *Ballroom Scene.* Imagining the heat of intoxication will divert blood to the skin's surface and dry up the lesions.

You will also benefit by learning to simultaneously remove smell and centrifugal force from reality. Katie, forty-three, a free-lance artist, was developing a severe case of agoraphobia. She wouldn't go out of her apartment for weeks and, since she lived alone, she was depressed from lack of social contact. After some probing I discovered her fears began with the non-stop media coverage of gang warfare. "You can't turn on the TV today without hearing about somebody getting beat up or raped," she said. "It doesn't matter who or where you are. These days they'll even attack in broad daylight in front of witnesses. Nobody seems to care anymore. You're helpless, even in a crowd."

First, I convinced Katie that she'd feel safer on the streets if she learned karate. She enrolled in a class, but soon had two objections. "I can't stand the smell of body odor," she said. "It's really hard for me to get into that kind of close physical contact, even though my class and instructor shower before and after each lesson. Can you imagine how I'd do if someone really filthy came after me? I'd surrender from the smell alone. Also, I think I'm just too small to do karate with any effect. I keep getting thrown around like a Frisbee."

I suggested that Katie practice the *Ballroom Scene* for a week. Then I told her, "Now that you have imagined removing smell and centrifugal force from your experiencing of water, I want you to imagine removing smell from your experiencing of your karate opponent and centrifugal force from your body. Practice an image in which your opponent is odorless and unable to throw you out from his center of rotation."

In three weeks Katie was happy to report, "The best way to take your attention off one thing is to focus on another. I don't even think of my opponent in terms of smell anymore. And when I stopped expecting to be thrown to kingdom come and instead expected not to be thrown at all, my body actually responded differently! I'm defying the physical laws of the universe. What amazed me even more, because I wasn't focusing directly on it like I was with smell and centrifugal force, is that I have a heightened sense of mass from practicing the *Ballroom Scene*. I feel denser, harder to throw, and my hearing is better, which is good. If my opponent tries to sneak up behind me, I'll be more apt to hear him before he gets the jump on me."

Practicing the *Ballroom Scene* improved Katie's methods of self-defense in four ways:

1. It prepared her to tune out any offensive odor of her opponent.
2. It removed her expectation of being thrown by helping her to conceive of herself as no longer subject to centrifugal force.
3. It expanded her hearing by allowing her to attend more to this remaining sense.
4. It heightened her sense of mass and indestructibility by allowing her to focus on this remaining property.

You too may find compounded benefits from a particular image such as the *Ballroom Scene.*

Becky, thirty, did typing out of her home to help defray the expenses of raising a family of five. Practicing the *Ballroom Scene* improved her typing skills immeasurably. "I used to make so many errors," she said. "Frankly I don't think I was able to type and look at what I was transcribing at the same time. I really didn't see the page clearly enough. That image really expanded my vision. I'm able to take in so much more material at a glance. And my touch is lighter. My fingers spring back from the keys more briskly. I can now type much faster, and with fewer errors!" The remaining sense of vision, and the remaining property of reflection, were expanded by Becky's mastery of the *Ballroom Scene.* She could better see the material she was transcribing and her fingers reflected more rapidly from the keys.

You will also see how heightening your senses and the properties they perceive makes you acutely aware of your own bodily functioning. Carmen, thirty-eight, an executive secretary for an entertainment lawyer, found a new practical application for this knowledge in relation to her use of the two-hole paper punch. "My work is becoming much less of a strain now," she said. "The images make me so aware of my body, I use only the muscle groups I need to finish a task. Now, when I use the paper punch, I relax all my body except my hand. Before I would have put my whole body into it and worn myself out before I needed to." You too will be amazed to discover how such fanciful images can lead to such pragmatic applications.

Car Scene

In the following image you learn to remove the property of inertia from water as well as your experiencing of it olfactorily. When you imagine a car in which you are drinking lemonade stopping abruptly, the liquid in the cup doesn't spill to continue its motion as it normally would. Because you eliminated inertia from water, the lemonade stops at the same time as the car. Water no longer has the property of staying in motion, once in motion.

When a yacht on which you are riding stops abruptly on impact with a cliff, your body continues its motion and you are thrown out, but the water in the yacht's swimming pool remains motionless because it stops at the same time as the yacht due to its lack of inertia. Waves go in all directions without benefit of wind or any external agent, because the water also lacks the property to remain at rest once at rest and therefore moves spontaneously.

Car Scene

You are driving late at night in your car across the desert. It's warm. The sky is deep purple. Black silhouettes of hills loom past you. The road and headlights are all you see before you. Miles pass to the constant, steady hum of the motor. Hear the road beneath you. You are drinking a cup of lemonade. Taste its sour sweetness. Sniff it. It has no smell. It feels cool and wet on your lips. Suddenly you see a roadblock ahead. Stop abruptly. Lurch forward. The lemonade remains motionless in the cup. It does not spill or lurch as you did.

Get out of the car. The road ends at a great fault in the earth like a phosphorescent Grand Canyon of intense iridescent shades of pink, rose, and purple. At the bottom of the canyon is a sea. Walk down a path to the water. A yacht is docked offshore. Bright lights are in view. Hear music. People are dancing. Take off your clothes. Swim to the yacht. The water has no smell. Make no ripples or splashing in the water. Climb up a ladder to the deck. There is a huge swimming pool. Japanese lanterns swing in the breeze, casting a warm glow over the boat. Soft lights and music.

The yacht starts to move . . . faster and faster. Dive into the pool. Surface to float on your back. The yacht continues to pick up speed. Suddenly it hits the side of a cliff. The pool water remains motionless. You are thrown out of the pool into the

*sea. The sea water moves spontaneously in all directions.
There is no wind. It tastes salty. It has no smell. It carries you
back and forth, to and fro, to one side and another, rocking
you into a deep, deep sleep.*

Reactions

Feelings of motion are often intensified by practicing the
Car Scene. "I could really feel the rocking," said a man in his
twenties. "I didn't want to stop rocking," sighed a thirty-year-
old housewife. You may also feel lightheaded, even numb in
that part of your body. "I feel a little numb in the head, not
too bad," reported a fifty-two-year-old shipping agent. "I feel
lightheaded," smiled a sixty-year-old social worker. Precognitive experiences may also arise. "I preceded you by a second
on the Japanese lanterns," laughed a forty-year-old businessman.

I was surprised to see a white light above Zack, a forty-
three-year-old merchant working on improving his self-image
and not worrying about getting acceptance from others, while
I was giving him the *Car Scene.* I saw the light only for a
moment and wondered what had been going on in Zack's mind
at the time it manifested. "I don't need others to determine my
self-worth, do I?" he said upon opening his eyes. "That comes
from a higher source." Zack had reacted to the *Car Scene* with
a profound insight from his higher self. In the last analysis
it was only he who chose to give himself approval. Choose to
give yourself unconditional love and approval and you'll find
it speaking with you a whole lot more, imparting wonderful
insights and divulging the secrets of creation.

Past-Life Regressions

On occasion an image will inadvertently trigger a spontaneous past-life regression, an experience as if you have lived
before, in another time, place, and body. Without any intention

to do so, you will suddenly be in this new state, independent of the image you are currently practicing. The most remarkable thing that I have noticed about such experiences is the tremendous amount of energy associated with them. There is a force, a drive, an involvement in the experiencing of a past life that is totally dynamic, charging you with energy to break old barriers, conquer new planes.

Adriana, a fifty-year-old advertising executive, suddenly found herself in a completely different setting while I was giving her the *Car Scene*. She later typed out the following relating her experience to me, as she wanted me to give it back to her in hypnosis so that we could cue the regression again and she could learn more about it:

"It is June. The sky is bright blue. The sun is a blazing yellow. You are sitting on a horse. There are ribbons braided into his mane. As the sun warms your metal helmet, you can feel the sweat—but there is no feeling of heat—no feeling of cold. You sit in a quiet place—completely alone—completely relaxed. In your left hand, you hold the reins—in your right hand, a gleaming weapon. Feel its weight. Suddenly—it is time. You lean forward in the saddle.

"Now, it's over. Let the reins drop from your left hand. A young man takes the weapon from your right hand. You raise the visor of the helmet and let the sweet, cool breeze dry the sweat on your face. Notice—for the first time—red and blue pennants, rippling on the towers. All about you—there is a steady roar of voices. Sit in the same calm, quiet place—as you slowly turn your head from side to side, nodding to the crowd."

You'll note that Adriana was blank for the event that is "over." She was not yet ready to deal with that aspect of her experience. As I continued to feed her regression experiences back to her while she was in a clear, receptive hypnotic state, she began to fill in the details of this originally spontaneous regression. The event she couldn't initially recall was a jousting match, and she had been killed on the field. As she explored more she came to recognize that many of her current attitudes toward men, including hatred of their macho, violent tendencies and propensity to settle things in combat, had come from that past life, at least the part of her represented by that past-life experience.

Hating the male aspect of violence, she was nonetheless drawn to it today and cultivated it in herself, projecting the image of a hard, ruthless businesswoman. Striving to become what she hated was definitely not the answer to a harmonious life and I worked with Adriana in helping her to love and nurture the yin, as the orientals call it, the female energy of her being, that she had so long repressed in her obsessive worship of the male energy, or yang. Visualization, the imagery progression you are mastering, will itself strengthen the feminine energy so necessary to creation.

As you continue to peel away the illusion of senses and properties using the negative hallucination as your vehicle, the related illusions of time, space, and motion are also lifted. There is then only Now. Past, present, and future coexist. All lives merge. Spontaneous past-life regressions are a beginning, an indication that the delusion of separateness is passing and you are on your path to the Indivisible.

Benefits

Removing smell and inertia from your experiencing of reality can yield many unexpected benefits. Greg, a thirty-one-year-old veterinarian, had trouble dealing with the smell of blood or the rot of infection when working with the animals he treated. He also experienced difficulty with his hand movements when doing surgery. "I can't believe I'm still so squeamish with smells," he said. "I thought I'd get over it in time, but so far I haven't and I've been practicing over five years now. Sometimes the smell of a wound doesn't bother me. Other times I break out in a sweat. That, plus one other problem, are all that is keeping me from being the best vet around. My surgery needs improving. Sometimes my movements are too gross. Like if I'm stitching a cut I seem to gather too much momentum. I don't have the control to stop in time, to tone down my actions and make finer stitches or maneuvers."

After Greg practiced the *Car Scene* for a week he reported, "It's uncanny! I not only no longer tune into the smells of blood and rot, I have more control when I perform surgery. I can stop a hand motion midway rather than going too far with it, such as when I'm making a fine incision. And my fingers don't slip as much." Through learning to remove the property of inertia, Greg's fingers, once in motion, did not have to remain in motion.

Greg also recounted benefits from a remaining sense and property that were expanded. "My hands are now more sensitive to pressure. I can perform more delicate operations. Not only that, my hands are steadier. They feel more grounded. In a way they feel heavier, but that's good because the feeling keeps them from wavering, providing a sort of ballast." Expanded touch made Greg more sensitive to the intricacies of surgery and expanded gravity made his hands feel heavier, thus steadying them.

Sterling, twenty-eight, a professional boxer, also benefited from an expanded sense and property when he practiced the *Car Scene*. "That image made me more aware of the taste of blood," he said. "I know you might think it's strange that I'd want to be more aware of that, but I do. Sometimes I get so focused on the heat of the battle that I go too long after I've been cut or hurt. I need to know immediately whenever I've been inflicted with some damage so that I can act accordingly, favor my right side or my left, stay away till the bell, whatever. The *Car Scene* heightened my sense of taste and really helped me to do that. It also gave me an increased feeling of mass, while letting me remain light on my feet. I feel impenetrable, like nobody can get to me."

Tent Scene

Combining the clearing of your sensory channels by negatively hallucinating reflection and smell with the eroticism of pouring wine over your bare flesh, as called for in the *Tent Scene*, makes this image especially sensual. Your sensuality is further enhanced by using the psychophysical principle of complementary colors to intensify the visual portion of your image. Orange and yellow tiger skins on the floor of your tent intensify the complementary purples and indigo blues of a desert sky, and vice versa.

Tent Scene

You are lying nude in an Arabian tent on the Sahara Desert. The walls are chiffon. See the desert night sky through the chiffon. Deep, deep blue. Feel soft, purple satin pillows beneath you. The smell of incense lingers in the air. Before you is a silver goblet of red wine. Sniff the wine. It has no smell. Drink. Taste the sweetness of the deep red-purple wine.

The floor is covered with orange and yellow tiger skins, stretched tight like a drumhead. Hold the half-full goblet above you. Tip it. The wine falls onto the taut animal skin. It does not splash or reflect. Take a pitcher of wine. Drink from the pitcher. Pour the wine over your naked body. There is no smell to the wine. The wine does not splash or reflect off your skin. It remains, simply to roll off.

Rhythmic waves of intoxication overtake you. Go out into the desert night. Walk through mountains of fine, shifting sand. Come to an oasis. In the center is a pond of clear, pure water. Run toward the pond. Jump. Bring your knees to your chest like a cannonball. Hit the water with a great splash. Sink slowly, deeper and deeper, to the bottom. Float to the top.

Swim among the rushes bordering the pond's shore. Take a hollow reed. Suck up water. Blow out through the reed with all your strength. A powerful stream of water hits against your right leg. As soon as it hits your body, it runs straight down. It does not bounce off your skin.

Leave the pond. Walk into the desert. Come to a great block of stone. Sit in the center of the block. It begins to rain. The raindrops do not splash or reflect off the rock surface. Listen to the sound of water against stone. Run through the rain back to the tent. Fall into the soft satin pillows. Smell the incense. Sip wine to the sound of rain against the tent roof. Drift . . . Sweet, sweet reverie.

Reactions

The overwhelming reaction to the *Tent Scene* is powerful sensuality. "The rain clings like a sheet," said Britt, a thirty-year-old tennis pro. "It feels so strange and marvelously sensuous!" With rising sensuality comes rising sex energy. You should begin feeling more energetic in all areas from practicing the *Tent Scene*.

Benefits

Benefits continue to accrue from your developing ability to remove senses and properties from reality. Monica, a twenty-two-year-old actress, was thrilled over landing the lead in her first feature film. "I've had good parts on TV before, but never in films. I'm going to be on the big screen. I'm so excited! There's only one thing wrong. I play a cowgirl and I have to ride a bucking bronco. I told them I knew all there was to know about horses. Otherwise they wouldn't have given me the part. The truth is I did used to ride, but I quit because I couldn't stand the way the horses smelled and I bounced in my saddle like a yo-yo. I can still feel the saddle sores when I think about it. I'm taking riding lessons every day now, but I still bounce and I still don't like the smell of horses."

I asked Monica to practice the *Tent Scene* for a week. Then

I suggested she create an image where she applied the technique she learned of negatively hallucinating smell and reflection specifically to riding. She was to envision herself riding a bucking bronco, sniffing the air, clear and fresh. Sitting firm in the saddle, flowing with the horse, her body water not reflecting like a rubber ball. Once she was able to clearly visualize the reality she wished to manifest, I told her to hold that image while she was actually riding horseback. Monica took a few spills, but in time, reality matched her image. She paid no attention to the aroma of horses and rode smooth in the saddle. She'd become the cowgirl the studio had signed her to play.

Patrick, a forty-one-year-old dentist, said he was chronically depressed because he hated his work. "I don't know whatever made me go into this field," he said. "I guess it was because my family dentist back in my hometown in Iowa encouraged me to do so. Just 'cause he loved standing on his feet all day drilling holes in people's teeth, that doesn't mean that I would. It's so damned boring. And smelling people's halitosis all day is no picnic either. The thing I hate most about it, though, is having to inflict pain on people. I feel like a sadist. It just kills me to know I'm hurting my patients."

I knew that with today's technology there was little need for dental patients to suffer, and wondered if maybe Patrick's technique couldn't stand some improving. I asked him to practice the *Tent Scene* for a week. Then I suggested he carry over the negative hallucinations from his image into the reality of his working on his patients. He was to imagine that their breath was odorless and that the water comprising his body did not possess the property of reflection.

"I noticed an almost immediate difference in the way my hands performed," he said. "They didn't allow the dental instruments to reflect the way I'd gotten used to letting them do. It can really hurt if a pick or a drill bounces a couple of times on a tooth's surface or in a cavity. I always try to keep my instruments steady, but they can only be as solid as my hands. When my hands stopped reflecting and bouncing around, so did my instruments. Tuning out the smell of bad breath was a lot harder. It took me a little over a month before my image of a fresh patient's mouth overrode the reality of halitosis."

Patrick also benefited from the expansion of his remaining sense of sight and remaining property of gravity. "I noticed while I was still practicing the *Tent Scene* that my hands started feeling heavier. The added ballast served as a stabilizer and smoothed out the way I handled my instruments. I next discovered that I could actually see better. It was like my vision was more focused on what I was doing. It was easier to maneuver because everything was more visible." With steadier hands and an expanded range of vision, Patrick's dental technique improved dramatically, and his patients stopped complaining that he was hurting them. When he no longer attended to their unpleasant breath and they no longer experienced his infliction of pain, dentistry became a positive occupation. He decided to stay in and enjoy it.

Lawn Scene

In this image you remove smell and the property of constant volume from your experiencing of water. Since water no longer has constant volume, one drop of tea expands to fill its entire container, a swimming pool, and lake water contracts, becoming denser when the volume of its basin is decreased due to an avalanche.

Lawn Scene

You are sitting on a rolling green lawn. It's a beautiful summer afternoon. You are drinking tea. Beside you is a large, empty swimming pool. Behind you is a mammoth white house. The lawn slopes to a lake surrounded by tall, sheer, snow-capped mountains. At the lake's edge is a dock to which are moored several rowboats of various bright colors.

Sniff the tea. It has no smell. Take a sip. Your entire stomach fills with hot liquid. The tea has a taste with a hint of lemon. Walk to the edge of the empty pool. Empty your cup into the pool. The entire basin instantly fills with tea.

Walk down to the lake shore. Pink and orange wild poppies grow along the way. Remove your clothes. Run along the dock. Dive headfirst into the water. The water has no smell. Float in the cold lake water. Hear a rumbling. There is an avalanche. The mountains crumble into the lake. The water gets thicker and thicker, denser and denser. The water level does not rise. Sink in and out of the water as you become more and more buoyant. Oozing in and out... in and out... in and out... Finally you no longer sink, but lie on the water's surface.

Stand. Feel the wetness of the water beneath your feet. Run along the surface of the lake one mile, to the other side. Hear the sound of splashing water as you speed along the water surface. Feel the hot sun on your back, a tingling sensation from sun and water and speed. Reach the far side. Turn around. Begin back, feeling the slippery water between your toes. The lawn and house loom ever larger as you reach the dock. Feel the grass beneath your wet feet as you bound up the poppy path to the tea-filled swimming pool. Dive headfirst into the great expanse of tea. Surface to float in a sea of tea under a summer sky.

Reactions

Controlling the senses and properties that comprise your reality will give you a wonderful sense of liberation. You are no longer a victim of the cosmos, but its creator. "It felt good running on water," said a man in his early seventies. "What freedom!" "It's amazing how it builds," said Laura, a thirty-eight-year-old real estate broker. "I have a growing sense of power with each image." You too will feel the energy of your spirit soar as you continue to lift the yoke of physical reality.

Benefits

The negative hallucinations of senses and properties that you are asked to do in these images vastly increase your power of concentration. Scott, a fourteen-year-old high school freshman whose phobia of dentists was putting his oral hygiene seriously at risk, was able to use the *Lawn Scene* to take his attention off his dentist's drilling. "I just asked my dentist to leave me alone for five minutes while I got into the image," he explained. "I also asked him to talk only to give me instructions, so that he wouldn't interrupt my concentration. I barely noticed the drilling and any discomfort was at an intellectual level. I'd say calmly to myself, 'Oh, that is a pain. Oh, I'll go deeper.' I used the discomfort to cue deeper concentration on my image. The more he drilled, the deeper I got into it. The texture of the tea, I could actually feel my body floating in it. It was warm to the touch."

Negatively hallucinating smell and constant volume can be an excellent tool to help you overcome anorexia. People with this condition often say they feel full even when they've eaten little or nothing. They also find foods they used to like disagreeable to smell and/or taste. Damon, a twenty-eight-year-old hairdresser, was down to 115 pounds from his normal 150. "I'm just not into eating," he said. "I'm never hungry. I always feel full. The thought of food doesn't appeal to me. In fact, I sometimes get nauseated just at the smell of food—like if I pass a takeout place or outdoor restaurant, I'll feel my stomach start to heave." One food that Damon was having special difficulty incorporating into his diet was boiled cabbage, a good source of vitamin A recommended by his nutritionist, but which Damon couldn't stand the smell of. "I don't mind the taste," he said, "but the smell of it makes me sick."

I asked Damon to practice the *Lawn Scene* for a week and then create his own image where he was happily enjoying eating boiled cabbage in his kitchen at home. Just as he imagined not smelling water in the *Lawn Scene,* he was to imagine not smelling cabbage in his image for anorexia. He was also to imagine the fluid in the cabbage to be minus the property of constant volume once it reached his stomach, where it would contract down to nothing. This was to prevent Damon from feeling prematurely full after a meal. After he had practiced this specific image for a week, I asked Damon to imagine odorless cabbage that contracted down to nothing when eaten, while he was actually eating cabbage. "It worked!" he said when I saw him a week later. "I didn't smell a thing and my stomach felt nearly empty, even after I finished the whole helping of cabbage. Eating cabbage is a piece of cake!"

Morgan, a twenty-six-year-old financially independent political activist on medication for high blood pressure, was terribly concerned over the environmental problems facing Los Angeles. "Whenever I smell smog my blood boils because I know they aren't enforcing the emissions codes. There's so much money under the table and illegal kickbacks it makes your head spin. Every year they tell us the smog is getting better and every year it just gets worse." The smell of smog had already given Morgan its informational value. She was warned of an ever-present danger to her health, but there was no need to perceive this danger signal around the clock. Morgan needed to learn to tune out the smell of smog until she could find a better way to deal with it, either by political reform or by leaving the city.

After Morgan practiced the Lawn Scene for a week, learning to negatively hallucinate smell and constant volume, I gave her the following affirmations while she was in a hypnotic state: "Just as you can tune out the smell of water, you can tune out the smell of smog. Just as you can make water shrink by removing its property of constant volume, you can make the blood in your system shrink. You will exercise these powers. Smog is without odor. Blood in your vessels is shrinking."

I had given Morgan two methods for reducing her blood pressure: negatively hallucinating the smell of smog that was making her so upset, and envisioning her blood shrinking, thus reducing the actual pressure in her vessels. She contin-

ued giving herself these affirmations while doing self-hypnosis three times a day, every day. A month later she reported,
"My blood pressure is down and I can't remember the last time
I smelled smog, although I'm as radical as ever on the subject,
still going after the crooked politicos." If you have high blood
pressure you might try this same technique as Morgan, practicing the *Lawn Scene,* and then giving yourself positive hypnotic affirmations that you tune out irritants and shrink your
blood to reduce its pressure.

Priscilla, thirty-eight, married to Collin, forty-seven, a successful entrepreneur, was plagued by severe sweating spells.
"They always come when I'm under a lot of pressure," she
said, "especially when I'm entertaining for Collin. He makes
a lot of his deals over dinner and I feel pressured to make it
all come off. Sometimes if he doesn't get an account I feel like
it's my fault. The sweating has gotten so bad that I worry
more about sweating than I do about what originally caused
the sweating, fear that Collin won't close the deal. The smell
of it makes me especially nervous. I can wear arm pads and
keep patting myself with Kleenex, but if I start to smell sweaty
it's a cue for sheer panic. I could die with embarrassment.
What an impression to make at a power lunch."

I instructed Priscilla to practice the *Lawn Scene* three times
a day for a week and give herself the following affirmations
immediately after the image, right before counting to three
to bring herself out of the hypnotic imagogic state: "Just as I
can tune out the smell of water, I can tune out the smell of
sweat. Just as I can make water shrink, I can make sweat
shrink. The next time that I am entertaining for Collin I will
smell fresh and clean throughout. Whatever sweat I emit will
immediately shrink to nothing." When the week was up, Priscilla said, "I realize now that I sweated because I expected to.
The *Lawn Scene* and the affirmations you gave me made me
come to expect that I wouldn't, and I didn't!" Tuning out her
olfactory cue for sweating, the smell of her own sweat, along
with envisioning her sweat immediately shrinking, kept Priscilla dry throughout her dinner parties. What you expect to
happen, often does. You can use these images involving your

control of senses and properties to condition yourself to expect a better reality, which will then manifest from your positive expectation.

Without the property of constant volume, water in the *Lawn Scene* not only contracts, it also expands. You can put your facility for visualizing the expansion of liquids to many uses. Sammy, nine, was allergic to certain of the flowering weeds that grew in the canyons where he lived. When his allergy was at its worst, Sammy's sinuses were so congested he couldn't breathe and he would have to be hospitalized, an event he dreaded even more than his suffocating allergy attacks. He was taking a liquid medication to help keep his sinuses clear, but it only helped to a point.

I asked Sammy to practice the tape of the *Lawn Scene* that I had recorded for him at his last session, including the following affirmations that I had inserted immediately after his image: "Just as you can tune out the smell of water, you can tune out the smell of flowering weeds. Just as you can make water expand, you can make your allergy medication expand. The air you breathe smells clear and fresh. The allergy medication you swallow expands infinitely in your bloodstream to vastly heighten its power. You are allergy-free."

Sammy's first positive results came from the maximization of his medication through his visualization of its expansion. "I was amazed," Sammy's mother told me. "We were able to reduce his dosage by half two weeks after he started practicing that image. That made me happy because the medicine has bad side effects like making Sammy drowsy and not able to do his homework properly. Not only that, he now gets better results from his half dose than he did his full one. He had only one attack last week and it was minor. It didn't last over a half hour and he was back outside playing."

It took Sammy another two weeks before he was able to master not smelling the weeds, but it was worth it. He never had another hospitalization. The importance of the mind in relation to asthma and allergies was dramatically documented in the now-classic "rose asthma" case wherein an allergic patient had a severe attack from a fake rose placed near his side.

His believing it was an allergen was enough to bring on the allergy, just as you may find that your not believing, not tuning into an allergen, is enough to fend off an attack.

The *Lawn Scene* worked similarly well to potentiate the effects of a liquid medication in the case of Candy, twelve, suffering from severe burns inflicted when her home burned down. Candy particularly couldn't stand the smell of the sulfur her medicine contained, and her mother was having a difficult time getting her to take it. "I'm at the end of my rope," said Candy's mother. "The poor child wakes up in the middle of the night screaming, but I can't get her to swallow her dose and sometimes it takes so much to give her any relief, several spoonfuls. I tell you it's like pulling teeth."

As with Sammy, I asked Candy to listen to a tape of the *Lawn Scene,* at the end of which were the affirmations: "Just as I can tune out the smell of water, I can tune out the smell of my medication. Just as I can make water grow larger, I can make my medicine grow larger once I have swallowed it. My medicine smells like nothing. My medicine grows inside my body. I like taking it. It makes me feel good." You'll notice again that you affirm what you want, not what you don't want. You say, for example, "It smells like nothing," rather than, "It doesn't smell bad." Soon Candy was no longer attending to the smell of her medication and was taking it without a fuss. She also required smaller doses, often getting by with a single spoonful at a time, much to her mother's relief. You can potentiate the effects of any medication, in liquid or pill form, simply by visualizing it dissolving in your blood which then expands to increase its power and effectiveness.

Visualizing your blood expanding, minus the property of constant volume, is also an excellent technique for increasing sexual arousal. A congestion of blood in the penis causes the erection in men, and a congestion of blood in the vaginal area of women also produces a sexual readiness. Blair, a twenty-one-year-old drama major, was very much in love with Nick, a twenty-three-year-old law student, and wanted to marry him. However, though she had been orgasmic with Nick at times, more often than not she didn't feel like making love with him and worried how she would feel in the long-term commitment of marriage. "When I think about him, I get really horny," she said, "but when we're together that feeling just seems to dry up. He's so cute and he's a good lover, very considerate, but you know what I think it is? I don't like his scent. Every man smells different, you know? Some I really love, but poor Nick, it turns me off. It's not that he smells bad. I'm sure some girls would really be turned on by him. I know this sounds shallow and stupid and I've tried to talk myself out of it, but I just haven't been able to."

Smell was our first sense and the most evocative. In animals it is still the primary elicitor of sexual arousal. The pheromones that give us each our individual scents are sexually powerful chemicals that normally arouse us to sexual passion. Sometimes, as in Blair's case, the chemistry just doesn't work. In therapy I always try to potentiate smell as an evoker of sexual arousal, but after several sessions with Blair I decided to help her tune it out as it remained a negative element in her relationship with Nick.

I requested that Blair practice the *Lawn Scene,* giving herself the following affirmations at the end: "Just as I can tune out the smell of water, I can tune out the smell of Nick during sex. Just as I can make water expand, I can make blood expand in my genitals. During sex Nick smells like nothing. During sex the blood in my genitals expands, grows, pounds, throbs, pulsates. I climax passionately with Nick. I love having sex with Nick."

As Blair continued to focus on the image of expanding blood, both as elicited by her affirmations and during actual lovemaking, her frequency of favorably responding to Nick increased. This focus also helped to take her attention off his scent, although she was not able to negatively hallucinate it directly until nearly three months after she started trying. At that point all was well between her and Nick. "Sex is all a matter of mind control, isn't it?" she said. "When I was able to direct my attention totally off Nick's smell and concentrate more on the hot, throbbing feeling of expanding blood in my vagina and clitoris, I had it made. Sex with Nick is now good every time, sometimes better than others, but never awful like it once in a while used to be."

I could go on explaining the practical uses you can make of the effects you are able to create by eliminating the various combinations of senses and properties that you will continue to work on, but I think by now you've gotten the general idea of the benefits to be gained. I'll therefore leave you the joy of discovering your own unique uses as you go on mastering the ongoing imagery progression. Here and there I'll still point out any outstanding practical applications of imagogic physics that may have cropped up over the years of my practice.

Watermelon Patch Scene

In this image you remove the receptors of taste and touch from your experiencing of water.

Watermelon Patch Scene

It's a warm, lazy, fall day. You are standing in a large watermelon patch surrounded by red and orange oak trees. The smell of burning leaves is in the wind. In the center of the patch is an old stone well. Walk to the well. Pull up a bucket holding red melon slices soaked in ice-cold well water. Smell the sweet, ripe melon. With a loud, juicy sound you suck the melon. It has no taste. There is no sensation of wetness or coolness. It's like eating watermelon-scented Styrofoam. Your mouth feels dry and warm.

Lean forward, looking down into the well. Fall forward, somersaulting downward into the depths. Smell the wet stone. Hear a loud splash. There is no sensation of wetness or water pressure as you continue falling... falling... falling. You are in an underground sea world. There are large silver bubbles floating underwater. Put one over your head to breathe the oxygen within. Swim underwater. Feel no sensation of wetness or pressure from the water.

The sea is filled with giant, luminescent pearls, iridescent tortoiseshells, salmon coral, and orange sea horses. Mount the back of a sea horse. He carries you to a castle of silver shells. Enter a large banquet hall. Drink seawater through a golden straw inserted into your head bubble. The water smells salty, but has no taste. Your mouth feels dry as you drink the water. The sea horse serves you octopus on a banquet table of opalescent abalone. It tastes like fried chicken.

The orange sea horse takes you to a bed of bubbles of green sea foam. Feel the bubbles beneath you, conforming to your body contour. Dream on a bed of bubbles in an underwater sea castle of shells.

Reactions

As you continue altering your perception of water you gain an emotional understanding that you are in essence its creator. Water is a function of your consciousness. With this realization you feel one with the water. You and it are inseparable. You cannot exist independently. Jan, a thirty-year-old travel agent, experienced the beginnings of this revelation. "The bed moved in and out with my breathing. How delicious. That was better than my waterbed. There's a glistening, ripply effect to reality which I am going to start applying right now. Everything is kind of diffused. The stimulus has to go through that in the process. The falling was absolutely euphoric. I felt different immediately when in water even though it wasn't wet or cool. It was a slow-motion effect, like a protective coating, like a mothering effect. It reminds me of the feeling I had during the *Séance Scene* where the sea says, 'We love you. You are home at last,' a oneness with the water. One image is now triggering a past image." When you feel one with creation, you will feel its overwhelming love for you, the same love that you, its mother, its creator, feel for it. You are

One. Jan's reaction also substantiates the fact that each image in this progression does in fact build on, and is enhanced by, the prior images. Jan called on elements of her various past images to further her experiencing of present images. You are being primed for greater levels of sensation.

Feelings of the excitingly bizarre, rising energy and profound time distortion continue to intensify as you peel away the illusions of reality. "Oh God, that was hard," breathed Gus, a thirty-five-year-old building manager. "It was really trippy." "My heart, it has an extra beat," said Florence, a forty-year-old secretary. "What energy I'm feeling!" "I don't remember how I got to the bed," said Dan, a twenty-eight-year-old TV repairman. "When you pause it's like four years. Every image gets deeper."

Electric Blue

"I saw an electric blue," said Don, thirty, a building contractor. "Veins of electric blue to purple, right after I got to the underground sea. There was a lava flow. Then I saw a magenta rolling cloud."

Just as a new purple is an indication that you are reaching ever higher planes of being and expanded perception, so is the appearance of what patients describe as an "electric blue." This new phenomenon usually appears only briefly, for a flash, often in the form of crackling energy or a lightning bolt. It's been my observation that it manifests later than the purple and is a sign of even higher development, direct perception of pure energy.

Benefits

Raising energy to the point where you can actually see it, even if only for a moment, as Don did, has wonderful effects on your mood. You feel up and filled with life, eager to explore new ideas and dimensions. There is nothing better for lifting the energy-depleted state called depression. Marilyn, a thirty-year-old mother of four, fell into a severely depressed state three years ago when her husband Arnie was killed in an automobile accident. At the point when she reached the *Watermelon Patch Scene* in this progression of images, she had raised her energy enough to lift her depression. "My parents are in awe of my progress," she told me. "My mother said, 'It's so good to have you back among the living. There for a while I'd thought we'd lost you. Now you've got enough energy for the two of us!'"

Anne found that the *Watermelon Patch Scene* not only heightened the senses that were remaining in the image—sight, sound, and smell—it expanded "extra" senses as well. "David decided to take the day off work so that he could fix up the house," she explained. "He went to the lumberyard for supplies, and while he was gone I suddenly 'knew' that someone at his job would be sick and he'd be needed. I called the lumberyard and told him to come right home. When David got home he called work and was told that three people were out and he was needed immediately."

Sensory expansion was also improving Anne's work performance. "I got the greatest review," she said. "My boss said I had no weak points. My evaluation was an itemized list of my strengths. I'm now typing over one hundred words a minute and I'm using my sense of removing inertia from water to increase my work efficiency. Whenever I'm typing and interrupted by a phone call, I imagine a huge quantity of water in my stomach. I then lean forward to answer the phone while imagining this water is without inertia so that it won't resist the movement of my body. Body water at rest does not therefore tend to stay at rest. Since my body is over eighty percent water, this leads to my feeling much less resistance or effort when I move. I not only move more easily using this method, I'm much better at knowing where I was before the interruption. The interruption takes less energy and is less disruptive. This works quite naturally now without my thinking about it.

"I also discovered that as my facility for removing a prop-

erty increases so does my facility for intensifying it. I'm able
to intensify a sensation of body water inertia and create a
ballast or inert liquid center that causes me to move more
gracefully and feel literally an 'inner calm.' There is something magic about seeing a stable liquid center. It gives me a
sense of peace."

Anne was also able to successfully use her imagery techniques to eliminate the pain of dentistry. "I've been to the
dentist twice since my last session," she said. "I have a bad
reaction to novocaine and am much better off not using it. My
first visit I told my dentist to leave me alone five minutes while
I got my imagery going. I regressed myself to childhood and
an experience of swinging over the river where mint grew. I
was able to divert my attention totally from any source of
possible discomfort without using any anesthetic. Then I gave
myself affirmations for time concentration: 'Ten minutes seem
like one. Time is going by very rapidly. It seems like an
instant.'

"Before I knew it the dentist was shaking me. The forty-
five-minute session was over. I told him I thought it had only
lasted a minute. The second time I saw him he insisted on
giving me a minimal amount of novocaine because he wanted
to do some root canal work. I recalled the *Watermelon Patch
Scene* and didn't even feel the novocaine injection, which is
amazing for me because I have extremely sensitive gums from
the diabetes. The more he worked on me, the deeper I went.
The bubbles of green sea foam were more real to me than his
office. Again it was over before I knew it. Believe me, this is
not like me at all. Normally I *hate* going to the dentist and
the pain is excruciating."

Not only was her work and health improving, Anne was
even playing better. "I had the greatest time at our company
picnic," she said. "I enjoyed myself immensely, swinging in
my long dress, watching the sun filter through the trees. I
feel like I have a childhood innocence again, only with past
knowledge." In keeping with her tendency to be precognitive
for the images, her next image, and yours as well, begins on
a swing. "My ability for precognition and 'inner inertia,' at-

taining that stable calm inside, are both still increasing," she went on. "My thinking has taken on an extra clarity and my intuition is stronger. I'm happier than I've ever been. My parents came to visit us and my mother, who has been very skeptical about hypnosis, imagery, and my sessions with you, paid me the extreme compliment. She said, 'I had a daughter bright as sunshine. Then she became morose. Now she's back.' This was the first validation from my mother. It was like her saying, 'Yes, I see it. You are a different person. I see the change.' My parents were awed by me all week. I evolved from a chronic complainer into a literal inspiration. I can't help being pleased with myself. We spent our time discussing suspensions and emulsions, quite a change from the topics of our usual conversations."

The discussion of suspensions and emulsions was a carry-over from a conversation that Anne and I had had our last session together, where I'd explained some principles of elementary physics in order to prepare her for future images and give her a better feeling for the universe and her place in it. Anne and I had defined and discussed three mixtures of matter in different states: colloidal suspension—a stable mixture of a solid and a liquid, such as ink, or water mixed with fine sand that will not settle out; emulsion—globules of one liquid suspended in another, such as milk, which is fat suspended in water; and foam—a gas suspended in a liquid.

I feel that a knowledge of physics changes your perspective of life and the cosmos. Understanding the science that deals with matter and energy and their interactions in the fields of mechanics, acoustics, optics, heat, electricity, magnetism, radiation, atomic structure, and nuclear phenomena gives you a sense of infinite harmony, order, and truth, especially if this understanding is emotional as well as intellectual. This is exactly what I've designed this imagery progression to provide you, an emotional understanding of the physics determining your reality.

Swing Scene

In this image you remove taste and hearing from your sensing of water. The smell, sight, and touch of water will therefore be more vivid, as you can now focus your attention on only three sense modalities.

Swing Scene

You are swinging nude on a rope-borne swing from a giant oak tree over a cliff by the sea. Up, up, up, into the blue, higher and higher. Smell the salt air. Hear the sound of creaking branches from the weight of the swing. The sea below is vast and silent. Go ever higher.

You are slipping. Fly off and up into the air. Come down to land in the sea with a great, silent splash. There is no sound. Drink the seawater. It has no taste, but smells very salty. Huge, silent waves carry you far, far away.

Come to a tropical lagoon, a pirate's cove. A Spanish galleon with white sails billowing in the sea breeze is anchored there. Swim to the ship. Crawl up netting on its side, and board. Go to the captain's room. It is large with round windows and red velvet chairs. In the center is a large ebony table. Sit at it. You are served hot rum. Sniff the rum. It smells of butter and cinnamon. Drink. It has no taste and makes no sound as you slurp it down. It feels hot and wet, sliding down your throat into your stomach.

The boat begins to rock. A storm is brewing. There is a bolt of lightning, a clap of thunder. Great silent waves lap against the sides of the boat. Lightning strikes the ship! Smell smoke. Jump out of the ship's window into the sea. Swim through the turbulent, silent water.

Reach a secluded cove where the water is still. The sand on shore is like powdered diamonds, sparkling in the tropic sun. Rock forming the cove is pearl, luminescent rainbow colors glistening in the water. Palms covered with glittering crystals fringe the beach. Float to shore. Sleep in the diamond dust, lulled by the trade winds.

Reactions

Sometimes people have difficulty *not* creating a sense or property. "For some reason I want to hear that sound," said Betty, a thirty-year-old teacher. However, responding specifically to the image will give you a marvelous sense of control. "I feel much more relaxed each time," said Melanie, a twenty-two-year-old lab technician. "It helps to think of myself as smiling. The image gives control back to me like, isn't it marvelous what I can do? Something you're accomplishing put control back into me and doesn't make life so grim." Your life always looks better when you feel you have control over it.

Ken, a fifty-one-year-old optometrist, described a series of responses, going from an extrasensory type of hearing, to moving out of this world, culminating in the appearance of a purple vortex, a new sensation inviting him to the next dimension. "In the beginning it was like hearing at different levels. Then when I was lying in the diamond dust I suddenly saw myself in outer space. Then the stars were gone. Then there was purple like smoke which kept opening in the middle. Then it became streaks." The yogis speak of the astral body, which hears without the benefit of physical ears, truly hearing on a different level. As you transcend the illusion of a physical reality you transcend the illusion of your physical body as well.

As the image takes you deeper into yourself you may come to feel a loving presence, the memory of which is lost on your complete return to ordinary reality. There were tears welling from the closed eyes of Tim, a burly forty-seven-year-old plant manager, during the *Swing Scene*. When I counted three to end his image, he opened his eyes briefly and then closed them again, lying perfectly still. "I don't want to come back," he whispered. "We'll see you."

I waited approximately five minutes, until Tim was ready to come out of his state naturally. Then I asked him why he'd said *"We'll* see you." "I said, 'I,'" he yelled emphatically. I believe that Tim's tears of joy and his plural reference were a function of his feeling close to a loving force that commonly manifests in deeper imagery states, but I let his denial ride. He looked at me rather sheepishly for having raised his voice and said, "No sound made the splash seem larger." Removing hearing had expanded seeing. That was as much as he was willing to allow into his awareness of reality for the moment. He would merge realities further when he was ready, as we all will.

Benefits

Practicing the *Swing Scene,* focusing on and intensifying sight, touch, and smell, heightens your awareness of reality as well, and you will be more alert and on top of what is happening. Chuck, a twenty-two-year-old medical student who was trying to develop better study habits, reported the following benefits after practicing the *Swing Scene* for a week: "I now see things better in recall than when I first see them. That's great for exams. And I notice different things. The professor I work for told me, 'You don't behave and work and act like any other student I've seen. You have an interest, a perception, an attention to details.' One response like that can make you feel alive, but it's happening all over. I'm getting compliments from everyone."

Living Within Your Imagery

The *Swing Scene* not only heightens your awareness of reality, it serves to make your imagery more vivid, not only the *Swing Scene* per se, but any imagery you may be working on or find yourself involved in. At the gathering that Dr. Kroger held at his home after the seminar described earlier,

Anne had run across my self-portrait, a large oil painting I had done of myself and left for Dr. Kroger to show to the owner of an art gallery who was considering exhibiting some of my work. She liked the painting very much. "I've been thinking about that painting a lot this week," she said, referring to the week she'd also spent practicing the *Swing Scene*. "I was especially involved with it this morning. The image of it became like a cone encircling me. I was almost inside. It was three-D. I wished I would have gone inside." Anne's imagery was becoming three-dimensional. It was so real to her that she felt she could inhabit it. In fact, she wished she could; it was more attractive than the reality she was presently creating.

Come along. Let us continue our journey through the progression. You will learn to imagine a better reality and dwell therein.

nine

Channeling Sexual Energy

In this chapter, you will learn how to create sexual energy and transfer it to different areas of your body. Not only does this give you increased physical and sensory control, sexual-energy transfers have several positive effects that will be discussed. Energy generated from this creation and channeling of your sexuality can be used for healing and for transcending your common five-sensory reality.

The transfer helps you channel sex energy so that you can use it for purposes other than achieving sexual satisfaction. A strong sexual desire is good, but there are other things you may want or prefer to experience as well. Explore and see what you think. Channeled sex energy still feels sexual, but it is a different kind of sexual feeling than you have ever experienced before, less lusty and carnal, more powerfully expansive and spiritual; less a manifestation of the physical body than one of pure existential energy.

A sex-energy transfer also serves to magnify and potentiate the energy being transferred by extending it throughout your body, and finally out of body, infinitely, without the restrictive illusion of the body boundary. You may already have had experiences when, after a particularly glorious episode of lovemaking, you felt transported out of your body, catapulted to a higher plane of consciousness through the sheer energy of powerful sexual release. After three days of practicing the *Swing Scene,* Anne reported she had had luck expanding her sex energy when making love with David. "I felt floating above the bed," she said. Her sex energy had carried her out of body. Learning to channel your sex energy can elevate your actual sexual experiences as well as serve to fuel your ascendance into higher levels of knowledge and being.

Energy transfers expand your sense of self, get you out of your formerly limited sphere of influence into an ever-increasing range of action. As you channel and magnify energy, you project yourself exponentially outward, breaking through the illusory compartments that encase your understanding.

Invisible Ocean Scene

In the *Invisible Ocean Scene* you create the sensation of orgasm in your head. Just as you learned to transfer the sensations of numbness and warmth in Chapter 3, you now develop the ability to transfer the sensation of the sexual climax. Any sensation you've ever experienced is recorded forever and you can recall it as vividly as the first time you experienced it. Also, a sensation you experience in one part of your body can be recalled and transferred to any other part of your body.

Since it is possible to transfer numbness to areas where you've never experienced it, it is also possible to transfer the sensation of orgasm to an area other than the genitals. In addition, you will remove taste and sight from your sensing of water.

Invisible Ocean Scene

You are standing before a vast area of white sand that slopes down thousands of feet. The sun is hot against your skin. You are unclothed. Feel the heat of the sand beneath your bare feet. Walk forward. Cross a band where the sand turns darker. Your feet feel wet. Smell salt. Hear waves lapping. Walk further. Feel like you are submerging in water. Feel an increasing pressure like you are underwater. Hear a ringing in your ears. Great silver bubbles float in the air. One covers your head. The air is easier to breathe. Fresh, pure oxygen in the bubble feeds into your respiratory system.

See great chasms, pointed pinnacles, and brilliant pink buttes. Walk further. Behold emerald coral, white oysters, and brightly colored fish appearing to float in midair. The light is bright like sunlight. Suck in. It feels like drinking water. Your mouth feels wet and cool. Feel water running down your throat and into your stomach. It has no taste. Feel the pressure on your body increase as you walk further.

Come to a ruby-red atoll like a butte, flat on top. Swim to the top. Lie there. A beautiful, naked man/woman [sex to which you are sexually attracted] swims toward you. Feel a strong sexual attraction. He/she cradles your head between his/her legs and begins massaging your head with his/her hands. Feel the heat of his/her thighs around your head. He/she strokes your temples and runs his/her palms around your cheeks. Your head is getting warmer and warmer. Face is flushing, pulsating. Feel an ever-increasing pressure in your head. A pressure building to a sexual climax ... throbbing ... surging ... climax! .... in your head; your genital area is cool, uncongested, unaroused.

Slowly float through bright sunlight to the surface of the sea. Drift. See no water. Taste no water. Smell of salt. Sound of rolling waves. Blue sky. Blazing sun. Sensation of wetness, coolness, and buoyancy.

Reactions

The *Invisible Ocean Scene* will definitely give you a sense of increased energy. It may take as simple a form as your being especially alert through the sexual part of the image. Scott, twenty-two, who often fell asleep through segments of his imagery, said, "I sure was awake during the orgastic part. I felt rested during all of it." Increased energy also manifests in your improved ability to focus; stray thoughts are eliminated and you concentrate only on the moment. "I had no sensory conflict," said Joan, eighteen, a high school senior suffering from psychotic ideation, bizarre thoughts that constantly entered her mind and kept her from studying and being socially acceptable. "That was the first time my mind didn't wander!" "I didn't have that little voice analyzing," said Debbie, a thirty-one-year-old newscaster plagued with worry and excessive rumination.

Energy is often experienced as heat. "My head got hot," said Edward, a twenty-eight-year-old data processor. "I felt heat into my hands," said Sarah, a fifty-two-year-old buyer for a major department store. "And water pressure on my legs." On occasion, as in the case of Sarah, and in that of Madeline, twenty-seven, a teacher who had just retired to concentrate on raising her family, sensation is felt in areas other than the head. "My genitals started," said Madeline. The energy may not only feel like heat, you might experience it as electricity. Charles, a twenty-two-year-old actor, said, "I ended with a crackling head."

Raising energy is a major step toward transcending the physical plane, and you may experience a great feeling of liberated lightness from practicing the *Invisible Ocean Scene*. Chad, a forty-two-year-old optometrist whose chronic worrying had produced a peptic ulcer, had the following reaction: "Right this minute I'm standing inside my head and it's yellow sunshine, yellow trees, yellow fields, yellow hair. I'm just standing there looking at the sun. I'm here and I'm there. I just turned around and saw my face. I'm grinning. Now I'm running. I think I'm back. God, what a yellow. I can't believe it! I think if I stood inside the sun that's the color it would be. I came out of your image and went into my own. I've never done that before. My head feels light . . . a champagney feeling! I wouldn't have had the yellow without the orgasm, like a migraine without pain, like it's going to blow right up and then head sinks into neck right after!"

Raising sex energy may cause a temporary vibratory awakening of one of the occult spinal centers, or chakras, the sacred goal of the yogi. It is through the seven chakras in the cerebrospinal axis that the yogi, by scientific meditation, escapes the physical prison of the body to resume his true identity as Spirit. It is said that the advanced yogi is able to transmute his cells into pure energy, causing his body to materialize and dematerialize at will. Drawing energy up the spinal column may result in the appearance of multicolored lights. The incredible yellow described by Chad indicates the manifestation of such dynamic spinal energies.

You too will experience that the effects you achieve from channeling your sexual energy do not ultimately feel sexual at all, but transcendent. Your channeled sex energy launches you into a higher level of experience, a positive spiritual realm where you've never been before.

AIDS

Sex energy can be used beneficially in the treatment of AIDS. It is important in treating this disease to not suppress sex energy through guilt concerning how the disease was acquired. Sex energy is one of the most accessible forms of energy available for strengthening the immune system. It is virtually the energy of life.

To love yourself, you must also love your sexuality and the

energy that gave you life. The early Christians, in their hatred of the competing religion of Paganism which treated sexuality positively in its cosmology, took the vital force of sex energy out of religion, and with it the pure knowledge that comes with direct perception of the creative energy that is the cosmos. The value of sex energy as a vehicle to mystical experience was well understood by many of the ancient religions.

The Babylonian goddess Ishtar was called the Mother of Harlots. She was the deity reigning over the temple prostitutes, harlots, or sacred whores revered for their sensual magic, learning, and healing of the sick. Centers of learning in Greece and Asia Minor honored the harlots like queens, and some, such as the Empress Theodora, wife of Justinian, and St. Helena, mother of Constantine, even became queens. Barbara Walker, in *The Woman's Encyclopedia of Myths and Secrets,* states, "The Tantric word for a sacred harlot was Veshya, probable origin of the Goddess's oldest names in Greece and Rome. Hestia or Vesta, the Hearth-mother, served by the Vestal Virgins who were originally harlot-priestesses." These harlot-priestesses were called "virgins" because they remained unmarried. Ishtar, whose Greek name was Athene, was not only the Great Whore, but also the Great Virgin. Athene's temple, the Parthenon, was attended by "promiscuous" women like other shrines of the goddess.

The Christian church vilified promiscuity centuries before medicine understood there was a connection between sexual activity and venereal disease. One of the reasons for the vilification was that the patriarchal church wanted to ensure that women had only one sexual partner to guarantee the husband's paternity. However, the double standard reigned supreme, and "real men" were encouraged to be sexually promiscuous as a testimony to their manhood. In the eighteenth century, Dryden described a gentleman as one who "eats, drinks, and wenches abundantly." Meanwhile, promiscuous women were called whores, hussies, and prostitutes, a long way from their original place as Holy Harlots, priestesses to the goddess Ishtar, vehicles to mystical enlightenment.

Sex energy, whether expressed monogamously or promiscuously, heterosexually or homosexually, channeled for healing or enlightenment, is the vital force of creation and is good. In treating AIDS it is imperative to view it as such.

Positive Expectation

Raymond, a thirty-eight-year-old gay businessman, had been diagnosed with HIV infection a month ago, and his T4 cell count kept dropping, although his physician had started him immediately on AZT. "I didn't have any symptoms," he said, "but one day I had a strong fever of 104 degrees and I thought I'd better check it out. I was over the fever in a day or two, but my test came back positive for AIDS. You know the statistics are really bad after that kind of diagnosis. One of my doctors said that out of fifty thousand cases diagnosed with AIDS only one hundred thirty still survived after five years."

To quote statistics like that to an AIDS patient is like handing him a death sentence. Why do we persist in giving ourselves and others fatally negative affirmations? My mother died of lung cancer in April 1981. The disease had been diagnosed a year and a half before as inoperable, although she did go through radiation therapy. I remember her doctor telling me, "She has six months to a year to live." When I asked him why he insisted on being so definite with his terminal diagnosis, he said that he didn't want to give my mother or those who loved her "false hope."

How can hope be false? There is no such thing as false hope. Hope is always true, always positive. Hope is faith in a positive outcome. It is a living, vital energy that propels us forward. Is hope false simply because what we hope for doesn't always materialize? Not at all. Hope, belief that our dreams will come true, is the foundation for all creation. Entertaining any image or affirmation contrary to your desired outcome is counterproductive and totally unnecessary. Don't listen to people when they tell you not to get your hopes up, or that you aren't facing reality when you refuse to accept the possibility that things may not turn out the way you want. Your desire *creates* reality.

When a cocaine addict asks me if he will be cured in one session, there are many times when I'd like to say, "No, that's impossible. Don't even consider it." That way if our first session together doesn't effect a cure he can't come back angrily at me saying, "You said I'd get well in one visit. You lied to me. You just wanted to string me along to get my money." But I know that telling my patients not to expect immediate cure is robbing them of positive expectation. I partially solve this dilemma by telling them that a one-session cure is possible, though it usually happens in only one out of ten cases— but they should expect positive results from the outset. Even this explanation leaves me unsatisfied, however, since I believe an authoritative statement such as "You will be cured today" increases the probability of the positive results manifesting.

In your own case, *always* give yourself positive images and affirmations of immediate results and don't be angry if these promises to yourself don't materialize instantly. If it makes you more comfortable, think of these images and affirmations as suggestions, not statements of fact. You affirm and visualize yourself positively not because you are, but because you wish to be—but the positive result should always be imagined as *now*. There is nothing false about envisioning a better reality.

I know that I had some trouble with this at first, especially when working with my mother. I had spent years lecturing, writing, and doing therapy extolling the positive benefits of imagery. Yet when I used imagery techniques with my mother, whom I wanted to save more than anything, she still died—maybe a few months or a year later than the doctors predicted, but still the outcome was not the one desired. For several years I stopped using imagery techniques for healing disease and focused on pain control and removal of habit patterns, conditions I knew responded to treatment and where it wouldn't be fatal if they didn't.

Eventually I came back around. I read of and saw the marvelous things that people were doing with positive imagery and self-healing. Norman Cousins's book *Anatomy of an Illness* described how he cured himself of a "fatal" illness using humor and positive imagery. Carl and Stephanie Simonton, Louise Hay, and Bernie Siegel, among many others, were using positive imagery to heal. The field of imagery was coming into its own and I realized it was time to rejoin the living on the cutting edge of the mind-body connection, the realm of the imagination.

Combining a Specific Image
with an Image in the Progression

I told Raymond to forget the statistics. He was going to get well. Any thoughts to the contrary he was not to allow to consciousness.

Then we worked on creating a specific image to destroy the AIDS virus. I told Raymond that conjuring an appropriate image was really a simple affair. He only needed to decide how he wanted to visualize his good guys, the T4 cells and macrophages of his immune system, and how he wanted to picture the villain, the AIDS virus. Once we had a suitable metaphor, it was just a matter of imagining the good guys totally annihilating the enemy. He mentioned a few possibilities that he'd heard about, such as a kindly PacMan devouring evil dots, but none of these possible scenarios appealed to him and he wanted me to help him out.

I ran a few suggestions by him, such as visualizing the T cells and macrophages as white light, as sunshine, as himself with an ax or gun, or as a giant bulldozer. Some of the considerations for the virus were a dirty green light, mud, grotesquely formed cells as viewed under a microscope, and ugly black bugs. The metaphor that Raymond finally chose is one that is also popular with my cancer patients. He felt comfortable visualizing his T cells and macrophages as white knights on chargers, and the AIDS virus as raw, rotten hamburger.

I next asked Raymond to think about making his knights

and hamburger as real in all five senses as possible. He had no trouble seeing them, and embellished his knights with lances to pierce the hamburger when they attacked. The smell of rotting hamburger was easy for him to recall, and I asked him whether he'd like to add a scent to his knights as well; maybe an after-shave or men's cologne. Women often imagine beautiful ladies or fairy queens smelling of lilac or other pleasant fragrances as the good force destroying their disease. Raymond decided to leave the knights scentless. Perfume and power didn't go together in his mind. For the moment he couldn't come up with a taste or sound.

As for touch, this imagery paradigm presents an interesting situation. If you imagine the good guys and the bad guys both as external agents, there will be no touch involved. You can't tactilely experience what another agent is doing, even though you can observe it through your other four senses of sight, sound, taste, and smell. This is okay. You don't have to use all five senses to get powerful results.

However, if you want to be able to incorporate touch into your healing imagery there are two ways to do it: Imagine yourself within your own blood stream destroying the negative agent by strangling it with your hands, chopping it with an ax, cutting it with a knife, whatever. Or imagine that you *are* the positive metaphor, the white knight, the healing angel, the white light, whatever form you have chosen to effect the healing. After all, you *are* the T cell or macrophage. You are *not* the virus. In either case, you will then be able to experience the healing image tactilely as well. Raymond felt more comfortable visualizing an external source to do his battle, and we therefore left touch out of his imagery paradigm.

The last thing we needed to decide was what form the attack would take. *How* were the knights going to destroy the raw, rotting hamburger? We decided that they were going to whack it into tiny pieces with their lances, piercing it to bits. Suddenly Raymond had another idea. "Why not burn the hamburger?" he asked. "Great," I agreed. "That gives us another olfactory element as well, aroma of smoke. And a sound! The singeing hiss of fire on flesh. We'll have a metamorphosis, a transformation of matter. The virus hamburger is cleansed by fire and dissolves into the air. At the end you can imagine that everything smells fresh and clean and healthy."

Raymond liked our mutual creation, and this is how it read the first time that I gave it to him: "You are going to create an image to cleanse and heal your body. You see your T4 cells and macrophages as strong white knights on powerful chargers wielding long, sharp lances. You see the AIDS virus as weak, confused, raw, rotting hamburger. Smell the vile putrefaction of the rot. The knights charge the hamburger, their lances poised for attack. The lances pierce the hamburger in great puffs of smoke. Hear the singeing hamburger hiss as it ignites in flames, burning to diffuse completely into the air and blow away. The air smells clean, clear, fresh. The knights are victorious. The battle is won!"

I gave Raymond the *Invisible Ocean Scene* right before this specifically tailored-for-AIDS image in order to raise his energy and give more power to the healing image. "It seemed real," he said, referring to the *Invisible Ocean Scene*. "On occasion I lost track a little. My mind sort of jumped. The image of my head between the man's legs was vivid, though. I transferred the orgastic sensation to my head. I felt warmth around my cheeks when you said the man was touching me."

Raymond did a hypnotic clearing procedure, a sex-energy-raising image, and a specific image, in that order, when he practiced on his own. The *Invisible Ocean Scene* was also intended to revive any sexuality that he may have repressed out of guilt or abhorrence of getting a socially stigmatized sexually transmitted disease. I wanted Raymond to feel good about his sex drive and use that energy positively to heal himself. I also wanted him to love and feel good about himself. His sexuality was an inseparable part of him that could only be denied by his denying himself as well. Most of all, I wanted Raymond to be and love himself in his full expression. That included his sexuality.

After three days of practicing the *Invisible Ocean Scene* coupled with his specific image of knights and hamburger, Raymond said, "I like this visualization. It gives me an alignment, a reconciliation between mental, spiritual, and emotional. I need that. It reduces the stress of my job, which is life in the fast lane, and it gets rid of a lot of anger. My brothers haven't been very supportive of my illness. One of them, whom I've financially supported for the last twenty years, took it as a joke. When I told him I was going to write my will, he laughed. When I got angry, he said, 'Everyone needs comic relief.' He says my being gay is 'not natural.' My mother is dead and my father remarried to a religious reactionary woman that I can't get along with. I can't even tell him that I'm sick. I have something everyone looks down on and that can lead to a schizophrenic life. It's important to not be afraid and hide and lead a double life. The imagery raises my energy, boosts my self-image, and makes me more forgiving." Raymond is still in therapy with me at the time I am writing this.

Creativity

It should not come as a surprise to you that raising sex energy, the creative force of life, increases your own creative powers. Melody, a thirty-two-year-old screenwriter, complained to me of writer's block. "I haven't been able to write a thing in months," she said. "It's like I've dried up. Nothing comes to mind. Ideas used to just pour out of me. I couldn't even get dressed or cook dinner without having to stop a dozen times to jot hot new ideas down. My mind was filled with new projects, story lines, character developments, dramatic structures."

"How's your sex life?" I inquired. "Not too good," she admitted. "I've been seeing someone for six months. The sex was fantastic at first but now it's wham, bam, thank you ma'am. He's got me so frustrated I haven't had a period in three months. It's easier just not to feel anything at all than to get excited only to be left hanging." Melody was repressing her sex energy rather than deal with sexual frustration. Unfortunately the price she paid was a damming up of her creativity which manifested itself in writer's block. Soon after our first session together she left the man she had been seeing, but her block remained.

I asked Melody to practice the *Invisible Ocean Scene* to raise her sex energy and free the creative force within her. A week later she reported, "I had my period the day I started practicing. It's all come back, that great flood of ideas that used to make me so mad because it interfered with my getting other things done. I'm so happy. I appreciate those thoughts a whole lot more now. I'm writing up a storm." If you wish to increase your creativity, try raising and channeling your sex energy using the *Invisible Ocean Scene* as Melody did. Sex energy often manifests in artistic expression. My asking you to experience an orgasm in your head is no small request, but it will become easier with practice. The important thing is that you try. Sooner or later the positive sensations that you are striving for will become a reality.

Rio Scene

The *Rio Scene* gives you a necessary breather from the intensity of your creating and transferring sex energy. In addition to learning to shut out taste and density from your reality, you gain from this image an emotional understanding of the limitations of your five senses and the relativity of your perception.

You cannot see all of the ocean. If it were only half its size it would still *appear* as large to you. Past a certain point, your vision cannot pick up on an increase in size, unless of course the object is moved farther away from you. Therefore, while a sand castle appears to grow larger and larger as you shrink, the ocean cannot appear any larger than it already is, further demonstrating the limitations of your senses and relativity of your perception.

Rio Scene

You are wearing a black bathing suit, walking along a great stretch of white, sandy beach in Rio de Janeiro. Behind you is Sugar Loaf Mountain. The sun is hot white, the water sparkling turquoise, the palms deep emerald green. Smell the salt in the air. It's one hundred degrees above zero. Hot. Heat waves rise and shimmer like spirits off the sand.

A block of fine sand extends to the water. Run through the hot, deep sand toward the water. Faster . . . faster . . . Hit the water. It offers no resistance. It has no density. It feels like cool, wet turquoise air. Run straight out till you are over your head. Hold your breath. Walk back to neck-deep water. You are surrounded by brilliant illuminated turquoise. Feel wet and cool. Drink. It feels like a mouthful of cool, wet air. There is no taste, but it smells very salty.

Walk back to the beach. Sit by the water's side. Begin to build a sand castle, a great castle with turrets, towers, and a moat. The water laps against the sand but the castle remains as the water offers no resistance. Build the castle way out into the water. The sun is getting warmer. Your skin is getting hotter and hotter.

Now the castle appears to be getting larger, growing. You are shrinking . . . getting smaller . . . and smaller . . . and smaller. The sand castle is miles up into the sky. A rivulet of sea water trickles through one of the sand walls forming a moat of turquoise around the castle. Walk through the moat. It feels like moist blue-green air.

Climb sand stairs to a tower. The sea looks the same. There are no waves. The water is still. The sea sounds the same. The sea smells the same. Only the sand castle has changed by your diminishing size. Sleep in a tower of sand by a sea of turquoise.

Reactions

Removing senses and properties continues to make your imagery more vivid. "It's unbelievable what it does," said Malcolm, a forty-year-old restaurant manager. "It's like magic. That was fabulous. Going through turquoise water was the most vivid imagery experience I've had so far." Many people also react to this image with feelings of peace and serenity. "I went back up in that tower," said Marilyn, a twenty-one-year-old secretary. "That's where I felt most peaceful, in that tower. Glassy, very glassy water, and very smooth. No ripples, no waves." Imagining vast bodies of still water often produces a calming effect.

"My logic says that if I shrink, the sea will look larger," said Brian, a thirty-two-year-old real estate broker. "But in the image it didn't. It made me realize how limited my perception really is." Everything is relative. In this case, the size of the castle is relative to the size of you, the perceiver. As you shrink, the castle appears larger. However, it is not possible for the sea to seem larger to you as it is already out of your range of perception.

Benefits

Practicing the *Rio Scene* puts you more in the sensory moment. Cora, a forty-eight-year-old private duty nurse, was worried that her attention was becoming too scattered to carry on her work responsibly. "I'm too preoccupied," she said. "My mind is continually tripping over trivia, thinking about something I read in the paper, a TV show I watched the other night, things I have to do. I'm so busy with that stuff I don't pay attention to what I am doing. I forget if I gave a medication, made up a bed, or even fixed a meal." After practicing the *Rio Scene,* she said, "Everything is right now. Everything I do at work, I'm in it, not thinking of the next thing I'll be doing.

That imagery helped me sense the world, not just see it."

Even though taste and density are the sense and property you learn to negatively hallucinate in the *Rio Scene,* your learning to tune out these facets of reality helps you to tune out additional ones. Therefore the benefits you realize from practicing the *Rio Scene* may involve your increased capacity to remove other components from reality as well. Alicia, a forty-two-year-old hairdresser, smoked over three packs a day for the past twenty years. Her system was so clogged from this habit that she could actually blow smoke from her lungs without a cigarette and her tongue had a constant white coating. She had chronic chest pain and neuropathy, numb fingers that looked pinched at the ends as if she'd kept them in water too long, the result of nicotine constricting her capillaries and draining blood from her extremities. When awakening in the morning she couldn't breathe and felt she was suffocating. Food had completely lost its taste. Worst of all, there was a persistent sore spot in her throat that had her worried that her tissues were diseased.

"I smoke at work when I'm stressed out or bored," she said. "My difficult clients make me want to smoke the most. The one I had yesterday drove me crazy. From one o'clock to five her mouth didn't stop. You know how when some people talk so much your ears start to thump? That's when I have to leave. I've always been a social smoker, smoking with my customers when they ask me to join them. Sometimes I think it's a subconscious suicide trip. I'm not getting anywhere financially. I have no car. If I hadn't gotten five numbers in the lotto, I wouldn't have been able to pay my rent. I'm always thinking about smoking. The urge never lets up."

I gave Alicia the *Rio Scene* and added the following affirmation at the end: "Just as you can tune out taste and density from water, you can tune out the urge to smoke. You are a nonsmoker." A week later Alicia reported a drastic reduction in her smoking; she hadn't had a single cigarette in three days. "When I first left your office," she said, "I had no desire to smoke at all. Then I saw my roommate smoke and I took a couple of puffs. It made me sick." That was the last time I saw

Alicia. She was through smoking. It's two sides to the same coin. Learning to negatively hallucinate one thing helps you negatively hallucinate another, including unwanted urges to smoke.

Boris, a fifty-year-old executive in the transportation industry, developed a severe phobia of flying from a traumatic incident that occurred on a flight to Miami. "I had the flu when I boarded the plane," he said. "I was taking antibiotics that I later learned I was allergic to, so I was already feeling poorly at the start of my trip. Although I flew first class, the plane wasn't a wide-body and I was upset at how small my seating compartment was. I would have had more room in coach. Also, the jet fumes in first class overload you more and that didn't help my flu and antibiotic allergy. I sat by the window and would have preferred an aisle seat because it gives you more space.

"The moment I heard the door shut, I wanted to fight my way out of that plane. I didn't care if I fell thirty thousand feet. Black spots started in front of my eyes. It started to get hot and I felt even more closed in. I thought, I can't breathe. I can't get out of here. I changed seats with the person on the aisle, trying to improve my situation, but I should have gotten off the plane the second those feelings began. Instead I kept trying to push the fear down. I kept taking deep breaths, but didn't feel like I was getting any oxygen. They gave me oxygen, but the walls still felt like they were closing in. I got nauseated. I put my head between my legs for the whole five-and-a-half-hour flight and didn't eat a thing. I was too sick to go to the meeting when I got to Miami and I made my wife fly to Miami to fly back to L.A. with me. I wouldn't do it alone, and even with her I'd only go on a wide-body. That's a pretty serious restriction if you have to do as much flying as I do. That was over a year ago and I've been afraid to fly ever since."

After giving Boris the *Rio Scene,* I suggested, "If you can tune out water, you can tune out an airplane. You fly easily, effortlessly, in a deep state of relaxation. You love to fly. The thought of it makes you happy." Boris taped his image and affirmations and practiced them for a month before making a plane trip to New York. He took a cassette recorder on the plane with him and listened through an earpiece during his flight. "I was so calm," he reported later. "Nothing bothered me. I was oblivious to everything. I could just as well have been home in bed for all I knew."

Since the *Rio Scene* ends with your sleeping in a tower of sand by a sea of turquoise, it's excellent for eliminating insomnia. Milton, thirty, had the pressure of working two jobs, as an advertising analyst by day and a musician at night, in order to get himself out of heavy debt incurred from his wife's medical expenses. "I can't afford not to sleep," he said. "When you work sixteen-hour days, every moment is precious. It's not like I can take a catnap the next afternoon to make up for lost sleep. But it seems like the more I try to fall asleep, the more I toss and turn. Sometimes it's time to get up before I've even dozed off."

After practicing the *Rio Scene* for a week Milton reported, "It's great. The image merges right into sleep. I recorded it on tape without the three count to bring me out. Usually I'm drifting off before I even get to the end where the sleep suggestion is." If you have trouble sleeping, do as Milton and tape the *Rio Scene* leaving out counting to three to end the image. You'll find your image will blend into deep, restful sleep and you'll awaken more refreshed than you would normally.

Imagining yourself shrinking down to a tiny size is also an excellent technique for weight control. Bernie, a forty-two-year-old air-traffic controller, needed to lose eighty pounds. "I just can't imagine being thin," he said. "All my life I've had a weight problem. I remember my mother had me on diets when I was still learning to talk. The thinnest I ever got was my senior year in high school when I got down to just a hair under two hundred pounds. Hardly anyone even noticed the difference. It was discouraging. Finally I just gave up and worked at accepting myself as heavy. But now my doctor says I need to take off weight for health reasons. I've got high blood pressure and the excess baggage is putting too much stress on my heart."

Bernie's problem was that he couldn't conceive of himself

weighing less than he did. I asked him to practice the *Rio Scene* in order to change that misconception, to gain the facility to think of himself as *much* smaller. Sometimes it helps to exaggerate your image of the effect you are after. Rather than simply imagining his weighing 80 pounds less, he was going to envision himself nearly 230 pounds less, the size of a thimble! Bernie practiced the *Rio Scene* diligently, at least twice a day, and he began losing weight. In a year and a half he was down to 150 pounds. "It was all a matter of my self-image," he said. "Amazing. As I kept focusing on myself as small, actually tiny, my body began to match the image I was creating. There was no need to keep eating so much, because this tiny body I kept thinking of didn't need it." Conceiving of yourself as weighing less is a major part of the battle for weight control.

Banquet Hall Scene

After taking a breather with the *Rio Scene,* you return to directly raising sex energy. You will learn to transfer the orgastic sensation and sex energy to your legs and feet in the *Banquet Hall Scene,* along with negatively hallucinating taste and gravity.

Banquet Hall Scene

You are looking out over a moonlit garden of trimmed hedges in a mazelike pattern from a large mirrored banquet hall. Twenty sparkling chandeliers hang from the ceiling. Before you stretches a marble table on which twenty glistening silver candelabras burn slim white candles. Smell the wax. Between the candles are silver vases of deep red roses. A rose fragrance mixes with the burning wax. The entire setting is reflected in the mirrored ceiling, walls, and floor. Shimmering fire and crystal.

In front of you is a crystal goblet of ruby-red wine. Smell the sweetness of the wine. Drink. It has no taste. It feels wet. Open your mouth to take another sip. The wine that you have already drunk floats back out of your stomach, out of your mouth, and through the air to the mirrored ceiling. Take a wine bottle and pour more. The wine goes up rather than down, rising to the ceiling. It knows no law of gravity.

Leave the banquet hall. Walk out onto a balcony over a pool on which silver swans glide in the moonlight among waxy purple water lilies. Take off your clothes. Jump headfirst from the balcony into the pool with a great, loud splash. The water continues going up forever, sparkling in the moonlight.

Suddenly hear the sound of splashing behind you. A beautiful man/woman [sex to which you are attracted] is swimming toward you, his/her wet skin glistening in the moonlight. His/her body is slim, supple, firm. Float on your back in the water. He/she begins caressing your feet and legs, rubbing . . . massaging. Feet and legs are getting warmer . . . throbbing . . . pulsating . . . pressure is building. They feel like they will burst. There's an overwhelming sexual frenzy in your legs. The genital area is cool. The pressure and congestion builds to a fever pitch. Higher. Higher. Your legs and feet climax! Swoon and float in the man's/woman's arms. The swans encircle you. You drift. You float. You dream, buoyant in your lover's arms.

Reactions

"If I move them, will they work?" Sam, a sixty-two-year-old dentist working on stress management and physical fitness, asked me about his legs after doing the *Banquet Hall Scene.* "That's weird. Funny I couldn't get that close with the head. My legs are still warm and tingling, like unbelievable. Is that part of it?"

A rush of blood to your legs and consequent tingling is definitely a part of what you also will experience from this image. On getting up from the couch, Sam gulped, "My legs feel very light, there's a spring to my walk. I feel limber at the joints, knees, and ankles. This image will be great for my tennis game." After Sam left my office, I stood at my window, watching him walk to his car. He unquestionably had added a spring to his gait. He walked like he was thirty years younger.

While your legs will almost always feel lighter when you walk on them, as Sam's did after the *Banquet Hall Scene,* they often feel swollen and/or heavier while you are still lying down, before you move them. "I'm so relaxed," said Janet, a thirty-year-old wife and mother. "My legs swelled up. I actually felt the climax in my head on the last image." "I can understand in the head, but in the legs?" said Frank, forty, a bartender. "They said 'What?' They felt heavy and warm." On occasion your leg muscles will actually contract. "My legs, I felt them spasm," said Leonard, a forty-eight-year-old dermatologist.

Even though you are focusing on your legs in the *Banquet Hall Scene,* you may experience pulsations, tinglings, and ticklings in other parts of your body as well as you generate more sex energy. "I was drifting," said Sharon, fifty. "My hands were pulsating again." "My fingers fell asleep," said Raymond. "The companion was the most vivid part of the image."

The intensity and automaticity of your response to this image may surprise you. "It was like I was sitting watching my body respond," said Marcia, a twenty-eight-year-old hairstylist. "Like I was sitting on the side watching it happen. Wild!"

You will begin to actually sense your rising sex energy. Murray, fifty-eight, a choreographer, sensed it as "a tickling inside my brain. It was a very pleasant feeling. A tickling of my scalp. It was a very ecstatic feeling, a feeling I usually have when I'm observing someone doing something or when they're explaining something to me. Little ants walking under my scalp, but very pleasant. It goes along with a certain state of being. Being relaxed, observant, floaty feeling. It's rare. I probably never experience it normally more than once every six months. My concentration is focused, my attention outwardly directed. There's no chatter in my mind." However you sense your growing sex energy, whether as a tickling in your scalp like Murray, yellow light like Chad, or throbbing pulsations throughout your body like many of my other patients, these phenomena are always associated with a feeling of pure, ecstatic, effortless concentration.

Benefits

You will find that raising sex energy will energize and potentiate any image for a specific problem that you are working on. Do the *Banquet Hall Scene* directly before your specific image, as I taught Raymond to·do with the *Invisible Ocean Scene* before his specific image for AIDS, and you'll discover your specific image is stronger, more real, more powerful. It should be. You went into it with more energy, the energy you generated first with the *Banquet Hall Scene*. Raymond reported, "I'm getting the image of the hamburger down a lot better now that I'm practicing the *Banquet Hall Scene*." Just as he'd done with the *Invisible Ocean Scene,* he was now practicing the *Banquet Hall Scene* and his *White Knights and Hamburger Scene* back to back, using the first to charge the second.

Like Sam, you will also feel lighter, more limber in your joints, knees, and ankles. There'll be a spring in your walk and you'll feel years younger. Suzie, sixty-eight, married to Kap, a retired seventy-two-year-old clothing merchant, suffered extensive damage to her right leg when Kap turned their car in front of another vehicle, running both cars off the road. Kap came out all right, but after several operations, including a knee and hip replacement, Suzie still had pain throughout her leg from her toes to her hip. The leg was stiff and hard to move, necessitating her using a cane or walker whenever she went out. The doctors who had performed her operations termed them a success and couldn't understand why Suzie still had so much trouble. Their only diagnosis was "nerve damage." "As if the pain weren't bad enough," Suzie said, "this accident has turned me into an invalid. I used to get out and play poker with the girls at least four times a week. Now all I do is sit. It's taken all the joy out of living."

As Suzie practiced the *Banquet Hall Scene* she started getting the results she wanted. "At first all I got was a little extra pep," she said. "Then, after about two weeks, I noticed my leg felt kind of like the joint had been oiled. It's a funny way to describe it, but there was a greasy feeling. My leg moved easier and it didn't hurt as much. I stopped clopping around too. I was nimbler on my feet. Imagining my leg climax really loosened it up."

Cal, a twenty-year-old college student, found that practicing the *Banquet Hall Scene* vastly improved his game of beach volleyball. "Me and a friend of mine have been thinking of making the circuit," he said. "Beach volleyball is really coming into its own. You can make some good money in the competitions. My only problem has been my jump. I wasn't able to get enough height on the ball to slam it down the way you need to, to put your opponents out of the running. When I did the *Banquet Hall Scene* I thought my legs and feet were going to explode. Then I thought, Wouldn't it be great if I could get that same feeling every time I jumped for the ball? I'd blast into outer space. I tried experimenting. Every time I jumped I'd think of the sensation I'd created in my legs from my practicing at home—that pulsing, frenzied, hot explosion and sexual power. In time I was able to recall it. The results are phenomenal. I not only jump higher and faster, I have so much energy I intimidate the other side to death. They're *afraid* to beat me!"

Kerry, a twenty-six-year-old dancer, was bothered by outbreaks of a rash of small pimples on his legs which was especially bad on the tender insides of his thighs and in the groin area. The condition was exacerbated by sweat, and the strenuous exercise of his profession made the condition more pronounced. "It's even worse if I have to wear a tight-fitting costume," he said. "Something like wool leggings puts me away. I try to stay dry and avoid tight clothes, but when you're in a show you have to wear what they tell you. No one is going to hire you if you ask for costume approval. Most stars don't even get that."

Using the *Banquet Hall Scene,* Kerry was able to divert blood to his legs in sufficient quantities to dry his skin eruptions and nourish and heal his damaged skin. "My skin totally cleared up in less than a month," he said. "It's terrific! Even the problem areas like the inside of my legs near the crotch where the seams ride are blemish-free." If you have a dermatological problem, try imagining a sexual climax throughout the affected area. Recalling sexual arousal causes blood to congest in the area you are focusing upon, just as does your recalling heat, a technique you learned in Chapter 3. The increased blood concentration dries your lesions and provides nutrients to heal your skin.

Selma, a forty-one-year-old clerical worker, reported that channeling sex energy to her legs in the *Banquet Hall Scene* burned the fat causing her cellulite and made her thighs and calves more shapely. "No matter how much I exercised," she said, "I was never able to get rid of that crinkly cellulite at the back of my thighs near the buttocks or that excess fat on the side of my upper legs and around the hollows of my knee joints. When it began to disappear I couldn't believe my eyes. At first I couldn't figure out what was causing it, but then I realized, it was channeling all that energy in my legs. I do the *Banquet Hall Scene* every day now to keep my legs in shape."

Not only are there benefits to be had from channeling sex energy in the *Banquet Hall Scene;* imagining wine float back up out of your stomach as a function of your negatively hallucinating the effect of gravity can be used to successfully treat the purging or voluntarily induced vomiting associated with bulimia. Such a treatment strategy follows the law of reversed effect or paradoxical intention, whereby the harder you try to do one thing the more you do its opposite. In this case you affirm or imagine the opposite of what you want to happen.

For example, if you're having trouble becoming pregnant,

you might suggest to yourself, "I don't try to get pregnant. The harder I try, the less chance I have. I relax. Every time I have intercourse, I assume I cannot conceive." Similarly, if you bite your nails, you might suggest, "I can increase or decrease biting any nail I select to the degree that I think is necessary." Such an affirmation is intended to make nailbiting a routine and boring chore against which you will rebel.

In many cases of insomnia, the harder you try to fall asleep, the more you stay awake. Following the law of reversed effect, you can give yourself an affirmation such as, "I need to keep awake!" The harder you then try to remain awake, the more you tend to fall asleep. The law of reversed effect is used only in difficult cases where the strategy of imagining what you want to happen has failed. In these cases, imagining what you don't want may give you what you do. Imagining food rising out of your stomach may result in its staying in.

Maxine was a beautiful twenty-two-year-old girl who forced herself to throw up at least once every day. "I've had a weight problem ever since I was nine," she said. "Mother blew the importance of food way out of proportion. She lights up just at the mention of the word *beauty*. All she wants for me is to marry rich. She sees looks as a career to be used to the max or you're a failure. Most rich men are older and I'm not attracted to older men. Rich men seem to be interested *only* in looks and that creates more pressure. Then I get down on myself and eat more. From childhood on I can hear my mother saying, 'She's pretty, but she's overweight.' She'd always start out gushing about me and then kill it by referring to my weight. She got me into a TV commercial when I was eight. I was just a little overweight and my legs rubbed together. She apologized about it to everyone who ever saw the commercial.

"I see myself fat now no matter what I weigh. Throwing up is my only salvation. It really isn't hard to do. You know you're doing it right if the food you started with comes out, like if you started with a salad. I've tried laxatives too, instead of vomiting. I took thirty once. The food came out in chunks. Purging makes my face puffy and it alienates me from people.

It's driving my boyfriend, Carlo, crazy. Sometimes we'll go out to dinner and I'll binge and then go to the washroom to purge. I feel so bad for doing it I completely lose all sexual feelings and won't make love to him. I've tried to stop, but not eating makes me feel deprived. I eat enormous amounts of food in front of people, like a defiant child. Once I see the food, even if I resist at first, the thought of it sticks in my head. Resisting creates a need that builds. I just feel so bad because I can't control my bulimia."

I tried the common treatment stratagems with Maxine first. She was skipping breakfast, and I encouraged her to eat three meals a day *on schedule* to establish control of her eating behavior. Next I created a specific image for her in which she imagined eating a normal quantity of food, feeling relaxed, and not bingeing afterward. Two weeks later, Maxine was still purging daily. I recalled she had said that she ate defiantly, rebelling against the dictum to control her eating, and I reasoned that an image employing the law of reversed effect was in order. After two weeks of practicing the *Banquet Hall Scene,* Maxine was neither bingeing nor purging. She rebelled against the image of food rising out of her stomach by keeping it down in reality! If you find yourself thwarted by orthodox imagery techniques, try incorporating the law of reversed effect into your imagery. Try visualizing what you *don't* want. Out of sheer spite and rebellion you may find yourself manifesting the opposite.

Restaurant Scene

Your last image in this chapter, *Restaurant Scene,* gives you another necessary respite from the intensity of concentration required of you for generating and channeling sex energy. In it you learn to negatively hallucinate taste and centrifugal force.

Restaurant Scene

You are sitting at a table in a restaurant in Venice on a moonlit night looking over the canals. Sweet violin music filters through the night to the glow of candlelight. On your table is an immense basket of pink carnations. Smell them. Beside the carnations is a fresh loaf of bread, a platter of cheese, a glass of beer, and a bowl of crisp pretzels. Drink the beer. It has no taste, but feels cold and wet and smells like strong beer. Drink glass after glass, getting drunker and drunker, hungrier and hungrier. The room is spinning. Swirling candlelight and moonlight.

The music grows louder. Gaze at the intensity of the silver moonlight streaming in upon the stark white tablecloth. Your body is condensing. You are shrinking. Growing smaller . . . and smaller . . . and smaller . . . Grab the tablecloth. Crawl onto the table. You are three inches high. Walk to the cheese. Sniff the cheese. It smells strong and tangy. Eat. It tastes delicious. Crawl up on top of the cheese. It feels spongy against your body.

Jump from the cheese into the pretzel basket. Eat the pretzels. Taste their salty flavor. Crawl up to the highest pretzel. You are eye level with the beer glass. It's full to the rim with golden beer. Jump. Feel the beer. You are floating in it. Guzzle it. It has no taste, but feels cold and wet and quenches your thirst.

A man picks up the beer glass. He begins moving the glass rapidly in a circular motion. The beer does not fly off, away from its axis. You are surrounded by the smell, sound, and sight of sparkling, golden liquid.

Reactions

It always amazes me how easily most people are able to visualize these images, no matter how bizarre the requirements. "I was small, hungry, thirsty," said Candice, a thirty-four-year-old high school teacher. "Incredible how real the

room was. I was hoping I would be allowed to smell the carnations." "I was definitely relaxed," said Rob, thirty-one, a
newspaper journalist. "Most memorable was smelling the
flowers. I had a sharp sense of smell. There was a definite
sense of coldness to the beer."

Sometimes people come up with new techniques on their
own to make their imagery more vivid. "It was terrific being
three inches high," said Mac, a forty-two-year-old computer
programmer. "I see a brown tan haze with nothing. Then I
look through it to the scene. That way I can shut out everything but the scene."

Playing with senses and properties in imagery will alter
your sense of time, space, and motion in reality. "I was sleepy
and my eyes were crossing," said Gene, a thirty-year-old
stockbroker, describing his reaction to the *Restaurant Scene*.
"I came very slowly to wake. It was an effort to open my eyes.
I had no trouble at all getting down to three inches. When I
finally did manage to get my eyes open my depth perception
had changed. Your desk was farther away than it looked."
Gene had experienced space concentration, bringing reality
closer than it appeared normally.

Benefits

Learning to negatively hallucinate a sense and a property
in the *Restaurant Scene* prepares you to tune out anything
you wish in reality, including stressors that are giving you
anxiety. Gabe, a forty-year-old assistant director, was under
severe stress from the constant demands of his job. "I always
feel on the verge of exploding in anger," he said. "If someone
cuts me off in traffic I have an unreasonable response. I go
overboard. I get chest pains and stress headaches and take
aspirins at least five days a week to relieve the dull, aching
pounding. I expand my schedule to the limit trying to do
things and need better time management. I dread work. The
movie business is a blame-placing, pointing-the-finger, cover-
your-ass society. I live in constant fear of making a mistake,

feeling someone won't like me. I'm working with a director now who's very sarcastic and loves making a fool of you in front of a crowd. My productivity falls seventy percent when I have that kind of pressure and I crave sweets and chocolates. The sugar rush calms me down, but I need a better way to cope. I'm so wound up I don't know if the sun is shining."

I suggested that Gabe practice the *Restaurant Scene,* giving himself the following affirmation at the end, "If I can tune out taste and centrifugal force from water, I can tune out distracting stressors from my job. At work I respond only to things that make me feel better. I feel more and more relaxed in all situations, under all conditions." "I didn't realize that I had so much control over my environment," Gabe reported after two weeks of practice. "I just ignore the jerks now. If someone points the finger or tries to blame me and pass the buck it doesn't even register. I'm beyond and above all that now. I only take in what I want to. For the first time in my life I can finally relax."

Lorraine, a fifty-two-year-old divorced receptionist with two grown children, was having difficulty getting Abe, a divorced sixty-year-old semiretired businessman, out of her mind after deciding not to see him anymore because he wouldn't commit to seeing her more than twice a week after dating her nearly a year. "I'm too old and tired for this bullshit," she said. "I want more than just seeing a man a couple of times a week. I don't need marriage, but I do need a real relationship. I love Abe and he's a nice, decent, stimulating man. If he could just get past the jams of *love* and *relationship,* the L and R words.

"I had lunch with my friend Jean. She's been dating Seth, Abe's best friend, for ten years now, since she was thirty. She sees Seth twice a week for what I call 'food and fucking' and says she's happy, happy. She thinks of herself as miss sex queen, yet she hasn't so much as a toothbrush at Seth's house. If I were her I'd tell Seth, 'I've been with you ten years and want a baby. I'm leaving you, asshole!' Seth and Abe spend their Sundays at the Beach Club together with their other two friends, Paul and Casper, watching sports and bragging about how macho they are. They're a bunch of sixty-year-old jerky men who all had women who cared about them, but they refused to commit to them. They claim they're asserting their rights. 'No woman is going to make me marry her or have a commitment.' Great, now they're all alone except Seth, who's got Jean.

" 'You're the only fool that's stayed,' I told her, ' 'cause you're willing to put up with shit!' I told Abe, 'I know what I want and if I don't get it from you, trust me, I'll get it from someone else.' Jean said men don't like ultimatums and I said, 'So sue me!' I'd rather be out of a twice-a-week arrangement so I can find a better relationship. I know I could manipulate Abe into marriage in a year or two if I was willing to work that hard. I'm not. I finally told him, 'You know how you worry about me being so in love with you? I want you to know I love you as a friend. Our sexual connection is the best. But I don't have a need to spend the rest of my life with you.' When I take control of my life like that I always feel better, and I know I made the right decision. I'm just having trouble abiding by it. I think about Abe more than I should."

I suggested that Lorraine practice the *Restaurant Scene* and give herself the following affirmation at the end: "Just as I can tune out taste and centrifugal force from water, I can tune out all thoughts of Abe. I think only what I want to think, when I want to think it. My mind is clear, calm, and peaceful." Thoughts of Abe began decreasing as soon as Lorraine started her imagery and affirmations. A month later, she said, "I have him truly out of mind. Once in a while he'll still call or I'll see something that reminds me of him, but that's all there is to it. I don't dwell on it." For further suggestions on how to stop thinking about someone, I recommend my book *Breaking Free: 90 Ways to Leave Your Lover & Survive.*

You can also use the *Restaurant Scene,* with a slight modification, to end cravings for alcohol. Instead of imagining drinking the beer, envision yourself surrounded by the golden alcohol and resisting it effortlessly, having no desire to imbibe. For the beer in this image, you may substitute whatever alcoholic beverage you wish to turn off to. Clarissa, twenty-eight, accountant for a catering service, would pass out nearly every night after work from drinking vodka. "It turns my mind off," she said. "Dealing with figures all day gets to you after a while. The booze just erases it all and leaves my mind blank. It's a mental anesthetic. The problem is, my mind is still off in the morning when I have to go back to work. I've been written up twice this week for not balancing the company budget properly."

I suggested that Clarissa practice the *Restaurant Scene,* visualizing herself surrounded by clear vodka and having no desire to drink it. "It worked better than just imagining resisting a glass of vodka," she reported, "because it was so overwhelming. There was so much liquor, it was too much for me. I didn't want any." This strategy, called "implosion" or "flooding," in which you imagine effortlessly resisting an overwhelming amount of the substance you wish to turn off to, is often effective in eliminating urges for alcohol, drugs, cigarettes, or foods not on your diet. If your image of easily resisting your normal portion of the unwanted substance fails to get the results you desire, try conjuring an image in which you easily resist an enormous amount of the substance. Implosive imagery of this nature may well give you the results that you are after.

Time, Space, Motion, and Love

As you continue using the negative hallucination to clear your channels of perception, you will not only experience an alteration of your five primary senses, but of your time sense as well. Time distortion becomes increasingly prevalent as your images progress. After practicing the *Restaurant Scene,* Sarah, forty-three, bookkeeper for an electric company, said, "That time expansion sure works for filing sales slips. My fingers move faster than I can see the numbers. I'm also developing a great memory for details."

By the point in the imagery progression where Anne had finished practicing the *Restaurant Scene,* she had developed such control over her time sense that she no longer needed

an alarm clock. She would awaken whenever she had decided
to. She was also getting spontaneous, automatic time expansion to prolong pleasant experiences in her life. "I was having
a wonderful time in the shower one morning," she said, "and
was afraid I'd been in too long and used up all the hot water
for David. I was sure I'd taken at least half an hour. When I
got out, he thanked me. I'd only taken eight minutes! It was
incredible. I've had the revelation that there is no such thing
as time. I no longer work in that framework."

Anne had had her difficult periods as well, and I don't want
you to be disheartened if you feel you aren't getting the same
wonderful results. We all excel in different aspects at different
rates and times. She had reduced cigarette smoking consid-
erably, but was concerned with her not stopping totally. "I
still have trouble with the last eight or ten cigarettes a day,"
she said. "I feel like this habit is my last step in a grasp on a
total sense of freedom." Incredible as Anne's results with imagery had been, she still hadn't been able to stop smoking
using the imagery techniques that I'd taught her.

Although she was happy with her telepathic experience of
knowing David would be needed at work when he went off to
the lumberyard, a dream she'd had a day later revealed she har-
bored some subconscious conflict over the development of such
powers. "I dreamed I was Mother Superior," she said, "and you
were a young priest tempting me to leave the convent. The devil
was working through you to influence me and I couldn't trust
you. The devil can only lie." Our roles had reversed from her
dream before in which she was the sultry island siren trying to
lure me. She was eventually to work these conflicts out as evidenced by what she wrote in the manuscript I gave her regarding these incidents: "It's so lovely and warming to have these
extremes regarding you behind me."

However, at the time, her conflict over her still smoking,
her unresolved sexual attraction toward me, and her development of "occult" powers that were forbidden or looked down
on in many religious circles, was further exacerbated by the
difficulty she experienced in producing the sensation of orgasm in her head with the *Invisible Ocean Scene*. She dis-

cussed this frustration with David and they decided she was trying too hard to please me and should relax and let happen what will, which is always good advice. She continued progressing rapidly at a practical level, finding ever-new uses for imagery in her work. "Whenever I need to figure something out," she said, "such as a means of calibrating a chart or flow diagram, I flash on an image and my logic vastly improves."

Then she had a dream she was a prophet. "I was like Jeanne Dixon," she said, "all alone in the world because of my psychic powers." I reassured her that she was afraid of something that would never happen. Her growth had been beautiful and would continue to be so. I knew she was still angry with me, feeling I was pushing her and inflicting my will on her, an outgrowth of her frustration over new imagery demands.

The next week, Anne sent me a card apologizing for accusing me of pushing her. When I saw her I thanked her for the card. I explained that I understood her frustration and no apology was necessary. "I don't get short with anyone anymore but you," she smiled. "I didn't do as well with the *Rio Scene* as I might have because my anger allowed negative thoughts to creep into my mind. I think David sensed I was having a hard time, because he asked me about when I would be ending my therapy. 'You can't go on with this forever,' he said.

"I tried to explain to him that you can't think of therapy as having a time framework. 'The doctor is growing also,' I told him. 'As I grow I give him information so I can grow more. You can take imagery as far as you wish. The system, like growth, is infinite.'" Anne was right. I was growing along with her. The feedback she gave me as she experientially progressed through the images was invaluable to me for exploring and discovering new cosmic phenomena. I didn't want that to stop. Yet I knew the purpose of her therapy was freedom, not dependence. I would have to be able to let her go when she was ready.

"David's had to stop house-dreaming because of the money we spend on my therapy. To David, money spent on imagery is money for something that isn't tangible. He was poor growing up. That's why he's so money-conscious. He sees diminishing returns while I see myself growing faster. I get more out of it now than I did a couple of months ago. I have more to apply even though it may be less dramatic."

A week later, Anne reduced her sessions from twice to once a week for what she described as financial reasons. She was doing so well in her present job, where she'd been employed only six months, that she was receiving a raise. "In fact," she said, "the rumor in the grapevine is that I may be promoted to administrative secretary for something I was told I might get fired for doing. I covered the walls near my desk with posters of flowers and animals. One of the other secretaries warned me that my area didn't look very professional and that the division president who would be inspecting the premises soon wouldn't approve. I trusted my feelings. Not only did I leave the posters up, I added more. When the president inspected, he remarked on them, and I told him, 'I spend a lot of my life here.' I heard he later told my boss, 'That's quite a girl you've got there.' "

By the time Anne finished practicing the *Banquet Hall Scene,* she was rolling with the imagery progression again and no longer frustrated by its demands. "Now that I look back it's all so simple, clear, logical. Imagery works all the time without my even being cognizant of it. I've got the tingliest legs in town. I can't get over it. I was able to produce a throbbing, a glow, a warmth, a feeling of blood moving to the surface of my legs, emotional attachment, and release. I think of the sweet ache prior to culmination while experiencing the first three sensations. I found myself grinning on coming out of each practice session. Overall, my slipping moments are so short in comparison to my growth. When I'm low physically there may be a chink in my armor and I fall back to a more comfortable, less adaptive habit pattern, but the growth continues even during these weak times. Recognition of the slip alone brings me out."

After practicing the *Restaurant Scene,* Anne recounted, "The better I felt the shrinking, the faster the whirling dervish went. Like a time tunnel." The smaller Anne felt, the faster the funnel seemed to spin. Reducing your space, getting smaller, speeds up your sense of motion. Space concentration produces motion expansion. Subjective speed or velocity is relative to the size of the perceiver.

As you watch a marble roll across the floor, it appears to move at a given rate. If you were now to shrink to the size of the marble, it would seem to be moving much faster. At first glance the hour hand on your watch doesn't seem to be moving at all. If, however, you shrank to the size of an atom, the hour hand would appear to speed by. Conversely, if you were the size of a giant, straddling the country with one foot in the Pacific and the other in the Atlantic, an airplane going six hundred miles an hour would take five hours to go from your left leg to your right, the time it would take to cross the country. The plane would certainly not appear to you to be moving very fast. Motion, like time, is an illusion, a product of limited perception. The *Restaurant Scene* gives you an emotional understanding of this.

Space concentration, getting smaller, increases your sense of motion and *decreases* your sense of time. Objects move faster and time moves slower. Remember how when you were smaller, in the wonderful days of childhood, time went so much more slowly? Waiting for your parents to come home or for a school holiday was an eternity. Adulthood seemed a million years away. A golden afternoon during summer vacation seemed to last forever.

Your perception of time, space, and motion are inseparably interlinked. Concentrating space concentrates motion and expands time. The faster you go through space (motion concentration) the slower time goes. If you go faster than light, you go back in time. If you go the same speed as light, time stands still. There is no more time. Light knows no time. If you *were* light, there would be time no more. To navigate without your physical body you *become* light. To do this you transcend time. Revelation 10:6 states, "And swear . . . *that there should be time no longer* (emphasis added)."

In order to transcend time it helps to comprehend it. Time is often referred to as the fourth dimension. Few people stop to ask themselves, however, "The fourth dimension of what?" Time is the fourth dimension of *space*. You can better understand the fourth dimension by learning what is known about the first, second, and third dimensions. A geometric figure of no dimension is termed a point. The tracing of a point, or path it leaves when it passes, is a one-dimensional line. The tracing of a line is a two-dimensional surface. The tracing of a surface is a three-dimensional solid.

In all cases these tracings must be in a direction not contained within the figure. The tracing of a line moving lengthwise would only produce a longer line. The line must move sideways, in the direction of the second dimension, width, in order for its tracing to make a surface. Likewise, a surface must be moved in the third dimension, up or down, before its tracing forms a solid.

The Russian philosopher, P. Ouspensky, speaks of a "supersolid," the tracing of a solid in a direction not contained within it. This figure of the fourth dimension must move in a direction that is neither lengthwise, sideways, nor up and down. Such a direction is time. The tracing of a body in time is what Ouespensky terms a supersolid.

If you were standing in front of a mountain in a two-dimensional world you would only see that mountain. You could cross the mountain and see the other side, but you could never see both sides of the mountain at the same time. If, however, you were then allowed access to the third dimension, depth, you could rise above the mountain and see both sides at the same time. Likewise, if you were now able to gain mastery of the fourth dimension, time, you would be able to see past, present, and future simultaneously. They would all exist *now,* just as both sides of the mountain exist *now* even though you may be aware of only one side at a time due to your limited vantage point. Paul, in his Epistle to the Ephesians 3:17–18, states, "That ye, being rooted and grounded in *love* may be able to *comprehend* with all *saints* what *is* the *breadth, and length, and depth, and height* (emphasis added)." Love is the force that enables you to scale the dimensions. Beyond time, space, and motion is love. Pure energy is love. God is love.

The pure energy of light is a supersolid. Height, width, depth, and time are contained within it. To attain light you must be grounded in the pure energy of love.

ten

Power

Y ou *are* the light. You *are* the energy. You *are* the power.
In the ancient tradition of the Hindu discipline of Tan-
tra, you will transcend the duality of masculine and
feminine, Shiva and Shakti, in the full realization that there
is only one energy—you.

Three images, *Cherry Orchard Scene, Marble Quarry
Scene,* and *Squirt Gun Scene,* will help you culminate the
channeling of your sex energy to reach new levels of power
for healing and accessing higher knowledge. You raise energy
without intermission now, building powerful momentum.

Continuing to use the negative hallucination as a vehicle for clearing your sensory channels, you will learn to combine your increasing clarity of thought with the creation of orgastic energy and sensation in your arms and hands, trunk, and finally your total body. Your result will be a surge of energy like you've never felt before, a burst of power that will take you into a new and higher dimension of your consciousness—a realm of limitless possibilities.

Cherry Orchard Scene

The *Cherry Orchard Scene*, in which you learn to simultaneously negatively hallucinate taste and inertia, teaches you to create sex energy throughout your arms and hands. You build power to such intensity that the aftermath is a sense of total freedom and relaxation.

Cherry Orchard Scene

It's a beautiful summer day. Miles of bright green cornfields stretch before you. Behind you is a pasture where cows and sheep are grazing. You are in the midst of a wild cherry orchard. Wildflowers abound, daisies, tiger lilies, forget-me-nots. Butterflies dart among the blossoms. Pick the plump, bright red cherries. Squeeze them in your hand. Sniff the sweet-sour cherry juice. Lick your hand. The juice is tasteless. Take a fistful of cherries. Squeeze them tightly. The juice squirts out in all directions and keeps traveling till it hits the ground, the trees, or the sky. Bite into a big red cherry. The juice squirts straight ahead, never stopping till it hits a cow. Keep eating and squirting the cherry juice, aiming at the cows. One cow is now white with pink polka dots.

Leave the orchard. Walk through the corn. Come out into a meadow where sheep are grazing. Mount the back of a fluffy white sheep. He takes you to a lake surrounded by silver poplar trees, glistening in the sun, shimmering in the breeze. Drink

*the lake water. It is clear and cool. It has no taste. Frolic with
the sheep, splashing water at each other. The water stays in
motion till it hits an object, traveling great distances through
the air, some of it going to the sun. The lake water moves
spontaneously in all directions. It carries you out, in, and
sideways. The sheep float one way past you as you go another.
Cows and ducks join you, all floating in different directions.
The water carries you across the lake to a big red barn.*

*Go into the barn. Lie in the hay with the sheep. A beautiful
man/woman [sex to which you are attracted] comes down the
ladder from the hayloft. He/she slowly undresses you. Standing above your naked body, he/she begins stripping off his/
her own clothes. He/she kneels behind you, pulling your back
to his/her hot, heaving chest. He/she begins running his/her
hands up and down your arms. Blood flows to your arms. They
are flushed, vibrant, glowing, pulsating, pounding. Your
arms are beating, growing larger on each beat . . . larger . . .
and larger . . . and larger . . . they climax! . . . Your two bodies
mesh in the hay. You sleep entwined in each other's arms with
the sheep around you.*

Reactions

The *Cherry Orchard Scene* is a good image to have fun
with, and people often respond with healing, endorphin-re-
leasing humor. "Squirting cows with cherries almost made
me laugh," said Greg, a nineteen-year-old college student.
"There are all kinds of cows in South Dakota where I visited
last year. They make funny noises." "I burst out laughing at
the three count," said Rachel, a forty-year-old mother and
homemaker. "I was wondering what was going to happen with
the sheep. It reminded me of Gene Wilder in the movie *Everything You Always Wanted to Know about Sex*."

A strong response of heat and pulsation in the arms can
be expected. "I felt a flush in the back of my arms," Greg also
reported. "I'm very relaxed," smiled Martha, thirty-three, secretary for a manufacturing firm. "I have to get up, but it'll be
an effort. My breathing was labored and excited during the

arms part. I was also aware of the genitals, but I felt quite a bit more in my arms. I can still feel it. There's a relaxed sort of feeling through the body. The heaviness is still there." "My arms were pulsating so much they hurt," said John, thirty-nine, an automotive mechanic. "In and out, that's what my arms are doing now," laughed Sharon, a thirty-one-year-old aerobics instructor.

Feelings of numbness in your other extremities may be even more pronounced than they normally are after practicing hypnotic imagery, because your recalling a sexual climax in your arms diverts blood to this area with resultant feelings of anesthesia in the body areas the blood has left. "I could feel the hot sexual energy," said Mark, a twenty-four-year-old TV repairman. "And my legs really fell asleep this time. They felt like bricks." "I have no headaches anymore," said Carol, a thirty-four-year-old cook for the public school system. "The temperature in both my arms has risen. That's the warmest they've ever gotten. I did well transferring the feeling."

Benefits

Diverting blood from your head to your arms as Carol did while using the *Cherry Orchard Scene* is an excellent technique for eliminating headaches.

Like Martha, you'll also be able to use this image to create a deep sense of relaxation. Hal, a twenty-two-year-old computer programmer trying to get over a case of "nerves," said, "That was neat. I feel wiped out, like a dishrag. Nothing is really working too good. I can't move a thing. It's great. I haven't a care in the world."

You will find that you are more focused when your sex energy is high. Luke, a twenty-seven-year-old car dealer, reported the following benefits from practicing the *Cherry Orchard Scene:* "For the first time in my life I'm 'really there' at work. My boss told me customers had been complaining that I wasn't really listening to their needs when I was trying to sell them a car. You know they say that to be a good salesman

you have to 'find a need and satisfy it.' Well I was too scattered
to even know what my customers wanted, let alone how to
give it to them. Now I'm grounded. My energy is high and
focused. I hear what people ask for and I act on it!"

More specifically, channeling sex energy to your arms
gives them added fluidity and power. This can help you in any
areas where you need added strength, from taking out the
garbage to lifting an overturned motorcycle to free an accident
victim. Lew, a twenty-one-year-old pitcher, wanted to make it
from the bush leagues to the majors. "My arm just doesn't
pack enough wallop," he said. "I don't want the batter even to
see the ball when I pitch. I want to throw hard, fast, and easy."

I encouraged Lew to practice the *Cherry Orchard Scene*
and a week later he recounted, "I can't believe how much that
image loosened my arms up. I recall that woman massaging
my arms when I'm winding up to throw, and I'm on fire! A
regular piston. I let loose with enough energy to bust the damn
bat right in half. When my teammates say I'm 'hot,' they don't
know how true that statement really is." Raising sex energy
and channeling it to his throwing arm gave Lew the added
punch he needed. He made it to the major leagues the following year.

Cathy, a twenty-six-year-old waitress, cut her fingers in
the meat slicer and required surgical repair. Her doctors called
the operation a success, but Cathy wasn't satisfied. "My fingers
are so stiff," she said. "They're hard to move. I can only do
gross movements. I can't do fine work like sewing or needle-
point. Sometimes I have trouble writing up my orders. I can't
seem to make the pen do what I want it to. I guess I should
at least be glad I don't have any pain like some people do after
these operations."

I started Cathy practicing on the *Cherry Orchard Scene,*
and in a couple of weeks she reported, "My fingers are actually
getting more nimble. That hot, throbbing sensation I'm able
to create by imagining a climax in my hands makes them more
alive. It's like they're reviving, getting their old feeling back.
My writing has gotten a lot better. I've even started to crochet
again." If you experience stiffness in your hands and arms

for any reason, try using the *Cherry Orchard Scene* to channel sex energy to the troubled area to revitalize it.

I'd worked with Brittany, a thirty-two-year-old representative for a pharmaceutical company, helping her lose thirty pounds. She was delighted with her weight loss, having reached what she considered her perfect weight, one hundred ten pounds. Her only remaining complaint was the loose skin on the underside of her arms. "I just can't seem to get rid of the flab under my arms," she said. "No matter how much weight I lose or how much I exercise it's still there. It jiggles like Jell-O every time I reach for something. I'm tired of having to wear long sleeves to cover it up."

The triceps is an area that many people, especially women, have trouble keeping firm. It is particularly difficult to tone after a weight loss, and one of the last areas to lose fat from dieting. I suggested that Brittany practice the *Cherry Orchard Scene* to direct sex energy to that part of her body. The energy would serve to burn off remaining adipose tissue as well as charge the muscles to tone them. Brittany found the sex-energy transfer easy to do, and within three weeks the flab around her upper arms started to disappear. "I can tell when I'm doing well," she said. "If I really concentrate and get my arms to flush and feel warm I can feel them start to firm up in a few days. It's terrific. It's the only thing I've tried that I've been able to get rid of arm flab."

Sex energy is not only good for burning excess fat and getting rid of flab, you can use it to build muscle as well, in the same way that any electrical stimulation increases muscle mass. Chet, a sixteen-year-old junior in high school, was depressed over his not being able to get a girlfriend. His self-image was low and he was beginning to withdraw from school activities. "What's the use?" he said. "Why go out at all? No girl will even look at me. I'm so puny. I tried lifting weights, but nothing happened. Maybe I should try steroids."

I knew that having a better body wouldn't be the answer to all of Chet's problems, but it might make him feel better about himself and it was worth a try. "I know something better than steroids," I told him. "Sex energy." Chet looked at me like I was crazy at first, but when I explained to him how diverting this powerful, primal energy to his biceps, triceps, and forearms could stimulate these muscles and increase their mass, he quickly became interested. I suggested that he start with the *Cherry Orchard Scene,* because he was especially concerned over developing what he called his "string bean" arms. In two weeks Chet started to notice a difference. "I'm doing curls with free weights to develop my arms," he said. "I can tell they're getting stronger. I'm able to do more reps and I'm adding weight. I wasn't able to get anywhere with this exercise before."

If you also want to work on developing your leg muscles, you can use the *Banquet Hall Scene.* To add mass to chest, stomach, and back muscles, your next image, the *Marble Quarry Scene,* is indicated. You should do the images in conjunction with weight or other exercises designed to develop your muscles, as Chet did. The sex energy potentiates the effects of the physical exercise. Most people prefer to do the imagery right before the weight training. Some actually create the image simultaneously with the exercise, although this takes excellent concentration. Experiment and see what works best for you.

You can also use sex energy for the healing of wounds. Joe, a forty-two-year-old gardener, was thinking of giving up his occupation because of continual infections in his arms and hands. "I try to wear gloves and long sleeves whenever I can," he said, "but I keep getting banged up anyway. The skin on my arms and hands is a mess of cuts and lacerations from thorns, and weeds, and scrapes. It's an occupational hazard, but it didn't use to bother me. I seem to be getting more sensitive. I bruise more easily and am more prone to infections. It seems like I'm always having trouble with a sore healing somewhere."

I advised Joe to practice the *Cherry Orchard Scene,* raising sex energy and channeling it to his arms and hands to promote healing. Diverting blood to those body parts would also help clean his cuts and prevent infection. "It's great," he reported. "I do the image at the end of each workday. I can feel the energy around the cuts. Sometimes my arms flush. So far I've stayed almost infection-free. I may not have to give up gardening after all." For directing cleansing, nourishing blood and healing energy to wounds, practice the *Invisible Ocean* (head), *Banquet Hall* (legs), and *Cherry Orchard* (hands and arms) scenes, or the upcoming *Marble Quarry Scene* (trunk), depending upon which part of your body is affected.

Using Expanded Senses to Recall Your Past

Your negatively hallucinating senses and properties continues to have the effect of heightening those remaining. Anne described how her sense of smell expanded as a function of her practicing the *Cherry Orchard Scene:* "The images are finally just fun. I'm not pushing anymore . . . finally! And they're becoming more real. At no point in my last image did I realize I was in your office. They even helped me immensely to enjoy the thundershower last night. I had a ball running through the water and rolling in the wet grass. David kidded me. 'You and your age regression,' he said. He thinks I'm acting more like a child every day and he's right. I love it!

"What was surprising was how acute my sense of smell was during the rainstorm. The smell of wet asphalt was so poignant it triggered many old memories. I went right into the house, put myself into hypnosis while holding the asphalt smell in my immediate memory, and used it to bring back all memories associated with wet cement or pavement. I vividly recalled a washtub in my parents' cabin. I was two years old, wearing white, rubberized pants. Then I remembered that I'd won the cutest-baby-of-the-year contest sponsored by the *Los Angeles Times*. The picture of myself, 'carrot top,' sporting red ringlets and sitting in a garden eating petunias, flashed clearly before me." You can use any vivid specific sensation such as the smell of wet asphalt to trigger sensational associations and exhume your memory bank.

Hattie, a twenty-two-year-old nightclub dancer, was accused of killing a man, a stranger she'd never seen before, with a gun in a bar two blocks from the club where she worked. Her mind was blank for the entire evening. Her trial was coming up soon and she needed to remember the evening's events in order to prepare her case. "I don't even remember going into that damned place," she said, "let alone shooting someone. The bartender swears I did it, though. Last thing I remember of that night, I had just gotten off work and was heading west in my truck. I can still feel the touch of my red velvet dress against my back."

I asked Hattie to perform an exercise that you can do too if you want to work directly on heightening your awareness in a specific sense modality. I asked her to devote five minutes a day to focusing only on her sense of touch. You expand a sense by directing your attention to it. Once Hattie was more aware of touch in reality, she was able to imagine it more vividly. The strongest and most recent sensations are the easiest to recall. I wanted Hattie to recall her memory of red velvet on the night of the murder as vividly as possible so that it would trigger further associations she had for that evening.

After Hattie spent five minutes a day for a week focusing on touch, I put her into a hypnotic state and painted an image for her of what happened up to her last memory, the touch of red velvet. "Gravel," she said. "I see gravel, and headlights. It's a parking lot. I'm parking my truck. There's a bar. A saloon-type swinging door. Oh my God! The guy at the bar's got a gun. He's laughing. He puts it on the bar and motions for me to come over. I don't want to, but I do. He buys me a drink. Now I've got the gun. I don't know why. I think he dared me to pick it up. I'm scared to death of guns. Oooh . . ."

Hattie began to shake and cry. I said nothing, waiting for her to go on. "The gun went off. It hit him. I'm out of there." I brought Hattie back. There was no need for her to experience any more of that unpleasant event. We had the data we needed. The shooting was self-defense. Although Hattie still had to prove her innocence, this knowledge, when told to the only witness, the bartender, changed his testimony. He had not, as he formerly thought, seen Hattie draw the gun and fire. He turned at the sound of the shot and saw Hattie holding the

gun. Her story was plausible, and by building her case around
it, she was acquitted. She was saved by a slender thread, her
memory of the touch of red velvet.

The memory of a sound got Hank, a twenty-three-year-old
medical student, a $400,000 settlement in a personal-injury
case. Hank and his family were vacationing in Canada when
they were in a bad automobile accident. He, his mother, father,
and sister were all badly injured. None of them could remember anything about the details of the accident. They had no
idea how it had happened. All the police report said was that
Hank was driving, the car had hit some markers on a left
curve, turned over, and landed upside-down on the other side
of the road.

Hank's last memory was a loud popping sound. As I did
with Hattie, I asked him to spend five minutes a day for a week
focusing on one particular sense. In Hank's case the sense was
hearing. This exercise expanded his awareness of sound so
that he could recall it more vividly. Then I hypnotized him
and conjured an image vivid in every detail of his last memory, the loud popping sound. "Shaking," he said. "The whole
car's shaking. I've got to make that curve. It's pulling me to
the right. The whole back of the car just dropped. There's a
grating sound like metal dragging." Then Hank's face whit-
ened and his eyes teared. "My mother is looking at me so
strange. She's upside-down." According to Hank's recall, the
tire had blown and the wheel had come off the axle. The tires
and the car were new, and he sued the makers of both. Hank's
hypnotic recall was not proof per se, but it provided enough
information to establish material proof.

Bree, a forty-eight-year-old real estate broker, was saved
from a charge of involuntary manslaughter by an expanded
taste that triggered the associations her conscious mind had
not been able to grasp. She had collided with another car in
an intersection, and the other driver had died instantly. She
insisted her light was green, but two witnesses reported
seeing a car that fit the description of the one she was driving
run two red lights less than a mile away from the scene of the

accident, going nearly twice the speed limit. Bree remembered leaving home to visit a friend. "Those two lights they say I ran are on the way I would normally take, but somehow I just don't think I went that way that day. My last memory," she said, "was tasting a cigarette. I think I was driving about a mile from where I was supposed to have run the first light."

I had her focus on taste, five minutes a day, for a week. Then I hypnotized her and took her imaginally up to her last memory. "I'm not smoking!" she exclaimed. "I want a cigarette so bad I can taste it. I go to the gas station on Seventh Street and get a pack of cigarettes." From this station there was no way that Bree would have taken the route where the witnesses claimed to have seen her car. Fortunately, she was a regular customer, and the attendant remembered her. She'd told him she was going to stop smoking tomorrow. Lucky for her she'd waited a day. The charges were dropped.

If you ever need to remember something—where you hid your money, where you put your keys, the make of the suspicious car you later learned burglarized your neighbors— try expanding the sense you remember most prominently before your memory lapse and use it as a trigger in self-hypnosis to cue the associations you are after.

Marble Quarry Scene

At this stage of your rising energy and power, you continue to build momentum, and you won't have any more breathers. The *Marble Quarry Scene,* in which you learn to negatively hallucinate taste and constant volume simultaneously, builds your power surge by teaching you to channel sex energy to the trunk of your body. The purpose of this channeling is to get the energy out of your genitals so that it manifests not in sexual arousal but in pure energy that can be used for other purposes.

At this point in your development, the energy you create

may be so intense that you can feel it as a separate entity passing through your body. It is often sensed as a throbbing or pulse.

Marble Quarry Scene

It's spring. You are basking in the sun in a quarry of white, glistening marble with jet-black streaks. Feel the heat of the sun reflect off the sheer walls of the quarry. Above you, on a ledge, sits a little boy drinking cream soda. He throws the empty bottle into the marble pit. Hear the glass shatter. See two sparkling drops of soda in the sunlight. The entire pit fills with cream soda, carrying you straight up with it. Smell the rich soda. Drink. There is no taste. Float in the cool, creamy soda. Suddenly you hear a rumble growing louder and louder.

The marble has been weakened by the soda. It begins to crack, filling the pit. The soda becomes thicker and thicker, denser and denser. The soda does not rise higher; it contracts. You are oozing in and out, becoming more and more buoyant. You can now slide on your stomach along the slippery, rubbery surface. Stand. Run and slide along the cream soda surface to the sound of splashing. It feels wet, cool, beneath your feet.

Leave the quarry. The sun is setting. Come to the ocean. The sky is pink. Lie on the sand. The tide is coming in. Waves are getting ever closer. A beautiful, naked man/woman [whichever you are attracted to] comes out of the sea, silhouetted against the sunset. He/she lies on the sand beside you. He/she removes your bathing suit. He/she presses his/her body against your stomach and chest, rubbing his/her chest back and forth against your flesh. His/her breathing quickens. Your chest engorges. Stomach and chest get hotter and hotter from his/her body friction. Your chest and abdomen are throbbing . . . pulsating . . . Chest feels ready to burst, getting closer . . . closer . . . closer . . . climax! . . . Waves wash over you as you cling to one another. The sun sets. Drift together to the eternal sound of the ocean.

Reactions

It always surprises me how easily people are able to channel sex energy to various parts of their bodies. "The sound of the water was the most real," said Pauline, a thirty-year-old dental hygienist. "It was easier to recall the orgasm in my stomach and chest than any other place besides my genitals. I liked the quarry. I'm still there." "I felt the heat definitely," laughed Bart, a thirty-eight-year-old health products distributor. "And the excitement. It was easy."

Pulses

Your energy may now have reached such magnitude that it feels like a pulse. The day I gave her the *Marble Quarry Scene,* Anne went more deeply than ever before. On the count of three she opened her eyes and lay motionless a few minutes. Then she rose and staggered to my desk, sinking into an armchair. "I'm having a little time coming out," she said. "It's like I could feel every pulse throughout my whole body, even behind my knees. It has to be a pulse point 'cause I feel it . . . now my neck . . . each finger . . . independent . . . ten different throbbings . . . now inside my elbows and my feet . . . inside my ankles . . . under my neck to the bone . . . now my toes are starting to separate . . . that's wild . . . inside my thighs. That's funny. I'm not sure of the small of my back. One pulse doesn't want to settle. It's making a circle around my waist. Pulsation is continual from my thighs all the way down my leg; it's not just pulse points. Now my mouth. Oooh! The palms of my hands, there's a spot in the middle of each. Now the backs of my hands, the wrists. Now the whole arm. Mmmm . . . Now I can feel my heartbeat. It's loud! Wow! Thud! Thud! I never felt that before, almost as if I could see it looking at me, tingling too. It's numb, tingling even though it's a pulse. It feels like my hands are asleep, but I still have pulse sensations. Feet too, they're tingling like they're going to go to sleep."

Anne was losing awareness of her physical body as her hands and feet felt numb, but growing was her sense of her astral body, herself as energy. She had come face-to-face with her heart chakra, a numb, tingling pulse looking at her. Sex energy had circled her waist from its source in the root chakra, and risen to her throat. She was truly rooted and grounded in love, connected electrically from the root chakra to the heart chakra, ready to comprehend the breadth and length and depth and height of consciousness.

Anne heaved a long sigh, "I'm just too relaxed to concentrate any longer." She slowly stood up and walked airily to the mirror hanging on my grass-cloth wall, to the left of the sofa. She stood transfixed, peering dreamily into the mercury surface. "I can stand in front of the mirror and bring color into my cheeks by recalling that image," she said. I could see that a sexual flush had spread from the trunk area of her body through her neck and up into her face to rouge her cheeks. "I did that, didn't I?" she murmured, referring to the flooding rose of the sexual flush that was blushing her skin. "I don't think I'll tell David about this," she laughed. "He'll say, 'What the hell do you need me for?'"

Anne left the mirror and sat before me in her chair. For a minute she said nothing. Then a bemused, enigmatic smile radiated her face. "I'm smirking," she said. "I'm now at odds as to which experience to call reality—the one I'm now recalling or the one I just had." Anne's image or recall of her experience with the pulses was as real as her actual experience. She was able to bring the throbs of electrical energy back simply by remembering them. Her face was flushing all over again. Her imagery was as vivid as her reality. We were both elated.

The next time I saw Anne, she looked marvelous. She wore an orange flowered sarong, off the shoulders, and her features glittered with a vibrant, vital energy. She brought me a bag of cherries to eat and I guessed that the *Cherry Orchard Scene* was still making an impact on her. "I've just come from a surprise birthday party for my boss," she beamed. "I feel really good about how well I fit in with his wife and family. We were all really at ease with each other. What's really amazing me these days, though, is my memory. I can remember even the smallest minutiae, like where I put a paper clip five months ago. It's incredible what extra energy can do for you. I've got something even more remarkable to tell you. When I work overtime and I'm late for a meal I usually get an insulin reaction. I decided I no longer had a need for those reactions, so after creating the *Marble Quarry Scene* I gave myself the affirmation, 'My body remains healthy and stable when I'm late for a meal.' I haven't had an insulin reaction in over a month!

"My powers of intuition and telepathy are still on the rise. David and I finish each other's sentences more now than could be coincidence. There are fewer and fewer blocks in our marriage now that our emotional and spiritual compatibility is increasing. Sometimes David says he thinks it's 'spooky,' but how can he not enjoy it?" You too will greatly enjoy the wonderful and often surprising effects of your ever-rising energy.

Benefits

You are using your sexuality to generate energy, and your positive results will be much more far-reaching than improving your sex life, which of course this imagery will also help you to do. Altered states of high energy such as you can produce with the *Marble Quarry Scene* provide excellent conditions for giving yourself positive affirmations as Anne did to modify her insulin reactions. The energy charges the affirmation and potentiates its manifestation.

You will also discover, like Anne, that this image will give you a growing awareness and heightened sensitivity that is especially good for improving your personal relationships. Jill, a thirty-two-year-old boutique operator seeking help with her seven-year marriage to Carlos, thirty, a musician, was pleased with the benefits she experienced from the *Marble Quarry Scene.* "The image made me more empathic," she said. "I found that I started anticipating Carlos's needs. As my sensitivity to him increased, so did our compatibility. I realized our blocks were due to a lack of understanding, and as my powers of perception increased so did my understanding of Carlos. I guess I became more compassionate as well as empathic. We're much happier now and growing closer every day."

The *Marble Quarry Scene* diverts blood and energy to your viscera, the vital organs of your body: heart, lungs, kidneys, liver, stomach, and intestines. It is an excellent image to use whenever there are diseases or disorders in any of these body parts. Everet, a fifty-year-old salesman, suffered from angina pectoris, a disease condition marked by brief paroxysmal attacks of chest pain precipitated by deficient oxygenation of the heart muscles. Such pains are often precursors of a heart attack, and Everet was beset with worry. "My doctors tell me to relax and take it easy, but how can I?" he said. "I have a high-stress job. My livelihood depends on commissions. I'd like to take a year off and travel, but I can't afford it. I'm still a good fifteen years from retirement. How do you relax under these conditions?"

Heart disease is the number-one killer in our country today. There's no doubt that relaxation would make us all less prone to this pervasive ailment. However, the heart needs more than just relaxation to be healthy and strong. It needs energy and a good blood supply. I suggested that Everet practice the *Marble Quarry Scene* to electrically recharge his heart with sex energy and give it a greater volume of the blood it needs to oxygenate its tissue. In two weeks Everet's attacks of angina had decreased by half. "I think I'm getting a handle on it," he said. "I feel much better knowing I have direct control over this organ and don't need to spend a year in the South Seas to improve its condition."

Royce, fifty-six, a marketing engineer, underwent surgery and radiation therapy for lung cancer. His physician told him he had an eighty-percent chance of complete recovery, but he wanted to do all he could to increase the odds. "Why take chances?" he said. "If there's anything I can do to make my lungs healthier, I want to give it a go. You just don't realize how important your health is until you lose it." I gave Royce the *Marble Quarry Scene* and told him to practice it at least once a day, vitalizing his lungs with blood and sex energy. Two years later there has been no recurrence of the cancer.

Miriam, a sixty-seven-year-old retired nurse, was debilitated by emphysema, a condition of the lung marked by air-filled expansion of the tissue and distention that frequently impairs heart action. "I can barely get around anymore," she said. "Just going from the bedroom to the kitchen leaves me panting. I have to sit down and rest four or five times in the course of fixing a meal. Thank goodness I'm on the route of a Meals on Wheels here in L.A. called Home Dining Delight that can bring my food to the door already prepared. I almost never go out anymore, certainly not alone. If it wasn't for my sister who does things for me like bring me here today, I don't know what I'd do."

Miriam's lungs needed energy and nourishment desperately, and I encouraged her to practice the tape I'd made for her of the *Marble Quarry Scene* three times a day. A month later I spoke to her by phone and she said, "I think it's working. I really do have more zip. I can actually make breakfast for myself now without a rest and I don't breathe so heavily when I'm doing it. The stairs are still a problem, but I can get down them now by myself. If I stop for a breather once I'm outdoors, I can actually take a little walk. It's so good just being able to get back into the world, to see people around me, and maybe have a chat or two. I feel like I'm back from the grave."

Maurine, a forty-four-year-old marriage and family counselor and recovering alcoholic, sustained kidney and liver damage that left her with a chronically low energy level. "I'm always so tired," she said. "Everything I do is an effort. My son Jim is a senior now and I know I won't have him home much longer. There are so many things I want to do with him this last year, but I'm just never up for it. By the time I see my clients I'm exhausted. I'm lucky I have a great husband. Dick usually cooks dinner and does the other household chores. He's a raging feminist. He says I'm a goddess and entitled by my superiority and power to give life, to be waited on by the male drone. He's really supportive. But frankly I'm too tired to even enjoy being taken care of. Besides, I *hate* being dependent, and that's what this lousy energy level has made me."

After Maurine practiced the *Marble Quarry Scene* for a week she started noticing a small rise in her energy level. "It was very subtle at first," she said. "Bursts that maybe only lasted a few minutes. I'd be at work dreading the grocery shopping I had to do afterward, when suddenly I'd actually feel like doing it. The feeling didn't stay, but it was nice while it lasted. I remember one night Jim wanted me to look at a report he'd gotten an A on and I was able to concentrate on the whole thing. Usually, by that hour I'm only good for watching TV and then I really don't know what I'm viewing." Maurine's energy continued to build as the months progressed. By the time Jim graduated, she was able to say, "I did all the things I needed to make his last year at home complete, thanks to sex energy."

Gastrointestinal disorders also respond favorably to an infusion of sex energy. Megan, a thirty-year-old second-grade teacher, had a severe case of colitis, inflammation of the colon, accompanied by painful bloating and flatulence. "My stomach blows up like a balloon," she said. "All that gas is not only painful, it's embarrassing. My second-graders don't miss a thing. If I blow wind in class I'll never hear the end of it. Kids live for that sort of thing. It's also hell on my waistline. I'm not overweight, but the gas in my stomach is destroying my figure. I'm tired of the pain and I'm tired of burping and belching my way through life."

Using the *Marble Quarry Scene*, Megan was able to channel sex energy to her stomach and intestinal area to aid in healing the inflammation. "It felt like my intestines were vibrating," she said. "Spots of hot energy tingled through my digestive tract. The gas went away."

In addition to using sex energy to eliminate diseases and disorders of your visceral organs, you can use it effectively to build the muscle mass of your chest, abdomen, and back through electrical stimulation. "I need an edge," said Gardner, a twenty-four-year-old competitive bodybuilder. "I'm doing what the other guys do, weights, routines, diets. I need something extra to put me out front ahead of the pack. I need a chest and stomach to die for."

Channeling sex energy to the muscles of his chest, abdomen, and back using the *Marble Quarry Scene* gave Gardner the edge he was looking for. "I'm impressed," he said. "I pump iron while imagining that lady rubbing her bare body against the trunk of my body, getting hotter and hotter, throbbing, pulsating, climaxing. It feels like the bar is going to melt. If I'm going to try a new exercise I do the image right before the weight exercise so as not to interfere with my concentration on learning the new routine. But if it's an exercise I know by rote I do it simultaneously with the image. I think I get the most power that way. My muscles are getting bigger and harder, growing faster. The other guys in the gym are trying to figure out what I'm doing different, but they can't see what's going on in my head."

Channeling sex energy to the body trunk can also be used for breast enlargement. Eve, a twenty-three-year-old actress, wanted larger breasts without the risk of injections or surgical implants. "My agent says it'll help my career," she said, "but I'm really doing it for myself. I've always wanted a more curvaceous figure. It's something I've never been able to get out of my head, so I guess it's time to do something about it. I've tried bust-enlargement exercises, but they didn't seem to do much except maybe firm up what I already have a little. I want to increase my measurements." In four months, practicing the *Marble Quarry Scene* at least once a day, Eve was able to increase the size of her breasts a full inch.

Sex energy is also healing to many conditions that are benefited by chiropractic, a system of healing that holds that disease results from a lack of normal nerve function that can be ameliorated by manipulation and specific adjustment of body structures such as the spinal column. Katerina, a forty-five-year-old switchboard operator, was diagnosed by her chiropractor as having cervicobrachial syndrome, a condition where the muscles on the right side of her neck and shoulder painfully contracted, restricting her motion. In the vernacular this condition is often called "student's neck," as it is frequently brought on by holding one's head down, as while reading or writing, over a long period of time. Secretaries, writers, and telephone operators are particularly prone to this condition. "My neck and shoulder muscles get tight and hard as steel," Katerina said. "It gets so I can barely move my head. It makes me claustrophobic. I hate not being able to move freely. What's worse, the muscles tighten up more if I exercise, especially if I lift something. I'm turning into a blob and an invalid."

I asked Katerina to use the *Marble Quarry Scene* in conjunction with her chiropractic treatments to direct blood and channel sex energy to nourish and charge the muscles and nerves of her trunk, where her spinal column as well as her injury resided. "I'm better," she said a month later. "My neck is finally loosening up. I have much greater freedom of movement. I'll be driving in my car and I'll think, 'My gosh, my shoulder feels good. It doesn't ache.' It's been so long since I've been without pain I'd forgotten what it felt like. I'd started hating so many things, like work and driving, because they'd become associated with the pain in my neck. I'm realizing now that work and driving are fine—when my neck feels good. The world looks bright again."

Squirt Gun Scene

It is the *quantity* of energy that determines the level of expansion you will achieve. It takes energy to overcome fears, eliminate unwanted urges, make relationships work, excel athletically, lift depression, retrieve data from your memory, rise above pain, achieve sexual satisfaction, work efficiently, process extra senses, and raise consciousness. The more energy you generate, the closer you come to accomplishing these goals.

Your final image in this book, the *Squirt Gun Scene*, in which you negatively hallucinate taste and reflection simultaneously, helps you to dramatically increase your quantity of energy. Here you learn to combine your facility for channeling sex energy to your head, legs and feet, hands and arms, and trunk into the uniform experiencing of sex energy throughout your entire body. This ups the voltage immeasurably, further contributing to the dematerialization of the illusion of your physical body and the sensing of yourself in your true form, pure energy.

This image asks you to age-regress to the dawn of puberty, a time before you experienced a sexual connection with another person. At this time the orgasm is a new experience, at its strongest and purest, uncontaminated by frustration or inhibition. Sex energy is high, pure, and unbridled.

Squirt Gun Scene

It is your first day of puberty. You are sitting under an elm tree on a hot summer day. You are in deep, deep shade. The smell of mint permeates the air. A river flows past the tree. Hear it babble as it runs to join the sea. A young boy/girl [sex to which you are attracted] is fishing by the river. You are going to sneak up on him/her with a squirt gun filled with grape juice.

Tiptoe stealthily through the grass till you are behind him/her. Holler, 'Boo!' He/she turns. Squirt him/her in the face. The grape juice does not bounce off or reflect from his/her skin. It just runs off. His/her face turns purple.

Now he/she whips out a squirt gun filled with pineapple juice. He/she fires. It hits your forehead, a hard stream of liquid. It does not reflect. It rolls straight down your face. Smell the sweet pineapple. It runs into your mouth. There is no taste. It feels wet and warm. Run back into the woods. Take your gun. Squirt the grape juice into your mouth. It hits the roof and clings to run down the sides of your throat and into your stomach. It does not reflect off the roof of your mouth. No taste.

Go back to the river. Lie on the shore. Waves hit you and then run down the sides of your body. They do not lap back. The young man/woman joins you. He/she lies beside you. The waves wash you together. The touch of his/her body sends a tingle down your arms . . . your legs . . . your back. This is the first time you have ever felt such a sensation. This is his/her first time too.

He/she undresses you, then himself/herself. He/she runs his/her hands along your chest. He/she kisses you gently on the lips and presses his/her body to yours. Your bodies join. Feel a thrusting . . . pulsating . . . throbbing . . . pounding . . . heat . . . beginning in your feet. A rush of sexual pleasure from your feet . . . to your legs . . . to your genitals . . . to your stomach . . . chest . . . arms . . . neck . . . head . . . and explosion! in your head which bounces back filling your whole body with a sexual surge from head to toe. Every muscle, every fiber, is totally aroused, alive!

Hear the roar of a giant wave approaching. It covers you, then recedes. Lie there together. Young. Gently washed into the water each time a wave recedes.

Reactions

Responses to the *Squirt Gun Scene* are dramatic. "You can change bodily sensation a tremendous degree," said Stephanie, a thirty-year-old restaurant manager. "I'm practically paralyzed," said Jim, a high school chemistry teacher. The illusion of yourself as possessing a physical body that moves through time and space begins to break down, which may result in a sense of physical immobility, as it did in Jim's case.

Along with the sense of a tremendous increase in energy comes a wonderful feeling that you have more control over reality. "I felt I was the cause, not the recipient," said Kent, a fifty-year-old investor. "I felt I had control of everything."

Since the *Squirt Gun Scene* involves your channeling sex energy through your entire body, including your genitals, it may produce sexual arousal along with extensively heightened energy. "I had a vaginal contraction when you described the tingling," said Mary, thirty-two, a legal secretary. The primary reaction to this image, however, is exponentially expanded energy, as demonstrated by the response of Terrence, a twenty-year-old college biology major: "How come there was no taste? So that I can tune out all distractions when I study? I sure could feel the sex energy. My legs got really warm. The energy went up and bounced off my head and then kind of covered everything. I was energized! If you want a color, it was yellow. I felt like I was glowing. The energy became yellow when it bounced off the top of my head. I guess it was because it increased then. I associate high energy with yellow. I felt energized, waiting for a focal point. What a great way to boost my energy!"

Generating high energy gives you a pure field, a tabula rasa, blank slate, from which to create a new reality—the focal point Terrence was waiting to manifest. This is an ideal state in which to give yourself positive affirmations and images pertaining to the specific goals you wish to actualize. First, do the *Squirt Gun Scene*. Then, before bringing yourself out of the state you have created, give yourself the affirmation and/or image you have targeted for materialization. Your expanded energy state will charge your suggestions and visualization into the matter that is reality.

Into Spirit

Anne lay motionless on the couch several minutes after I gave her the *Squirt Gun Scene*. Then she grabbed onto the windowsill and slowly pulled herself up. She whispered, "Ask me now about my sense of touch. How many pulses are there on the body? Hundreds. Thousands. God! It's like they're all competing. Just like the last image, only there are more of them. I feel like a walking throb. There is not one inch of me that isn't throbbing. They're strong, all of them. My heart is beating very slow. It's so amazing I can count the beats like that. That's really great.

"Mmmm . . . That age regression works great. I can even remember what I said the first time I made love. 'Hey the bed's moving.' Tim. I can even remember his name. I remember what he said. 'You're right.' That's weird. I was visiting my grandmother in Minnesota. I had just turned fifteen. He lived next door. He had an attic room, and we went up to listen to records. Funny the mixture of kid and grown-up adult of those years. We raced each other up the stairs laughing like children. I have a different afterglow from this image. A sharp, vivid memory of how special I was then. I keep thinking how cherished all that was, how sweet and uncomplicated, but I have no regret, no need to go back and repeat the event. The memory of today's experience seems so complete in itself." Anne was letting go of sensory bondage. The illusion of the senses was dear, but outgrown. It was time to move on. Into energy. Into spirit.

A fundamental Taoist principle is: Sex energy can be transformed into spirit. The thousands of "throbbing pulses" that Anne created from raising her sex energy showed she had attained a higher vibratory rate, the path to dematerialization of the illusion of the physical body and awareness of the self as pure energy, spirit. Anne was learning to navigate without her physical body, a lesson she would lovingly complete with the help of visualizations further along in the imagery progression, beyond the scope of this book.

Spirit, matter in equilibrium, is yearning to be free in all of us. It cries out to return to its true identity, pure energy. I pray that, grounded in love, the imagery progression in this book will help you to raise your own vibratory level to spiritual liberation. Joy be with you.

Index of Specific Problems

If you want to focus on particular areas, here is a list of some of the most common ones I've covered, along with the images most suited to working on them. I use the word *specific* below to denote imagery that is not a part of your natural sequence of images—i.e., special images pertaining only to certain problems. Please keep in mind that *all* the images I've given you in your imagery progression will reduce your stress and increase your peace, confidence, relaxation, concentration, energy, and motivation.

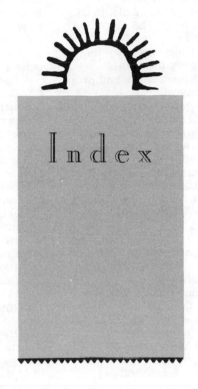

Index